COMPUTER SCIENCE, TECHNOLOGY AND APPLICATIONS

ADVANCES IN CLOUD COMPUTING RESEARCH

COMPUTER SCIENCE, TECHNOLOGY AND APPLICATIONS

Additional books in this series can be found on Nova's website
under the Series tab.

Additional e-books in this series can be found on Nova's website
under the e-book tab.

COMPUTER SCIENCE, TECHNOLOGY AND APPLICATIONS

ADVANCES IN CLOUD COMPUTING RESEARCH

MUTHU RAMACHANDRAN
EDITOR

New York

For permission to use material from this book please contact us:
Telephone 631-231-7269; Fax 631-231-8175
Web Site: http://www.novapublishers.com

NOTICE TO THE READER

The Publisher has taken reasonable care in the preparation of this book, but makes no expressed or implied warranty of any kind and assumes no responsibility for any errors or omissions. No liability is assumed for incidental or consequential damages in connection with or arising out of information contained in this book. The Publisher shall not be liable for any special, consequential, or exemplary damages resulting, in whole or in part, from the readers' use of, or reliance upon, this material. Any parts of this book based on government reports are so indicated and copyright is claimed for those parts to the extent applicable to compilations of such works.

Independent verification should be sought for any data, advice or recommendations contained in this book. In addition, no responsibility is assumed by the publisher for any injury and/or damage to persons or property arising from any methods, products, instructions, ideas or otherwise contained in this publication.

This publication is designed to provide accurate and authoritative information with regard to the subject matter covered herein. It is sold with the clear understanding that the Publisher is not engaged in rendering legal or any other professional services. If legal or any other expert assistance is required, the services of a competent person should be sought. FROM A DECLARATION OF PARTICIPANTS JOINTLY ADOPTED BY A COMMITTEE OF THE AMERICAN BAR ASSOCIATION AND A COMMITTEE OF PUBLISHERS.

Additional color graphics may be available in the e-book version of this book.

Library of Congress Cataloging-in-Publication Data

Advances in cloud computing research / editor, Muthu Ramachandran.
    pages cm
Includes bibliographical references and index.
ISBN 978-1-63117-192-5 (hardcover)
1. Cloud computing--Research. I. Ramachandran, Muthu.
QA76.585.A38 2014
004.67'82--dc23
                    2014000022

Published by Nova Science Publishers, Inc. † New York

CONTENTS

PREFACE

INTRODUCTION

Cloud computing has evolved to address the availability of computing services and resources anywhere, anytime, and on any device. In particular, computing hardware and software often gets outdated and, hence, it is wise to outsource computing resources and to manage their IT infrastructures outside of their company premises, which is more cost-effective than is the case at present. Cloud computing is emerging rapidly and software as a service paradigm has increasing its demand for more services. However, it is crucial to maintain and manage this growth in such way that the cloud technology remains cost efficient.

To this end this book is dedicated to keep up with current and future research directions in cloud computing and its applications.

Microsoft white paper (2012) claims that their cloud technology is cost effective to build your own private cloud solutions that are licensed on a per processor basis with unlimited virtualization. This helps to lower costs than charging per virtual server as well as the physical machines.

RESEARCH ADVANCES & FUTURE DIRECTIONS

Cloud computing provides opportunities and challenges how effectively we can manage computing resources in a large scale. The research challenges on cloud computing includes scalable and elastic architecture, virtualisation management including hypervisors, load balancing, resource management, fault tolerance, interoperability, availability, data integrity, trust worthiness, and security. Some of the key research challenges are explained in details:

- *Best practices on cloud computing: Cloud security, service development and cloud management*. Best practices on developing, deploying, and managing cloud services and deployment models are the key to success. According to Microsoft (2012) Application Service Development & Management should consider developing secured cloud services, deploying and operating your business applications. Service Delivery & Automation should be standardised and automating service and resource provisioning, managing change and access controls need to be optimised.

Infrastructure management should be deploying and operating the entire underlying infrastructure on which your business applications and services run. Currently, security related flaws are being found on daily basis are fixed by adding security patches. This is simply unacceptable paradigm for sustainability of cloud computing. Therefore, we need to develop and build cloud services with build in security of services (SaaS, PaaS, IaaS), data centres, and cloud servers. This chapter aims to provide a number techniques and methods for developing cloud services systematically with build in security. It will also cover a range of system security engineering techniques have been adopted as part of a cloud development process. A number of examples of scenarios have chosen from Amazon EC2, to illustrate with, emerging cloud system security engineering principles and paradigm (Ramachandran 2013 and 2014).

- *Energy efficient techniques.* Green ICT has become more popular research topic since the emergence of cloud computing as it consumes more energy than traditional computing. Baliga et al. (2010) have illustrated that energy consumption in transport and switching can be a significant percentage of total energy consumption in cloud computing. This largely due to cloud's high dependency on large internet bandwidth. Therefore, current & future research should focus on developing energy efficient technologies for software, algorithms, servers, storage, processors, and communications.
- *Business models and infrastructures for cloud services.* We need to make a balance amongst different delivery models: private, public, and hybrid.
- *Architecture and patterns for cloud computing.*
- *Bid data paradigm and techniques.*
- *Cloud paradigm and SaaS/PaaS/IaaS/BaaS development techniques & environment.* In this sub-topic is paramount to success & sustainability of cloud technology. We need to keep discovering new paradigm for cloud service development and at the same time to address design for availability, design for scalability, design for energy efficiency, design for elasticity, design for security, and design for reusability, customisability, and dynamic re-configurability of services.
- *Future research directions and emerging service technology innovation.* The future direction of cloud computing will dominate cost effective cloud solutions providers and more energy efficient cloud providers. Jeffery and Neidecker-Lutz (2010) discuss future perspective on cloud computing with technological aspects such as achieving scalability, performance, and elasticity and with non-technological aspects such as multi-tenancy, control over data, security, trust, and privacy. The future trend will look into providing and extending cloud infrastructures and platforms to business areas such as telecommunications, ERP systems, medical, manufacturing, financial systems, travel, IT services, other service sectors, scientific computing, Green Cloud, and disaster management systems, etc. The technical areas include elastic scalability, data management, and SaaS development & programming models.

READERSHIP & BOOK ORGANISATION

One of the main aims of this book is to collate current state of the art and future research directions on cloud computing. This book also aims to provide energy efficient practices, new paradigm, and service development techniques that can be employed. This book is useful for industrial experts, learners, and researchers.

BOOK ORGANISATION

This book consists of two parts: cloud applications and cloud energy efficiency. Part 1 consists of six chapters and Part 2 consists of two chapters.

Part 1 Cloud Applications
Chapter 1 - Challenges of Using Cloud Computing in Medical Imaging
Medical imaging is an important tool for medical diagnosis and treatment. Historically, this tool has been taking advantage of the computer technology advances. In fact, medical imaging has been more and more supported by computers. An example is the creation of image acquisition processes based on computational methods, like magnetic resonance imaging and positron emission tomography. Another example is the appearance of Picture Archiving and Communication System (PACS) concept, which is an umbrella term that embraces the systems responsible for the medical imaging acquisition, archive, distribution, visualization and management. This chapter identifies the challenges of using cloud in demanding medical imaging scenario and consequent strategies to solve or minimize them. Furthermore, it has proposed an architecture that combines distinct technological approaches to deal with data privacy, communication latency and protocol interoperability.

Chapter 2 - Cloud Computing in Business
Cloud Computing as an emerging model for delivering information technology services will most likely have major impact in ICT in the years to come. This research looks at the phenomenon of cloud computing from the business viewpoint; we classify common business models applied in cloud computing, discuss major advantages and drawbacks of cloud, and argue whether enterprise management is fully aware of what cloud computing actually is and what measurable benefits it can bring. Further, we present the state of the art in the area of cloud integration in business, and discuss ways in which the development of cloud computing will promote economic growth, increase productivity, and shift the type of jobs and skills required by industry.

Chapter 3 - Consulting as a Service – demonstrated by Cloud Computing consultancy projects in the Greater China
The objective of this paper is to highlight Cloud Computing projects with mutual interests for both mainland China and Taiwan, which present the a strong case of Consulting as a Service (CaaS) as an innovative way for generating profits and delivering services for clients. This paper explains the IT and Cloud development in the Greater China and presents three projects that Taiwanese have been involved in the design, implementation and research. The first project presents a case for Teradata and Shanghai Stock Exchange (SSE), where Taiwanese collaborators have been closely involved. The second project is about two

sandstorm simulations in the Inner Mongolia of mainland China and investigates its impacts to the environment and health of the populations. The third project is the Universe Computing which responds to mainland China's call to develop space programme and to explore the unknown territory. Universe Computing includes simulations for satellite orbiting, galaxy formation and galaxy explosion. The author is an investigator for the second and third project and uses Cloud Computing Adoption Framework (CCAF) to design and deploy Software as a Service (SaaS) and Consulting as a Service (CaaS). Taiwanese research and development outputs have been influential to the IT development in the Greater China. This is important to move away any differences and work together to establish more and better research and development results to create a mutual win-win and maintain a high GDP growth.

Chapter 4 - Cotinuous Delivery In The Cloud: An Economic Evaluation Using System Dynamics

The continuous delivery paradigm has been recently introduced to help facilitate the speedy deployment of working software into production and shifting software delivery exercise from a major event culture to an effortless activity. Recent advancements have made it possible to practice continuous delivery in the cloud. However, many practitioners are still sceptical about the economic profitability of practicing continuous delivery in the cloud. This work investigates the economic profitability of carrying out continuous delivery in the cloud and compares it with on-premise continuous delivery adoption using system dynamics. Results show that the continuous delivery in the cloud environment over a six year period has a Net present Value over twice that of the on-premise continuous delivery.

Chapter 5 - Financial Clouds and modelling offered by Cloud Computing Adoption Framework

Cloud Computing Adoption Framework (CCAF) is a framework for designing and implementation of Could Computing solutions. This paper focuses on how CCAF can help to address portability in Cloud Computing implementations in Finance domain. Portability involves migrating entire applications from desktops to clouds and between different Clouds in a way which is transparent to users so they may continue to work as if still using their familiar systems. Reviews for several financial models are studied, where Monte Carlo Methods (MCM) and Black Scholes Model (BSM) are chosen to demonstrate portability between desktops and clouds. A special technique in MCM, Variance-Gamma Process, is used for error corrections while performing analysis of good quality. Coding algorithm for MCM and BSM written in MATLAB are explained. Simulations for MCM and BSM are performed on different types of Clouds. Benchmark and experimental results are presented and discussed, together with implications for banking and ways to track risks in order to improve accuracy. We have used a conceptual Financial Cloud platform to explain how this fits into the CCAF, as well as Financial Software as a Service (FSaaS). Our objective is to demonstrate portability, speed, accuracy and reliability of applications in the clouds, while demonstrating portability for CCAF and FSaaS.

Chapter 6 - Review of Cloud Computing and existing Frameworks for Cloud adoption

This paper presents a selected review for Cloud Computing and explains the benefits and risks of adopting Cloud Computing in a business environment. Although all the risks identified may be associated with two major Cloud adoption challenges, a framework is required to support organisations as they begin to use Cloud and minimise risks of Cloud adoption. Eleven Cloud Computing frameworks are investigated and a comparison of their strengths and limitations is made; the result of the comparison is that none of them is able to deal with all the Cloud adoption challenges thoroughly and a new, comprehensive framework is required if organisations are to overcome these challenges. This ideal framework would ensure that benefits of Cloud adoption are maximised whilst minimising the risks of Cloud adoption.

Part 2 Energy Efficient Cloud

Chapter 7 - Estimating Emission Reductions from Low Carbon Information Technology: the Geochronos Relocation Project

In this chapter we present an information and communications technology (ICT) project that involved moving virtualized applications between data centres in order reduce greenhouse gas emissions. The emission reductions have been accounted for according to a protocol that is conformant with ISO 14064-2, an international standard for quantifying and reporting emission reduction projects. While the total amount of emission reductions attributable to the project were relatively small, the results of the article are important and illustrative as this may be one of the first examples of trying to quantify a specific project that aims to reduce emissions through the provision of low carbon ICT services. With rapid growth being experienced in the ICT services sector generally and rising energy and environmental impacts of the industry, the topic of low or zero carbon ICT services is of increasing importance from a number of perspectives. Two are subsequently discussed in this chapter, including the possible place of ICT within carbon markets and also the role of such ICT projects for helping large users of data management services reduce the environmental impact of the services that they require.

Chapter 8 - Energy Efficiency Of The Cloud Computing System

Cloud computing has been hailed as the achievement of the long-held dream of computing as a utility and has the potential to transform a large part of the Information and Communication Technology (ICT) industry. Cloud computing is currently the buzz word of the Information Technology industry. But cloud computing has had its share of controversy; ranging from the definition of cloud computing to its energy efficiency. This chapter looks at one area of controversy; the energy efficiency of cloud computing. While some are advocating and touting the energy saving potential of cloud computing, other have questioned all the hype on the energy efficiency of cloud computing. The energy demand of data centres, communication networks and the Internet are predicted to frow. We outline previous contributions to the discussion on the energy efficiency of cloud computing and investigate the energy efficiency of cloud computing through simulations.

I hope you enjoy reading this book.
Muthu Ramachandran
12th December 2013

REFERENCES

Baliga, J et al., (2012) Green Cloud Computing: Balancing Energy in Processing, Storage and Transport, Proc. IEEE, vol. 99, no. 1, 2010, pp. 149–167

Buyya, R., Broberg, J., and Goscinski, A (2011) (Eds) Cloud Computing Principles and Paradigms, Wiley, NJ, USA.

Kurtz, L. R, and Vines, D. R (2010) Cloud Security: A Comprehensive Guide to Secure Cloud Computing, Wiley, U.S.A

Microsoft (2012) Microsoft Private Cloud White Paper, January.

Rimal, P. B et al., (2009) A taxonomy and survey of cloud computing systems, Fifth International Joint Conference on INC, IMS and IDC, IEEE CS Press.

Ramachandran, M (2012) Software Security Engineering: Design and Applications, Nova Science Publishers, New York, USA, 2012. ISBN: 978-1-61470-128-6, https://www.novapublishers.com/catalog/product_info.php?products_id=26331

Ramachandran, M (2013) Business Requirements Engineering for Developing Cloud Computing Services, Springer, Software Engineering Frameworks for Cloud Computing Paradigm, Mahmmood, Z and Saeed, S (eds.), http://www.springer.com/computer/communication+networks/book/978-1-4471-5030-5

Ramachandran, M (2014) Systems Engineering Processes for the Development and Deployment of Secure Cloud Applications, Encyclopaedia of Information Technology, IGI Global.

Jeffery, K. and Neidecker-Lutz, B (2010) The Future of Cloud Computing Opportunities for European Cloud Computing Beyond 2010, Expert Group Report, European Commission, Information Society and Media.

ABOUT THE EDITOR

Dr. Muthu Ramachandran is currently a Principal Lecturer in the Computing, Creative Technologies, and Engineering School as part of the Faculty of Arts, Environment and Technology at Leeds Metropolitan University in the UK. Previously, he spent nearly eight years in industrial research (Philips Research Labs and Volantis Systems Ltd, Surrey, UK) where he worked on software architecture, reuse, and testing. Prior to that he was teaching at Liverpool John Moores University and received his PhD from Lancaster University. His first career started as a research scientist from India Space Research Labs where he worked on real-time systems development projects. Muthu is an author of two books: Software Components: Guidelines and Applications (Nova Publishers, NY, USA, 2008) and Software Security Engineering: Design and Applications (Nova Publishers, NY, USA, 2011). He is also an edited co-author of a book, Handbook of Research in Software Engineering (IGI, 2010) and has edited the book KE for SDLC (2011). He has also widely authored published journal articles, book chapters and conferences materials on various advanced topics in software engineering and education. He received his Master's from Indian Institute of Technology, Madras and from Madurai Kamaraj University, Madurai, India. He is a member of various professional organizations and computer societies: IEEE, ACM, Fellow of BCS, and Fellow of HEA. He is also invited speaker on several international conferences. Muthu's research projects and books publications can be accessed on www.se.moonfruit.com

Dr. Muthu Ramachandran, PhD
Leeds Metropolitan University
Leeds LS6 3QS UK
Tel: +441138124743
M. Ramachandran@leedsmet.ac.uk

PART 1. CLOUD APPLICATIONS

In: Advances in Cloud Computing Research
Editor: Muthu Ramachandran

ISBN: 978-1-63117-192-5
© 2014 Nova Science Publishers, Inc.

Chapter 1

CHALLENGES OF USING CLOUD COMPUTING IN MEDICAL IMAGING

Carlos Viana-Ferreira[*] and Carlos Costa
DETI/IEETA, University of Aveiro, Portugal

ABSTRACT

Medical imaging is an important tool for medical diagnosis and treatment. Historically, this tool has been taking advantage of the computer technology advances. In fact, medical imaging has been more and more supported by computers. An example is the creation of image acquisition processes based on computational methods, like magnetic resonance imaging and positron emission tomography. Another example is the appearance of Picture Archiving and Communication System (PACS) concept, which is an umbrella term that embraces the systems responsible for the medical imaging acquisition, archive, distribution, visualization and management.

In general, public cloud computing services have many advantages. They have potential to support medical imaging services and processes in distributed environments. For instance, they can be used to support centralized storage of medical imaging data, including the establishment of regional archives, releasing the healthcare institutions from the duties of maintaining an infrastructure capable of storing a huge amount of data. Another scenario is to support a broker of communications between institutions, taking advantage of cloud services availability and scalability. Nevertheless, such technologic choice has several risks, due to specificities of medical imaging scenario, especially about security and data access latency.

This chapter identifies the challenges of using cloud in demanding medical imaging scenario and consequent strategies to solve or minimize them. Furthermore, it has proposed an architecture that combines distinct technological approaches to deal with data privacy, communication latency and protocol interoperability.

Keywords: Medical imaging, cloud, system architecture

---

[*] Corresponding Author address: Email: c.ferreira@ua.pt.

INTRODUCTION

In healthcare provision services, medical imaging plays an important role in both diagnostic and treatment support (Sylva, 2010; Rengier et al., 2010), since it contains important biomarkers and provides a view of the anatomy and physical processes (Bui et al., 2007). This importance is increasing in the last decades, following the tendency of the computational resources availability that brought new imaging tools such as computed tomography, magnetic resonance imaging, Doppler ultrasound, positron emission tomography and single photon emission computed tomography (Ishikawa et al., 2009). Besides the fact that computers are creating methods of acquiring medical images, they are also changing the storage, visualization and transmission of images and other medical data. For that, much is due to the appearance of Picture Archiving and Communication Systems (PACS) concept, which is an umbrella term for systems that gather a set of technologies of acquisition, storage, visualization and distribution of medical image and data through a computer network (Huang, 2011; Ribeiro et al., 2010, Costa et al., 2011).

With the wide spread of Internet, it was soon realized that it was possible to broaden the horizons of PACS concept, promoting the data access from other departments or even from other institutions. In this context, two main scenarios appeared: (1) the outsourcing of the storage facility and (2) inter-institutional collaboration. In both scenarios, we believe that cloud computing can be a valuable asset.

In fact, many healthcare centres have only few modalities available. Therefore, sometimes the patient needs to visit other medical institutions, in order to be undergone to the required exams. Not to mention the natural mobility of patients from one institution to another for several situations and reasons. These reasons cause the dispersion of data and the consequent problems of access it when and where it is needed. In contrast with this dispersion, there is the physicians' side in which, the physician must need to use medical data that was produced and stored in another institution.

For this problem, traditional solutions proved to be ineffective, such as mail, email, patient and private solutions over virtual private networks (VPN). For instance, (1) VPN can be hard to set up and manage, for bureaucratic and technical reasons; (2) traditional mail can take too long; (3) the patient can forget, lose or damage the exams; (4) through email it is either necessary to previously know where the data will be needed, or to wait until the responsible for the data answers the request.

This inter-institutional collaboration is, not only related with disassociated institutions that share the interest of providing a better health care service provision, but also related with federations of small imaging centres or even a PACS at a regional level that merges the information of institutions of a geographical area.

Using a cloud service as a storage facility, it is also possible to avail the data to other institutions, in order to provide a better healthcare service provision, with all the advantages that such a system can bring, for instance:

- Possible reduction of the radiation dose to which the patient is submitted. If the physicians from one institution may access the exams of one patient carried out in another, it is possible to avoid another similar exam.

- The time that would be wasted by a new exam could be saved, which may lead to a faster diagnosis and treatment.
- The equipment acquisition may be more efficiently used, if they were only used for the exams that have not already been carried out in another institution.

As the volume of medical imaging data raises, the repositories of the healthcare institutions also needs to grow, increasing their costs. Therefore, cloud computing may be used as a storage facility, making the healthcare institution unaccounted for the responsibility to maintain the data storage system. Besides, in this way it is possible to reduce the Information Technology (IT) infrastructure in the healthcare institution. In fact, there are some implementations of this kind of services that use the cloud computing service to store the medical images and availing an interface to access the medical images stored in the cloud.

In some cases, the healthcare institutions' network is not prepared for other solutions such as VPN. This becomes critical when it comes the time to deploy those solutions. Cloud uses well known and universally used communication protocols, which facilitates the deployment of cloud-based solutions. For this reason, cloud technology becomes a good candidate for supporting a bridge of communications between distinct healthcare institutions, allowing two machines in distinct institutions to communicate with each other.

PICTURE ARCHIVE
AND COMMUNICATION SYSTEMS

PACS appeared somewhere in the 1980 decade in the shape of small islands, each one composed mainly by: (1) the acquisition equipment, i.e., the equipment responsible for the extraction of data and consequently for the construction of an image representative of the collected data; (2) visualization workstation and (3) printer. However, soon this concept started to proliferate associated with the need of different modalities for each department of the same institution and nowadays, PACS concept evolved to systems capable of managing medical imaging data of an entire enterprise. As an example, Figure 1 shows a current typical PACS instance.

A PACS is generally composed by the image acquisition equipment, a PACS controller and archive, and display workstations linked by a network. Some years ago, there was also an image and data acquisition gateway, which was the bridge between the imaging modality (image acquisition equipment) and the PACS controller. This component associated the image acquired by the imaging modality, with the related data of the patient from the Hospital Information System (HIS) and Radiology Information System (RIS), so that the radiological exam could be sent to the PACS controller. The translation between the language spoken by the imaging modality and the one spoken by the PACS controller was then assured by this component.

Nowadays, most part of the image acquisition equipment already speaks the same language of the PACS controller (Costa et al., 2009), so the image and data acquisition gateway, in most cases, became obsolete. Thus, the image acquisition equipment uses the data received from the RIS through the modality worklist, docking that data with the image and sending it to the PACS controller (also known as PACS server).

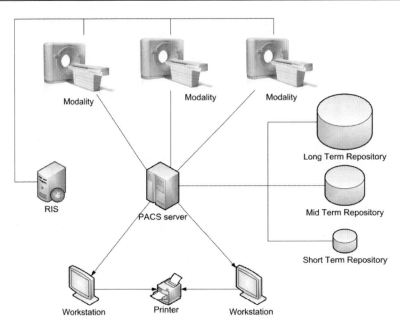

Figure 1. Main components of a current typical PACS instance.

Digital Imaging and Communication in Medicine

In the beginning of PACS concept, the interoperability was restricted for equipment of the same fabricant, being urgent to make the equipment of different providers interoperable. In this context, a normalization effort resulted in international Digital Imaging and Communications in Medicine (DICOM) standard (ACR-NEMA, 2011). Among others, DICOM defines the network communication layers, the services commands, the persistent objects coding, the media exchange structure and the documentation that must follow an implementation (Pianykh, 2012). This standard was well accepted, being implemented on most medical imaging equipment. As a consequence, during last years, much DICOM data has been created and stored in medical institution's repositories (Costa et al., 2009).

For what concerns the way of representing Real-World objects, DICOM uses the Information Object Definition (IOD) concept. An IOD is a way to encode information about digital medical images and related data. However, in the Real-World the objects are not isolated islands. Instead, the objects are related to each other. DICOM also takes this into account, for that it uses relationships between objects. An IOD that includes information about other Real-World Objects is called a Composite information object. DICOM normalizes an Entity-Relationship Model that relates the components or Information Entity (IE) of the IOD, instead of arbitrarily aggregating them.

DICOM standard also contemplates the way the IOD instances are encapsulated into files. According to the standard, these files must begin with a meta-information block followed by a stream representing the data set (see Figure 2).

Meta information part of the file begins with 128 bytes of preamble (available for specific implementations, usually padded with zeros) followed by the string "DICM", the size in bytes and other relevant data. Except the preamble and the string "DICM", all other fields of a

DICOM file are represented in a TLV (tag length value) structure, that means that each element of the file is divided into three fields: the tag (the identification of the field), the length (the number of bytes of the value field) and the value (ACR-NEMA, 2011).

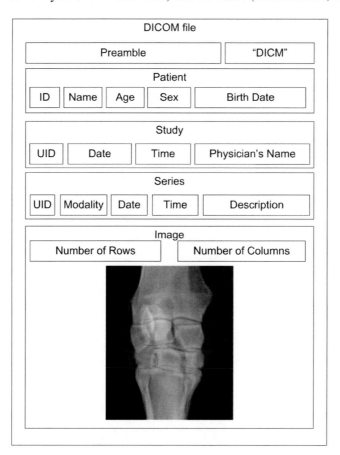

Figure 2. Structure of a DICOM file.

USE CASE SCENARIOS FOR CLOUD IN MEDICAL IMAGING SERVICES

Cloud for Infrastructure Outsourcing

Traditional PACS solutions have their IT (Information Technology) infrastructure hosted indoors. This forces institutions to dimension the infrastructure according to the hours when the need for IT services is greatest, which causes underuse of the resources at certain hours of the day, for instance, at night. Another disadvantage is the space occupied by the IT infrastructure in the healthcare institution building and also the maintenance and technical costs of this paradigm.

The main goal of the cloud computing paradigm is to provide computational resources on-demand, with high quality services. In fact, they can substitute the core of the IT infrastructure in the healthcare institution. As an analogy, hospitals usually do not produce their own electricity, on a regular basis. In this way, it is possible to pay only for the resources used since the allocation of cloud resources can be made according to needs, leaving concerns about the scaling of the infrastructure to the cloud service provider. Such technology choice gives to a PACS solution numerous advantages, such as:

- The healthcare institutions become unaccounted for the maintenance duties of the data storage system. Usually, there is a legal amount of time, in which data must be stored. For instance, in Portugal, medical data must be stored for at least 10 years.
- Some public cloud computing services have a geo-distributed infrastructure. This means that the quality of service is more uniformly distributed around the world, than if the service was only hosted in one location. Besides, this characteristic makes the service more disaster-proof, since even if a disaster (for instance: fire and earthquakes) occurs in one of the places where the cloud service is hosted, it will have other servers running in other parts of the world that will keep the service available.
- Most cloud computing services, automatically, backups the data in multiple repositories. In this way, the healthcare institution becomes also freed from the duties of backing up the data, since it is automatically carried out by the cloud service.
- Medical imaging services become accessible anywhere and anytime, promoting inter-institutional processes.
- Low initial investment: since cloud's business model is based on "pay what you use", healthcare institutions do not need to invest in an infrastructure designed to scale accordingly to the expected needs in the next years. Instead, they will pay only for what they use in the present (Abadi, 2009).
- Cloud scalability makes the systems built on top of cloud services able to grow according to needs (Fox et al., 2009).

In fact, there are already some implementations of this kind of services. Silva et al. (2012) described a system that stores medical imaging studies in multiple cloud services. The architecture of the system has three main components:

- The master index is the one responsible to implement the access control policies, being the element with access to the keys with which data stored in cloud services is encoded. This component is also responsible to maintain an index of all resources stored in the system. Because of its duties, this component must be hosted in a trustworthy place, for instance, a private server or a private cloud.
- The cloud slave is the component responsible to store encrypted chunks of data related to the DICOM data. Since the data is encrypted, this component can be hosted in a public cloud computing service.
- The gateway is a component that makes the translation between DICOM communications and the web services interface of the master index and cloud slaves.

In this way, the gateway serves as an intermediary between any DICOM-compliant PACS and the other components of the system.

Teng et al. (2010) described a system designed especially to be hosted in Microsoft Windows Azure [1]service. This service communicates with other PACS directly through TCP communications. In the Azure service, they hosted three components: (1) DICOM server, which acts as a normal PACS server; (2) DICOM image file indexer, that is responsible for parsing the header of the DICOM files and maintaining an index; (3) Web UI is the web-based user interface of the system, in which the user can upload, search and browse images.

Yang et al. (2010) described a medical image file accessing system (MIFAS) that uses a private cloud computing system to replace a traditional PACS solution. This solution uses the Hadoop platform to support query, storage and retrieve of medical imaging files.

Another example of the cloud used as a storage facility, with numerous advantages for the healthcare provision service is presented by Hsieh and Hsu (2012), in which the Microsoft Azure platform is used to store electrocardiograms from multiple sources, availing ubiquitous access to them.

Cloud for Bridge of Communication

Many healthcare processes involve shared provision of services. For instance, some healthcare centres have only a few modalities (i.e., medical imaging acquisition devices). Therefore, sometimes the patient needs to visit multiple institutions in order to undergo the required exams, as well as the natural mobility of patients from one institution to another for several situations and reasons. Previous scenarios cause dispersion of patient data, making it very difficult to access in an integrated way. This is particularly critical for physicians that usually need to have access to patient's data stored in several institutions.

This inter-institutional collaboration is, not only related to disassociated institutions that share an interest in providing better health care services, but also to federations of small imaging centres or even a PACS at a regional level, that merges the information from institutions in a geographical area.

In this context, using the cloud to support a centralized multi-institutional repository, or promote remote access to medical imaging data is a promising scenario. In the last case, the infrastructure is maintained inside the institutions, as in the current traditional system, and the cloud service is used as a bridge between the user that needs to access the data and the PACS.

Commonly, healthcare institutions are protected by firewalls with restrictive rules, in order to protect medical data, allowing only the traffic of "well-behaved" protocols, such as HTTP or HTTPS. Although these restrictions are needed, they may also block communications of licit applications. For instance, typical TCP ports needed by the DICOM communication protocol are usually blocked. Moreover, even some kinds of messages from "well-behaved" protocols are blocked. Some firewalls block HTTP requests from the institution's outside to the inside. These restrictions hinder the communication between institutions, but without firewall configurations, the level of security of the institution's network would decrease.

---

[1] http://www.microsoft.com/azure/.

One of the solutions to promote collaboration between institutions, by easing the communication process (without lowering the security level), is the creation of a service that acts as a bridge between institutions. This service would be responsible for receiving Web 2.0 compliant messages sent by the institutions, and delivering them to the right destination. Hosting such a service in a cloud would bring several benefits, for instance:

- The scalability provided by cloud providers is a great advantage in a service responsible for delivering messages, since it has to be prepared to deal with peaks of message traffic. In this way, the bridge hosted on the cloud would be able to grow and decrease according to needs.
- In some countries, legal issues oblige the storage of medical imaging data inside medical institutions. Nevertheless, by using a cloud service to act as a bridge, it is possible to integrate multiple data sources in real-time. Data would be accessible from anywhere and, at the same time, the security level of the institution's network would not be changed.

There are already some implementations of such services. Viana-Ferreira et al. (2012b) describe a relay service developed for Google App Engine[2] that allows the query and transference of images between the peers that are connected with the relay service. It uses a proprietary message protocol that allows more complex searches than the traditional PACS queries. Silva et al. (2013b) describe another relay service that acts as bridge of DICOM messages between institutions.

A Single Repository for a Federation of Clinics

In previous work, we developed a system capable of supporting medical imaging services for a federation of two clinics (Silva et al., 2013a). In this federation, each clinic had image acquisition equipment and all studies should be accessible from any clinic. Nevertheless, the images are stored only in one of the clinics. This means that when a study is created, it must be sent to the clinic with the storage infrastructure. Daily, both clinics create about 250 studies of three distinct modalities: Computer Tomography (CT), Ultrasound (US) and Computer Radiology (CR).

The main difficulties with this scenario were related to the Internet connection of the clinics, because they were simply domestic connections with no more than 12 megabit per second upstream bandwidth and 100 megabit per second of downstream bandwidth. This brings numerous problems, such as:

- The imaging data transference between two distinct clinics was limited to 12 megabit per second, which is a very restrictive transference speed, taking into account the size of the studies that can reach a size greater than 150 megabytes.
- As most domestic Internet connections, sometimes the Internet connections of the clinics become unstable which conditions the quality or, in worst cases, the

---

[2] https://appengine.google.com/

availability of the system, since with nothing else but one repository, the clinic with no repository when the Internet connection fails would not have access to the studies.

This is a real scenario in which cloud technology can be used as an intermediary, in benefit of: (1) availability, since there are public cloud services with more than 99.99% of availability and (2) quality of service of the system because, with no intermediary, the system is only able to transfer at 12 megabit per second (in the best thinkable scenario), even though the clinics have a contract with a downstream bandwidth of 100 megabits per second.

CHALLENGES

Although cloud computing has potential to revolutionize how medical imaging services are provided with numerous advantages, some challenges have hindering the use of cloud as supporting technology of such services.

The Impact of the Communication Latency

For the sake of healthcare service's quality, it is important to maintain medical imaging data with high availability, keeping the time needed to access the images, as short as possible. This length of time, also known as latency, may have a severe impact in some institution's workflow, especially, in those institutions whose quality of service depends on how fast the service is granted. This is one of the main issues of using public cloud services to support medical imaging.

The main reason for this to happen is related with the geographical location of the communications equipment: the cloud services may be hosted at, virtually, any part of the world. On the other hand, in a typical current approach, most communications are only among equipment in the same intra-network associated with a high performance IT infrastructure. Therefore, the communications in a typical current approach are more likely to be quicker than the ones supported by public cloud services (Philbin et al., 2011).

This problem is critically aggravated with the typical data profile of medical imaging, since in this scenario files can reach sizes of hundreds of megabytes. This means that image retrieval from a public cloud service is a task that can last for several minutes, which is much more than physicians are willing to wait to access such files.

It is necessary to create mechanisms to decrease the communications latency. Nevertheless, at the some point, decrease even further the latency may become technologically unfeasible, so the goal must be also to decrease the impact of communications latency.

Keeping the Service Always Available

Another problem related to cloud computing services usage is concerned with the availability of cloud computing services. Theoretically, the architecture of cloud computing services gives them a significant level of resiliency and availability. In practice, although they are actually capable of being running most of the time, even the greatest cloud computing service providers have their services sometimes unavailable (Cachin et al., 2009). As such, relying in a cloud computing service may cause temporarily unavailability of the system. This can bring some problems, since it is desirable that one system, which human lives may depend on, is available at all times.

Another cause of the unavailability problem is concerned with the Internet access of the institution. As previously mentioned, usually the storage facilities are placed in the institutions indoors. Nevertheless, moving them to public cloud services makes data only accessible with an Internet connection. In this way, the Internet connection of an institution can be a point of failure of the system.

Data Security

Since medical imaging data is a very critical, requiring the assurance of the patient privacy (Cao et al., 2009; Shini et al., 2012), one of the main problems of using the cloud for medical imaging purposes is about the data privacy. Using public cloud computing services, we are using the Internet as communication platform and, at the same time, we are storing the data in a third-party infrastructure. Therefore, it is important, not only to take into account the security of the communications, but also to avoid the access of the third-parties into the medical data.

We might say that this problem has a trivial solution: send and store the data encrypted. Actually, the solution passes through the storage of the data in an encrypted form. Nevertheless, the system must allow the lookup of the data that became more difficult when the data is encrypted.

A similar problem was faced by the Peer-to-Peer (P2P) file sharing communities. The P2P networks and their members were sued for sharing intellectual property. As such, Freenet[3] appeared.

It has a decentralized topology, in which each peer avails some storage capacity that is used by the system to store encrypted parts of a file, in such a way that the user does not know what he/she is sharing, so they cannot be sued for sharing it.

Actually, storing encrypted data in a cloud service may not solve all problems of data privacy. This is because security, as we know it today, is settled in assumptions like the computational power of today's computers. Therefore, it is not possible to guarantee that if the cloud service provider captures the data stored in its service, it will not be able to decrypt it in some point in the future.

Besides privacy, there are other fields inside the security problems: integrity of data and access control (authenticity). A system that handles with such critical data, as medical imaging, cannot afford to make assumptions about the security of the cloud services' security. As such, mechanisms must be developed so, not only the integrity of the data, but also the control of who has access to data are assured.

---

[3] https://freenetproject.org/

Alternatives for the Pushing of Data into the Cloud

Until now, the goals were described as if institutions would agree with pushing all the imaging data into the cloud. Nevertheless, for practical and legal reasons, it may be difficult at some point, for instance:

- When an institution with 10 years of imaging data wants to join the system, it would represent the upload into the cloud service of dozens of Terabytes, which could take a significant amount of time until the system is fully deployed.
- When an institution already has the IT infrastructure needed to support all its needs, it may have no sense wasting that infrastructure and replace it by the cloud computing service infrastructure.

As such, it could be wise thinking about alternatives for the storage of medical imaging data in the cloud.

Data Migration

Storing data in public cloud computing services may bring some problems and challenges that need to be solved. One of them is the possibility of the service becoming permanently unavailable.

Another problem associated with the migration of data is concerned with the possible need to migrate the data from one service to another, for instance, if one cloud service becomes cheaper than the currently used ones. One problem of the cloud computing services is about the lack of interoperability mechanisms between different cloud services. As such, transferring data from one service to another may become a non-trivial task.

A POSSIBLE SYSTEM ARCHITECTURE

Even with the numerous challenges and adversities for the usage of cloud services to support medical imaging services, cloud is still an advantageous technology to support such services. Our experience in developing systems for medical collaboration and outsourcing (Costa et al., 2009; Costa et al., 2011; Monteiro et al., 2012; Silva et al., 2010; Silva et al., 2012a; Silva et al., 2012b; Valente et al., 2012; Viana-Ferreira et al., 2012a; Viana-Ferreira et al., 2012b) have led us to an architecture (shown in figure 3) that explores some solutions to the described challenge. This architecture has four key components: (1) the main cloud service; (2) the redundancy services; (3) the security server and (4) the gateway.

Security Server

The greatest public cloud services providers are known as honest but curious. This means that we can trust the services in terms of not intending to damage the system.

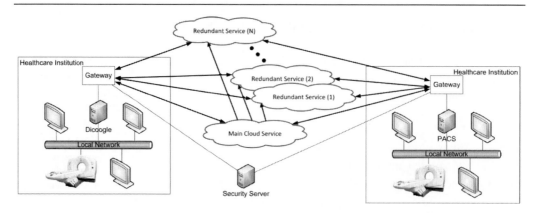

Figure 3. Diagram of the system architecture.

But, at the same time, they are curious because they want to have access to as much data as they can (Li et al., 2011). Taking into account the privacy needs of medical data, it is needed to send only to the cloud, data in an encrypted form, without giving to the cloud services the ability to decrypt the data.

Data is always sent in an encrypted form to the cloud services, in order to maintain data privacy. Nevertheless, aiming to make different institutions able to store data in the cloud and access it. It becomes clear the need to have a service accessible by all participants of the system that stores and provide the encryption/decryption parameters of the data stored in the cloud. This service is provided by the security server that must be hosted in a trustworthy server.

Gateway

One of the issues took into account, when designing this architecture, was related to its universality. Due to some characteristics of most healthcare institutions, it was needed to choose a communication protocol that would be supported by most institutions' networks. Moreover, this protocol should be also supported by public cloud services. In this way, HTTP and HTTPS were selected as the communication protocol between healthcare institutions and public cloud services. Nevertheless, as previously mentioned, inside a healthcare institution the most commonly used communication protocol is the DICOM communication layer. For this reason, a gateway is needed to translate between HTTP(S) and DICOM. Besides this translation, the gateway is also responsible for data compression/decompression. This mechanism reduces the latency of communication, since the length of messages is decreased.

Another mechanism of this component is the encryption and decryption of messages that are sent to and received from the cloud, respectively. For that, this component passes through an authentication procedure with the security server, and as a result, the gateway receives the encryption/decryption parameters. So that only legit gateways have access to the data stored in the cloud. A characteristic of this mechanism is the ability of the gateways to communicate with the cloud services, encrypting and decrypting data. To minimize a hypothetical problem of temporarily unavailability of the security server this authentication process is only needed when the gateway joins the system.

A vital mechanism to reduce the impact of communication latency is a cache mechanism that is embedded in the gateway. It is a small repository that is able to temporarily store medical imaging data for further usage.

In order to efficiently use the cache storage capacity, it is needed to wisely choose the population and eviction policies, since the cache is as efficient as its capability of having the needed data. For that reason, the gateway is endowed with a pattern recognition component that is responsible for predicting which medical images will be soon needed from those who are not. This involves not only data that is already stored in the cache, but also data that, in case of being needed, must be pre-fetched.

The pattern recognition component cannot act without data about the current context. Thus, the gateway is endowed with sensors that obtain relevant data about the context such as characteristics of the last DICOM requests, communication latency, and patient appointments.

The sensor that is responsible to measure the communication latency between the gateway and the distinct services (i.e., main cloud service and redundant services) also collaborates with important data that is used to choose which service to contact in order to obtain the data, in case the needed study is present in more than one service.

Main Cloud Service

The main cloud service is the component responsible for data storage and search mechanisms. Therefore, the main functionality of this component is to receive medical imaging studies and store them in its infrastructure. Nevertheless, ethically and legally, the cloud service provider should not be allowed, under any circumstances, to access medical imaging data. For this reason, it is not an easy task to develop a service in the cloud for data storage and search.

A traditional PACS solution gets the information about the studies from the DICOM file fields. With that information, the PACS server populates a relation database that is used for searching DICOM files based on attributes such as patient ID, modality or study date. To support this kind of search in a cloud environment, we also need to have a database with this kind of information, the challenge here is to support file searching and, at the same time, not have that kind of information in the cloud. One solution to that problem consists of using an encryption schema that allows the comparison of ciphered words, allowing us to populate the cloud database with ciphered fields, instead of the real words. Therefore, it is necessary to cipher the data using a symmetric key encryption. In this way, if the different users have access to the encryption parameters, such as the key and initialization vector, the result of ciphering the same word will be equally independent of the user who is ciphering the word. There are already some implementations of this kind of databases, like the one published in (Ribeiro, 2013).

Since the keys are shared by the security server, the already authenticated users have access to the encryption keys and send the query with the encrypted fields. Afterwards, the cloud sends, in return, the results of the search without access to the data. Nevertheless, this strategy uses symmetric encryption, which means that the keys must be shared among the users of the system, in this case, through the security server.

Another function of the main cloud service is to manage the redundancy services, either in terms of instantiation, or in terms of population. The idea is to send the images that are more likely to be requested to the redundancy services.

Redundancy Services

The redundancy services are services very similar to the main cloud service, the difference is that they have the components that are responsible for the instantiation of new redundancy services and their population deactivated. They are only activated if for any reason, the main cloud service becomes unavailable, in this way, the overall system is functional, even if the main cloud service is unavailable. In this way, the system becomes independent from a specific cloud service provider. Another advantage of this strategy is about the efficiency of the system. Although theoretically cloud services have unlimited capabilities, the quality of service is variable accordingly to the usage of the cloud service in certain time of the day. For this reason, sometimes they are overloaded and then the quality of the service becomes lower. With multiple cloud services, it is possible to redirect the requests through the distinct redundant services, avoiding those with a lower quality of service in the moment.

The downside of this strategy is the increase of maintenance costs. Even though, there are strategies that can be used to work around this problem, for instance, the redundant services may have only a partial replica of the data stored in the main cloud service.

CONCLUSION

Medical imaging can significantly benefit from cloud services, not only for promotion of inter-institutional collaboration, but also as outsourcing of IT infrastructure and to improve the performance of remote access of medical imaging repositories with limited Internet connection bandwidth. Nevertheless, for that to happen, some challenges must be overcome, such as communication latency, service availability, data security, data migration and allowance of the cooperation between institutions that are willing to send the images to the cloud and those who rather store the images in their own infrastructures.

The proposed system architecture intends to solve or minimize the following problems:

- Compression algorithms, cache mechanisms, replication and load balancing to minimize the communication latency impact on the system performance;
- The service replication and cache in the gateway to maximize the system availability;
- Data security is assured with encryption algorithms, authentication procedures, a trustworthy server and encrypted databases;
- The services in the cloud may be designed to act as hybrids storing the data and/or acting as bridge of communications between institutions in order to solve legal or feasibility issues that prevent institutions from storing data in the cloud;
- Creating mechanisms of self population of redundant services, also prepares the system for a possible need to migrate from one cloud service to another.

ACKNOWLEDGMENTS

This work has received support from the EU/EFPIA Innovative Medicines Initiative Joint Undertaking (EMIF grant n. 115372). Carlos Viana-Ferreira is funded by the FCT grant SFRH/BD/68280/2010.

REFERENCES

Abadi, D.J. (2009) 'Data Management in the Cloud: Limitations and Opportunities', *IEEE Data Engineering Bulletin*, vol. 32, no. 1, pp. 3-12.

ACR-NEMA (2011), *Digital Imaging and Communications in Medicine (DICOM)*, Rosslyn, VA: National Electrical Manufacturers Association.

Bui, A.A.T., Morioka, C., Dionisio, J.D.N., Johnson, D.B., Sinha, U., Ardekani, S., Taira, R.K., Aberle, D.R., El-Saden, S. and Kangarloo, H. (2007) 'Open Source PACS: An Extensible Infrastructure for Medical Image Management', *IEEE Transactions on Information Technology in Biomedicine*, vol. 11, no. 1, pp.94-109.

Cachin, C., Keidar, I. and Shraer, A. (2009) 'Trusting the cloud'. *ACM SIGACT News, vol.* 40, no. 2, pp. 81-86.

Cao, F., Huang, H. and Zhou, X. (2003) 'Medical image security in a HIPAA mandated PACS environment', *Computerized Medical Imaging and Graphics*, vol. 27, no. 2, pp. 185-196.

Costa C., Freitas F., Pereira M., Silva A. and Oliveira J.L. (2009) 'Indexing and retrieving DICOM data in disperse and unstructured archives', *International Journal of Computer Assisted Radiology and Surgery*, vol. 4, no. 1, pp. 71-77.

Costa C., Ferreira C., Bastião L., Ribeiro L., Silva A. and Oliveira J. (2011) 'Dicoogle - an Open Source Peer-to-Peer PACS', *Journal of Digital Imaging*, vol. 24, no. 5, pp. 848-56.

Fox, A., Griffith, R., Joseph A., Katz, R., Konwinski, A., Lee, G., Patterson, D. Rabkin, A. and Stoica, I. (2009) 'Above the clouds: A Berkeley view of cloud computing', *Dept Electrical Eng and Comput Sciences, University of California, Berkeley, Rep UCB/EEC*, vol. 28.

Hsieh J. C. and Hsu M. W. (2012) 'A cloud computing based 12-lead ECG telemedicine service', *BMC Medical Informatics and Decision Making*, vol. 12, no. 1, pp.1-12.

Huang, H. (2011) *PACS and imaging informatics: basic principles and applications,* 2nd edition. New Jersey, USA: Wiley-Blackwell.

Ishikawa, H., Kim, J., Friberg, T.R., Wollstein, G., Kagemann, L., Gabriele, M.L., Townsend, K.A., Sung, K. R., Duker, J.S., Fujimoto, J.G. and Schuman J.S. (2009), 'Three-dimensional optical coherence tomography (3D-OCT) image enhancement with segmentation-free contour modeling C-mode', *Investigative ophthalmology & visual science*, vol. 50, no.3, March, pp. 1344-1349.

Li, M., Shucheng, Y., Ning, C. and Wenjing, L. (2011) 'Authorized Private Keyword Search over Encrypted Data in Cloud Computing'. *31st International Conference on Distributed Computing Systems (ICDCS)*.

Monteiro, E.J.M., Silva, L.A.B. and Costa, C. (2012) 'CloudMed: Promoting telemedicine processes over the cloud', *7th Iberian Conference on Information Systems and Technologies (CISTI)*, Madrid.

Philbin, J., Prior, F. and Nagy P. (2011) 'Will the Next Generation of PACS Be Sitting on a Cloud?', *Journal of Digital Imaging*, vol. 24, no. 2, pp.179-83.

Pianykh, O.S. (2012) *Digital imaging and communications in medicine (DICOM)*, 2nd edition, Berlin: Springer.

Rengier, F., Mehndiratta, A., Tengg-Kobligk, H., Zechmann, C.M., Unterhinninghofen, R., Kauczor, H.U. and Giesel F.L. (2010) '3D printing based on imaging data: review of medical applications', *International Journal of Computer Assisted Radiology and Surgery*, vol. 5, no. 4, pp. 335-341.

Ribeiro, L.S., Costa, C. and Oliveira, J.L. (2010) 'A proxy of DICOM services', *Medical Imaging 2010: Advanced PACS-based Imaging Informatics and Therapeutic*, vol. 7628.

Ribeiro, L. (2013) *Posterior Playfair Searchable Encryption (PPSE)*, [Online], Available: https://github.com/bioinformatics-ua/PPSE [30 September 2013].

Shini, S.G., Thomas, T. and Chithraranjan, K. (2012) 'Cloud Based Medical Image Exchange-Security Challenges', *Procedia Engineering*, vol. 38, pp. 3454-3461.

Silva, L.B., Costa, C., Silva, A. and Oliveira, J.L. (2011) 'A PACS Gateway to the Cloud', *6th Iberian Conference on Information Systems and Technologies (CISTI)*, Chaves.

Silva, L.B., Costa, C. and Oliveira, J.L. (2012) 'A PACS archive architecture supported on cloud services', *International Journal of Computer Assisted Radiology and Surgery*, vol. 7, no. 3, pp.349-58.

Silva, L.B., Costa, C. and Oliveira, J.L. (2013a) 'An agile framework to support distributed medical imaging scenarios', *IEEE International Conference on Healthcare Informatics 2013 (ICHI 2013)*.

Silva, L.B., Costa, C. and Oliveira, J.L. (2013b) 'DICOM relay over the cloud', *International Journal Computer Assisted Radiology and Surgery*, vol. 8, no. 3, pp.323-33.

Sylva, P. (2010) 'A Situation Analysis on PACS prospects for a Developing Nation', *Sri Lanka Journal of Bio-Medical Informatics*, vol. 1, no. 2, pp.112-117.

Teng, C.-C., Mitchell, J., Walker, C., Swan, A., Davila, C., Howard, D. and Needham, T. (2010) 'A medical image archive solution in the cloud'. *IEEE International Conference on Software Engineering and Service Sciences (ICSESS)*, Provo, UT, USA: IEEE.

Valente, F., Viana-Ferreira, C., Costa, C. and Oliveira, J.L. (2012) 'A RESTful Image Gateway for Multiple Medical Image Repositories', *IEEE Transactions on Information Technology in Biomedicine*, vol. 16, no. 3, pp.356-364.

Viana-Ferreira, C., Ferreira, D., Valente, F., Monteiro, E., Costa, C. and Oliveira, J. (2012a) 'Dicoogle Mobile: a medical imaging platform for Android', *Studies in health technology and informatics*, pp. 180:502.

Viana-Ferreira, C., Costa, C. and Oliveira, J.L. (2012b) 'Dicoogle relay - a cloud communications bridge for medical imaging', *25th International Symposium on Computer-Based Medical Systems (CBMS)*, Rome, pp. 1-6.

Yang, C-T, Chen, L.-T., Chou, W.-L. and Wang, K.-C. (2010) 'Implementation of a Medical Image File Accessing System on Cloud Computing', *IEEE 13th International Conference on Computational Science and Engineering (CSE)*, pp.321-326.

In: Advances in Cloud Computing Research   ISBN: 978-1-63117-192-5
Editor: Muthu Ramachandran   © 2014 Nova Science Publishers, Inc.

Chapter 2

CLOUD COMPUTING IN BUSINESS

Dragan S. Markovic[1], Irina Branovic[2], Ranko Popovic[2], Dejan Zivkovic[1] and Violeta Tomasevic[1]*

[1]Faculty of Informatics and Computing,
Singidunum University, Belgrade, Serbia
[2]IEEE Member

ABSTRACT

Cloud Computing as an emerging model for delivering information technology services will most likely have major impact in ICT in the years to come. This research looks at the phenomenon of cloud computing from the business viewpoint; we classify common business models applied in cloud computing, discuss major advantages and drawbacks of cloud, and argue whether enterprise management is fully aware of what cloud computing actually is and what measurable benefits it can bring. Further, we present the state of the art in the area of cloud integration in business, and discuss ways in which the development of cloud computing will promote economic growth, increase productivity, and shift the type of jobs and skills required by industry.

Keywords: Cloud computing, business models, sustainability

1. INTRODUCTION

Current convergence of information, communication, and media technology and services is at the basis of highly integrated e-infrastructure that will shape the future of the society. The future e-infrastructure will be the key platform for the development and deployment of innovative, efficient and attractive society services. The development of this infrastructure poses some important challenges. Besides network connectivity, this infrastructure should

---

* Corresponding Author: email: dsamarkovic@singidunum.ac.rs.

also include basic application services. The successful development of this e-infrastructure must bring together public and private interests, complex coordination and governance issues.

For many companies, technology is taking on a new role—as a driver of revenue and enabler of new business models. Inevitably, mobile devices, social networking, cloud computing, and other progressive technologies are profoundly transforming the relationships between businesses and their customers. Industrial society of the past two centuries is shaping into an information society. The transformation to the so-called digital economy keeps gathering speed, as we transition from the *connected* economy of PCs, browsers and web servers to our increasingly *hyper connected* economy of smart mobile devices, cloud computing and broadband wireless networks.

Cloud computing is a technology whereby computing is delivered as a service over the Internet, meaning that data and applications do not need to be located on the user's machine or even the company's local servers. Instead, data and applications are located on a cloud computing vendor's servers and delivered to the enterprise as and when required. Also, any member of staff is able to access organization's data and applications from any Internet-connected computer. There are numerous benefits that this model brings to the system, but one of the most touted is the ability pay for server and infrastructure capacity as and when it is needed.

Cloud computing has recently received considerable attention in industrial community, driven by idea that users in industry can access cloud computing resources anytime, anywhere, on-demand. It remains a big IT trend, keeping the readership interest high since its beginnings. As a leading part of ICT, it now has the opportunity to make further significant productivity improvements, helping us transform the world to a more sustainable and more resource-efficient future. Development of cloud technology also calls for regulatory frameworks covering issues such as ownership of personal data, open standards, intellectual property rights, and competitiveness in the market.

We have several objectives in this review. Section 2 summarizes Cloud computing, and discusses possible models of implementations of cloud services in business. Section 3 introduces various prospectives of cloud integration in business that must be considered. Focuses of this section are economics of cloud computing, its social repercussions, energy efficiency, as well as the new management challenges introduced through adoption of this new model. The final, seventh section is devoted to a review of the state-of-the-art in cloud integration in the business world.

2. CLOUD COMPUTING

Cloud computing describes a broad movement toward the use of wide area networks, such as the Internet, to enable interaction between IT service providers of many types and consumers. Service providers are expanding their available offerings to include the entire traditional IT stack, from hardware and platforms to application components, software services, to whole applications [1].

The term "cloud" is used as a representation of the Internet and other communications systems as well as an abstraction of the underlying infrastructures involved. What we now commonly refer to as cloud computing is the result of an evolution of the widespread adoption of virtualization, service-oriented architecture, autonomic, and utility computing. Most end-users no longer need to thoroughly understand or control the technology infrastructure that supports their computing activities. In brief, economic rationale in cloud computing is equally important as its success in overcoming technical limitations.

Definition of cloud computing proposed by the National Institute of Standards and Technology (NIST) has gained fairly broad acceptance [2]. NIST defines cloud computing as a model for enabling convenient, on-demand network access to a shared pool of configurable computing resources (e.g., networks, servers, storage, applications, and services) that can be rapidly provisioned and released with minimal management effort or service provider interaction. The NIST definition of cloud computing includes five essential characteristics:

- *on-demand self-service* (users can subscribe directly to gain online access to cloud services)
- *broad network access* (users can access cloud services anywhere and anytime on the Internet)
- *resource pooling* (the infrastructure used to provide cloud services is pooled as a shared resource)
- *rapid elasticity* (services can be scaled up or down in response to the user's changing capacity needs)
- *measured service* (users pay only for what they use, which is tracked through metering systems)

Two items which are not specified as requirements in the NIST definition - virtualization and multi-tenancy - are likely to be commonplace in cloud computing. Virtualization is the technology that hides the physical characteristics of a computing platform from the users, instead presenting an abstract, emulated computing platform [3]. This emulated computing platform for all practical purposes behaves like an independent system, but unlike a physical system, can be configured on demand, and maintained and replicated very easily. A related concept is that of multitenancy, whereby a single instance of application software serves multiple clients. This allows better utilization of a system's resources (in terms of memory and processing overhead), whose requirements could otherwise be considerable if the software instance had to be duplicated for individual clients.

In a simple, topological sense, a cloud computing solution is made up of several elements: clients, the datacenter, and distributed servers. Each element has a purpose and plays a specific role in delivering a functional cloud-based application [4]. Clients in cloud computing are typically desk computers; generally, clients are devices that the end users interact with to manage their information on the cloud.

The datacenter is the collection of servers where the application to which clients subscribe is housed. It can reside locally, but can also be on the other side of the world and accessed via the Internet. A growing trend in the IT world is server virtualization, when software is installed on multiple instances of virtual servers running on one physical server.

In practice, the servers are not housed in the same location, but instead are distributed in geographically disparate locations. But to cloud subscriber, these servers seem to reside right next to each other. This approach gives the service provider more flexibility in options and security.

2.1. Cloud Services

Cloud computing is the ultimate frontier of various technologies such as grid computing, distributed computing, and Service-oriented Architecture (SOA) [5]. Cloud computing involves three types of stakeholders i.e., providers, adopters, and users. Providers are the IT industries that provide the facility of cloud services to the adopters, i.e., business organizations. The users are involved in the use of provided services. Nowadays, cloud computing mainly provides three types of services to clients: Software as a Service (SaaS), Platform as a Service (PaaS), and Infrastructure as a Service (IaaS). At the moment, SaaS is the most popular model [6].

2.1.1. Software-as-a-Service (SaaS)

Refers to on-demand use of the software over the Internet. Applications are provided as a service from the cloud, with end-user licenses procured or "released" in line with changing demand. Businesses are moving steadily towards this model, shifting from licensing software to subscribing to services, typically on per-user, per-month basis.

Typically, software that performs a simple task without much need to interact with other systems makes them ideal candidates for SaaS model. Customers who are not inclined to perform software development, but have need of high-powered applications can also benefit from SaaS. Some of typical business applications suitable for SaaS model are:

- Customer resource management
- Video conferencing
- IT service management
- Accounting
- Web analytics
- Web content management

SaaS applications differ from earlier distributed computing solutions in that SaaS software is natively Web based and aimed at using web tools, like the browser. It was also built with a multitenant back end in mind, which enables multiple customers to use single application. On the other hand, there are certain cases when SaaS is not the most appropriate approach, such as:

- Applications where extremely fast processing of real time data is required
- Applications where legislation or other regulation does not permit data being hosted externally
- Applications where an existing on-premise solution fulfills all of the organization's needs.

According to a recent Gartner report [7], three most popular SaaS solutions deployed are Customer Relations Management (49%), Enterprise Content Management (37%), and Digital Content Creation (35%). The three most-replaced on-premise applications are Supply Chain Management (35%), Web Conferencing, teaming platforms and social software suites (34%), as well as Project & Portfolio Management (33%).

2.1.2. Platform-as-a-Service (PaaS)

Refers to tools and environments to build and manage cloud applications and services. Includes platform software services (such as web, application, database servers, enterprise service buses and other middleware, with associated security mechanisms) on which web service-based applications can be built.

In PaaS model, cloud serves as a platform for the creation of software, delivered over the web. PaaS supplies all the resources required to build applications and services completely from the Internet, without having to download or install software. PaaS services include application design, development, testing, deployment, and hosting. Other services include team collaboration, web service integration, database integration, security, scalability, storage, state management, and versioning [4].

PaaS is especially useful in situations where multiple developers are working on a development project or where other external parties need to interact with the development process. Also, it has proven invaluable when companies with existing data sources, for example sales information from a customer relationship management tool, want to create applications which leverage that data. Finally, PaaS is useful for automating testing and deployment services.

On the downside, there are certain situations where PaaS may not be ideal:

- Application that must be highly portable in terms of hosting
- In cases where proprietary languages or approaches would impact the development process
- When proprietary language would hinder later moves to another provider – concerns are raised about vendor lock-in
- Where application performance requires customization of the underlying hardware and software

Popular public PaaS solutions include Heroku, Engine Yard, Windows Azure, Google App Engine, Force.com, CloudFoundry, CloudForge, AppFog, Cloudbees and others.

2.1.3. Infrastructure-as-a-Service (IaaS)

Refers to storage and/or computing resources as a service, implemented as virtual machine services accessed over the network. It is sometimes also referred to as hardware as a service (HaaS). IaaS cloud model allows renting resources such as server space, network equipment, memory, CPU cycles, storage space. Conceptually, this model provides a standardized virtual server. The consumer takes responsibility for configuration and operations of the guest operating system, software, and database.

IaaS makes sense in following situations:

- Where demand is very volatile – any time there are significant spikes and troughs in terms of demand on the infrastructure
- For new organizations without the capital to invest in hardware
- Where the organization is growing rapidly and scaling hardware would be problematic

- Where there is pressure on the organization to limit capital expenditure and to move to operating expenditure
- For specific line of business, trial or temporary infrastructural needs.

Examples of situations where caution with regards IaaS is advised include:

- When regulatory compliance makes the offshoring or outsourcing of data storage and processing difficult
- When the highest levels of performance are required, and on-premise or dedicated hosted infrastructure has the capacity to meet the business needs.

Popular IaaS solutions include Amazon EC2, Rackspace, Windows Azure, Joyent, BlueLock, OpenStack and many others.

2.2. Cloud Business Models Revisited

Cloud computing represents a set of approaches that enable organizations to quickly and effectively engage and free up resources in real-time. Unlike other approaches, cloud computing is both a business model and technology. In terms of the economic environment, from the perspective of users services, cloud computing is a new business and economic model, whereas for the service provider this concept is a technology. On the opposed sides there are cloud providers, motivated by profit that can be achieved offering these types of services, and users - companies, attracted with the possibility to reduce costs.

While cloud computing makes sense for some areas of company business, it usually cannot be applied across all of company IT infrastructure. Although many managers and IT executives understand the general benefits of cloud computing at this stage, they need to take a closer look at their specific business needs, coupled with their existing IT infrastructure and make an assessment about what makes sense for the company. For each application or business service, it is always necessary to create a business case that evaluates and justifies the migration to cloud, and then to review it throughout the lifetime of the service. It is also important to note that the achievable benefits vary for each application or business service that is being migrated to the cloud, depending on several factors: the size of the service and its efficiency, the cloud variant being migrated to, and the nature of the business itself.

Companies perform by achieving their goals and satisfying customers. Common questions that managers are facing in their quest to improve business performance are [8]:

- How well do we perform?
- What is the efficiency and effectiveness of our operations in meeting business objectives and satisfying customers?
- How do we compare with our competitors?
- What can we do to improve the performance of our business?
- How can we monitor progress and recognize the areas of strong or poor performance?

Overall business performance depends on the effective allocation and use of resources in order to produce some level of output with the least cost and with the desired quality. Traditionally, business performance is measured by money and expressed by numerous financial ratios, but the essential business performance indicator is profitability.

Business agility is the ability of a business to adapt rapidly and cost-efficiently in response to changes in the business environment; the benefits of agility include faster revenue growth, greater and more lasting cost reduction, and more effective management of risks and reputational threats [9]. Forward-thinking CIOs are deploying cloud computing as a strategic weapon—not just for IT, but to enable full business transformation, eventually changing how they operate their business.

Summarizing existing cloud services, Weihardt et al. proposed a holistic business model framework [10]. The Cloud Business Model Framework is mainly categorized in three layers, analogously to the technical layers in Cloud services, such as the IaaS, PaaS and SaaS application layer on top.

In CBMF model, the infrastructure layer comprehends business lifecycle from development to productive provisioning, while the application layer is what most people get to know from Cloud Computing as it represents the actual interface for the customer.

Paper [11] investigates business models empowered by Cloud technologies and concludes that the amount of investment in cloud services is still more than the profits received from these investments. This illustrates the importance of classifying the right business strategies and models for long-term sustainability.

The Cloud Cube Model (CCM) proposed by The Jericho Forum (JF) is used to enable secure collaboration in the appropriate cloud formations best suited to the business needs [12]. The JF points out that many cloud service providers claim themselves to be able to deliver solutions, so cloud customers need selecting the right formation within CCM suiting their needs. Within CCM, four distinct dimensions are identified (Figure 3). They are:

- External and Internal (internal means private clouds, and external means public clouds).
- Proprietary and Open (Proprietary means paid services or contractors. Open stands for open source services or solutions)
- Perimeterised and De-Perimeterised (Perimetrized means IaaS or Paas, while De-Perimetrized means SaaS)
- Insourced and Outsourced (Insourced means in-house development of clouds. Outsourced refers to letting contractors or service providers handle all requests; most of cloud business models fall into this).

For example, a typical Enterprise Cloud model would take on all parts of the CCM; it has areas overlapped with both outsourced and in-house options, which is introduced as a dark purple color. Therefore, all parts of CCM are in light purple colors except for internal clouds, which has joint characteristic of outsourcing and in-house development and is in dark purple color (left cube in Figure 1). On the contrary, entertainment and social networking focus on SaaS, who are typically proprietary and outsourced solutions. Therefore, in this case occupies only outsourced parts (in light purple) within the cube are occupied in CCM (right part in Figure 1).

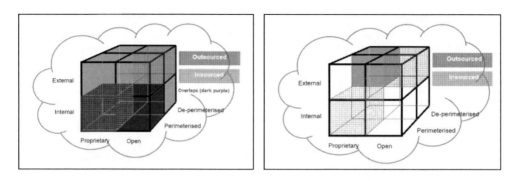

Figure 1. CCM applied to a typical Enterprise and Social Networking cloud business model [11].

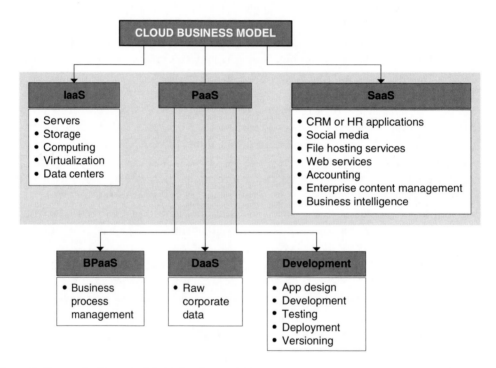

Figure 2. Current business models in cloud computing.

Summarizing existing research results, Figure 2 illustrates our view of business models in current use in cloud computing. The PaaS service is further extended with two new categories:

- *Data-as-a-Service (DaaS):* Data or information delivered from the cloud either as raw data sets or consumed through an analytics interface.
- *Business Process-as-a-Service (BPaaS):* Cloud-delivered business services that are aligned to business processes and associated measurable business outcomes.

However, naming convention has been open to abuse: vendors often append the "as-a-service" tag to any new network-based product and service, even not related to cloud or even "cloud-ready". This confusion is compounded by the same terms being used to define different elements of cloud. For example, DaaS can mean Desktop-as-a-Service as well as Data-as-a-Service. Data-as-a-Service is further confusing due to some people referencing it as Content-as-a-Service, which typically refers to media and/or social media related data, such as videos, sound files, blog posts, etc. Furthermore, Data-as-a-Service encompasses both unstructured content (i.e., Content-as-a-Service) and structured data.

Although the cloud computing architecture can be divided into layers as shown in Figure 2, same services can be deployed on different levels. For example, SaaS can be deployed directly on IaaS, instead of PaaS. Also, some services can be considered as a part of more than one layer. For example, data storage service can be viewed as either in IaaS or PaaS.

2.3. Cloud Deployment Models

Cloud providers offer different types of cloud deployment models to an organization according to their business requirements. From a business prospective, the way cloud is deployed can make a huge difference. Usually there are four different types of cloud deployment models: public, private, community, and hybrid cloud.

- *Public* model provides the highest degree of cost savings while requiring the least amount of overhead. In this model, cloud computing services are offered by vendors and are accessible over the Internet or a private network. This model uses data centers shared among multiple customers, with varying degrees of data privacy and control.
- *Private* model addresses the security and privacy concerns that are inherent in other cloud computing models. Private clouds are modeled after public models, but are managed and used internally by the company. Private clouds are popular mostly because they give businesses direct control and major confidence in data security, i.e., data is controlled within the organization.
- *Community* model is shared across organizations that have similar objectives and requirements, such as security or legal compliance. It can be managed by the member organizations or by a third party provider. Community clouds are usually setup by using public clouds to enable collaboration.
- *Hybrid* model combines advantages of the other models, and offers organizations the most flexibility. This is a mix of public cloud services, private cloud architectures, and classic IT infrastructure. For most enterprises, the hybrid cloud is the most economical model. According to recent VMware and EMC research, hybrid cloud deployment reduces typical total IT spend by approximately 20 to 30 percent [9, 13].

As cloud computing continues to gain acceptance, corporations must look at each of the existing models to determine which one best suit their specific requirements. Since no single model provides all of the advantages of cost reductions and security protection, the hybrid model is currently the most popular [14]. The question for executives becomes: Is the public cloud model safe enough to rely on or should we retrench to private cloud computing to gain safety and control? [15] The right answer to this question is to implement private cloud only when public model does not fulfill company's requirements for service levels, security, compliance etc.

2.4. Advantages and Drawbacks of Cloud Computing

Cloud computing is essentially a more efficient way to deliver and consume IT services. Its key benefits include:

- *Cost efficiency:* The benefits of the Cloud come from its economies of scale. Statistics data confirm that 80% of organizations adopting cloud computing achieve cost savings of at least 10-20% [13].
- *Smaller initial investment:* The advantages of cloud technology in this sense depend on the size of the company, and are more visible in small and medium companies. By adopting cloud, such companies get the opportunity to stand side by side with large companies, using cutting-edge technologies to achieve market competitiveness. There is no need for large initial/capital investment, and the decision to use new technologies to increase productivity in the primary business is easier
- *Reducing IT resources* (hardware, software, human): This is the case in large companies, where the reasons to use cloud computing are different. Large companies have modern information systems and their own ICT departments responsible for development, maintenance, quality, and support. Hardware and software resources are in most cases oversized, while human resources are almost always minimal.
- *Pay-per-use:* Many enterprises provision computing resources for peak loads, which often exceed average use by a factor of 2 to 10. One key benefit of cloud computing is that it spares companies from having to pay for underutilized resources. Executives often judge cloud's ability to reduce fixed IT costs and shift to a more variable "pay as you go" cost structure its top benefit [16].
- *Focus on business:* without the issues of server upgrades, hardware fixes, and similar, companies can focus more on business needs and thus improve their operational performance.
- *Enabling multiple users to collaborate on projects or documents.*

Whether or not use cloud computing in some business depends on a number of factors, including [4]:

- Cost/benefit ratio
- Speed of delivery
- How much capacity will be used
- Whether data is regulated
- Corporate and IT structure of the organization

However, on the dark side, there are some limiting factors to consider when deciding whether to use cloud computing, especially in public cloud models [18]:

- *Data security:* The distributed nature of cloud computing alters many notions about residency and ownership of data and information. In converting to cloud computing, companies are essentially handing over their data to third-party service providers, who store and process such data in the cloud [19] and whose physical location could be anywhere in the world. This could potentially be a problem. Also, the standardized interfaces of the cloud providers might not be amenable to very fine levels of security policy administration details for different users and processes, thereby increasing the risks of breach [20].

- *Absence of Service-Level Agreements:* The absence of common standards and clear contracts still keeps many potential users from adopting cloud solutions. Cloud providers and users are looking for clearer rules for delivery of cloud services, meeting legal requirements, moving data and software between different cloud providers, data security and application interoperability. There is an urgent need for the government and international agencies to be proactive in dealing with the unique challenges presented by the cloud computing environment. To avoid privacy and confidentiality risks, cloud providers should be able to adapt to different legislation, and the cloud community should define some standards for good practices, policies, and procedures.

- *Loss of control over data (data audit):* while most user companies recognize the value of being able to audit cloud computing, they have very little understanding of what should be audited [15]. Some of the largest cloud providers do not even allow their customers to conduct inspections [17].

Ultimately, the cloud is neither good nor bad: it's just a new paradigm with its own advantages and disadvantages. Over time, some of these concerns will be solved or the risks will be reduced to acceptable levels. For most organizations, the question of whether to move into the cloud will be a matter of weighing the pros and cons [18]. The adoption of cloud is therefore not just an IT issue; it is of concern to and impacts all parts of the business. Numerous commercial and regulatory considerations must also be evaluated before a cloud solution can be implemented; including the location of corporate data and the consequences it will have on legal jurisdiction and compliance. The impact on business processes and the ability of the business to react to changing market conditions after a cloud service has been implemented must also be assessed. Report [21] outlines the business benefits of cloud and highlights which particular cloud services can provide that benefit. It is important to note that the magnitude of the benefit will depend on the maturity of an IT department's outsourcing commitments.

3. CLOUD COMPUTING IN BUSINESS

3.1. Cloud Computing: Economics

To be competitive in today's tough economy climate, IT organizations need to find ways of delivering innovative business services while taking cost out of their operations. IT costs are normally categorized as operating expense and capital expense, and effective cost containment requires the right balance between the two. To reduce capital expense, many IT organizations have turned to virtualization, the ability to pool and share IT resources. Pooling resources reduces capital expense of hardware, software and facilities. Fewer infrastructures, and correspondingly, less energy are required to deliver the same quality of service.

The interoperability between clouds is important not only for the protection of the end user investments, but also for the development of the cloud ecosystem and market. The main aim of interoperability is to allow the achievement of the full advantage of the cloud properties like elasticity and pay-as-you-go, instead the exploitation of a vendor infrastructure, platform or service. Nowadays, many companies still do not tie their critical applications to specific cloud provider services due to the underlying proprietary technology [22].

Addressing standardization and virtualization is crucial to reducing infrastructure costs, while meeting the dynamic needs of the business. With increased infrastructure standardization, organizations are able to achieve greater economies of operating expense. Similarly, IT organizations that leverage virtualization within their infrastructure realize greater economies of capital expenditure. Standardization also helps vendors to provide additional higher level services like orchestration, apart from normal cloud services that are needed by the users. Standardization will thus pave the way towards realizing the true potential and benefits of cloud computing.

To meet the emerging cloud computing needs of a diversified customer base with varied workloads, applications and I/O connectivity requirements, the cloud provider's platform must be flexible. The decision to add new capacity or services depends not only on the hardware being deployed, but also on the acquisition cost. The quicker a company can recoup the capital expenditure for new hardware, the quicker they can begin the deployment for the next new service or new customer being added [19].

Implemented appropriately, the cloud computing economic model can drastically reduce the operations and maintenance cost of IT infrastructures. Research [23] concluded that a cloud computing approach could save 50 to 67% of the lifecycle cost for a 1000-server deployment.

In study [23], authors considered hosting options offered by two prominent cloud providers: Amazon and Windows Azure, including both IaaS (EC2 instances) and SaaS options (Amazon RDS and SQL Azure). They investigated the migration costs of several deployment options using popular benchmarks. Application characteristics such as workload intensity, growth rate, storage capacity and software licensing costs produce complex combined effect on overall costs, so they conclude that a complete migration to today's cloud is appealing only for small/stagnant businesses/organizations.

Although many potential benefits of migrating to the cloud can be enumerated, some benefits may not apply to a specific case in question. Also, there can be multiple ways in which an application might make use of the facilities offered by cloud providers. Answering these questions requires an in-depth understanding of the cost implications of all the possible choices specific to particular circumstances.

At the current level of cloud technology development, risks of moving to cloud are numerous and can be classified as:

- technical (migrating existing complex information systems is not automatic or easy process)

- legal and administrative (there are restrictions for some forms of business on where data can be stored and where should be available)
- economic (if not used properly, clouds can be more expensive than owning a classic Information System)
- safety and serviceability (service providers are typically protected; they pay a penalty only if the value of the service was compromised, but not if the lack of service damaged business).

All cloud service providers are not created equal. Companies as Amazon.com have an advantage in the market because they jumped in early and established dominance—especially among emerging "born on the Web companies." Even traditional businesses use Amazon.com's cloud services because of their low price. But others have opportunities to get into the act by offering more security and protection. IBM has created a cloud service that will indemnify customers against legal challenges based on service interruption. HP is the latest company to try to upend Amazon's market position by offering a similar service [24].

The politics of migrating from legacy platforms to the cloud is inherently complicated because the adoption of cloud computing affects the way many people—not just IT professionals—do their jobs. Over time, cloud computing might drastically change some roles so that they are no longer recognizable from their current form, or even potentially eliminate some jobs entirely. Thus, the human-economic implications of adopting and migrating to cloud computing platforms and processes should not be taken lightly.

Research [25] deals with the definition of key business value of cloud computing models and compares them with traditional business values on-site computing model. Key findings of the survey demonstrate that it is possible to quantify the value that the company tends to cloud computing model, and that the acceptance of cloud computing yields an increase in some critical values that are used in on-site business model. Even though the evaluation of the business model tends towards cloud computing, users still need to carefully examine certain types of cloud services before making a final decision.

However, large companies usually align their business processes with certifications for quality systems such as ISO9000, ISO27001. Consequently, respecting security policies can be crucial when deciding which services can be outsourced and which not.

According to a recent study by the London School of Economics and Political Science [26], the development of cloud computing will promote economic growth, increase productivity and shift the type of jobs and skills required by businesses. Cloud computing is likely to extend economic growth by increasing the efficiency of information technology (IT) in developed economies and could foster growth in economies where IT penetration is not yet fully mature. Cloud computing will give individuals and enterprises access to a vast processing power at a low cost that has not been possible before. In the US, researchers project that the productivity growth enabled by cloud computing will contribute almost one third of total US GDP growth in the coming decade. For developing countries, researchers expect even larger gains, because in these countries the adoption of IT is less mature: the factor share of IT capital in these countries is only 3%, as opposed to 11.7% in the developed ones [27].

3.2. Cloud: Social Implications

In the early stages of the computing evolution, IT was mainly restricted to business use. However, today's convergence of business and Internet has changed the whole computing paradigm and the way people make use of it to collaborate and communicate. Cloud Computing has already had an impact on the lifestyle of people in many important ways and interesting trends are taking shape across wide areas of society.

The most obvious example is people's use of social networking to connect, share and leverage the IT technology to enhance their life experiences. Through its different facets, Cloud Computing has enabled emergence of a number of popular platforms for various everyday life situations: file hosting services (e.g., Dropbox, Google Drive), image hosters (e.g., Flickr), video hosters (e.g., YouTube), location-based services (e.g., navigation software) and many more.

Social media such as Facebook, Twitter, LinkedIn and other virtual platforms have transformed traditional one-to-many communication models to support interactive communications. A social media user, for example, can post a message or picture and thousands of people can respond to raise a voice in reaction. This has implications not only to the quality of leisure time of people (for better or worse), but the consequences can be more serious on a global level in the form of shaping political issues or reputations of products and people.

In [28] it is emphasized another social effect of Cloud Computing through new forms of participation for civil society factors such as NGOs, journalists or individuals who benefit from the lower access hurdles to computing resources. There are already cloud solutions specifically for the target group of non-profit organizations (e.g., The Humanitarian Cloud) and NGOs have initiated their own Cloud Computing projects like The NetHope Humanitarian Cloud Services Portal [30]. This may not only help to reduce IT costs but also to ease information flows (possibly in combination with applications for mobile devices). This aspect is particularly interesting for journalists, because Cloud Computing technology has fostered the new field of data-driven journalism. With services like DocumentCloud.org, allowing for analyzing and publishing primary source documents, it is possible to combine computational resources and human expertise to support more efficient and effective investigative journalism [31].

An unsettling social consequence of Cloud Computing, as argued in [32], is that it has the potential to disrupt the IT workforce. Cloud Computing clients' data center downsizing effect has, at a first glance, the potential to eliminate the jobs of many data center workers of large and small businesses alike. The truth is, however, that some job roles will likely have reduced demand, some will have more demand, and even some new jobs will be created – both within and outside of IT. On the one hand, there will be less demand for jobs such as system administrators and database administrators. IT professionals with these skills would likely be in demand from cloud providers, rather than the companies using the system. Also, due to the ability to scale, there may be less demand overall. On the other hand, there will still be demand for IT project managers, business analysts, and software developers – companies will still need projects executed and teams will still need to be managed; companies will need software and systems that reflect their requirements and business processes; and, software will still need to be created. Of course, the knowledge of these IT professionals will need to expand and include concepts of cloud computing, but this will come with experience. Finally, new jobs will be created as a result of the new companies that will be launched to provide Cloud Computing and other related services. Also, more jobs will be moved from individual organizations into the cloud service providers. This means that new skills may be needed – so IT professionals may wish to improve their knowledge on cloud services and relationship management.

The norms and values that have been established over many years to protect assets in the physical world are not clearly established in the digital world. With Cloud Computing, we will need new rules for data and computing "everywhere all at once, and nowhere in particular" [33].

3.3. Cloud Computing: Energy Efficiency

Energy-efficiency has been widely explored for similar architectures such as Cluster and Grid Computing. However, it is still a challenging issue in the Cloud model due to the dynamicity of its components and flexibility of services supported by virtualization.

As the demand for IT products and services grows exponentially, in the US, Europe and particularly in developing economies such as India and China, so does the amount of data businesses produce globally. That information requires physical storage and access to reliable electricity. In our technologically interconnected world, data centers are the factories of the 21st Century.

Statistical data inform that nowadays 1.2 zettabytes of digital information (zettabyte =1 trillion gigabytes) is already generated by tweets, YouTube videos, Facebook status updates, iTunes downloads, emails, and other data transfers [34]. Additionally, there are five billion mobile users worldwide, and over 50 billion mobile connections are predicted by 2020 as smart meters and other smart devices are added to online networks [35].

The data centers that house this explosion of digital information currently consume more than 3%of US electricity, and approximately 1.5% to 2% of global electricity, growing at a rate of approximately 12% annually [36]. Electronic devices account for 15% of home electricity use, and are predicted to triple by 2030, equivalent to the electricity demand of the US and Japan residential market combined [37].

Clouds can be made more energy efficient through techniques such as resource virtualization and workload consolidation. Some of the techniques and information commonly investigated and applied at a macro-level or Resource Management System (RMS) level to achieve workload consolidation and energy-efficient scheduling include [39]:

- Applications workload estimation
- Relocation and live-migration of virtual machines
- Gathering precise information about server-racks, their configurations, energy consumption and thermal states
- Heat management or temperature-aware workload placement aiming for heat distribution and cooling efficiency
- Study of application dependencies and creation of performance models
- Load balancing among computing sites

Data center spaces can consume up to 100 to 200 times as much electricity as standard office spaces [40]. With such large power consumption, they are prime targets for energy-efficient design measures that can save money and reduce electricity use. However, the critical nature of data center loads elevates many design criteria, especially reliability and high power density capacity, far above energy efficiency. Many existing data centers were designed without a 'green' design brief; priorities were focused around infrastructure redundancy. By analyzing where energy is used in the facility, improvements can be targeted, most of which have short payback periods. This results in massive reductions in energy (and sometimes capital) costs, while still delivering a reliable service [41].

There are two opposing views on the energy efficiency of cloud computing. Cloud providers commissioned studies from Koomey, Pike Research, Nucleus Research, and Accenture that claim that cloud computing is more energy efficient than desktop computing. However, researchers challenged this assertion when they looked at the impact of data transport, storage and processing on the energy efficiency of cloud computing [42]. The assessment of the energy efficiency of cloud computing cannot be based only on data centers due to the importance of the intermediate communication networks that support the overall activity of providing cloud computing services and the devices used to access cloud services.

Virtualization is widely applied in modern data centers for cloud computing as a key technology to achieve energy-efficient operation of servers. Server consolidation and live migration of virtual machine are two important methods to achieve load balancing and energy savings. The technique of dynamic reallocation of virtual machines and switching off idle servers brings substantial energy savings and is applicable to real-world Cloud data centers.

Under some circumstances, cloud computing can consume more energy than conventional computing where each user performs all computing on their own PC. Even with energy-saving techniques such as server virtualization and advanced cooling systems, cloud computing is not always the greenest computing technology. For this reason, cloud computing services are offered through thin clients. Thin Computing is the use of a powerful datacenter focused strategy like Cloud Computing or Client Virtualization accessed by simpler, more energy-efficient desktop or mobile appliances, instead of a traditional PC. This proven model delivers the productivity people need, at a lower cost than traditional methods, while improving security and manageability. Research [43] indicates that replacing a PC environment with thin clients and required datacenter infrastructure can reduce energy consumption by 70 to 90%.

3.4. Mobile Cloud

Mobile Cloud Computing (MCC) provides mobile users with the data processing and storage services in clouds. The mobile devices do not need a powerful configuration (e.g., CPU speed and memory capacity) since all the complicated computing modules can be processed in the clouds. According to a recent study by ABI Research, more than 240 million businesses will use cloud services through mobile devices by 2015. Mobile cloud has additional advantages over those already mentioned, as stated in [44]:

- extending battery life of mobile devices (due to computation offloading)
- improving data storage capacity and computing power
- improving reliability (since data and application are stored and backed up on a number of computers)

Various mobile applications have already taken the advantages of MCC:

- mobile commerce (e.g., mobile transactions and payments, mobile messaging, and mobile ticketing) mobile learning (to enhance the communication quality between students and teachers)
- mobile healthcare (health monitoring, emergency management systems, pervasive access to information)
- mobile gaming.

Bandwidth is one of the big issues in MCC since the radio resource for wireless networks is much scarce as compared with the traditional wired networks. Although many researchers propose optimal and efficient ways of bandwidth allocation, the bandwidth limitation is still a big concern because the number of mobile and cloud users is dramatically increasing. Also, service availability becomes more important issue in MCC than that in the cloud computing with wired networks because mobile users may not be able to connect to the cloud to obtain service due to traffic congestion, network failures, and the out-of-signal.

4. CLOUD APPLICATIONS IN BUSINESS

Many people think of industry as the collective large-scale manufacturing of goods in well-organized plants with a high degree of automation and specialization. Although this is a common example of industry, it can also include other commercial activities that provide goods and services such as agriculture, transportation, hospitality, and many others. Industry is often classified into different categories or levels (usually three or five) for a better understanding of its different types. If a company participates in multiple business activities, it is usually considered to be in business in which most of its revenues are derived.

Businesses, educational institutions, governments, community organizations, and individuals are looking at cloud offerings to be able to focus on managing information instead of infrastructure.

There are various guides, reports and *success stories about cloud adoption and integration* in the business world [16, 38, 45]. Every type of business can benefit from cloud technology; however, the usage differs depending on respective business models. In the following we present insights on some typical cases in which cloud hosting platform has been adopted.

4.1. Healthcare

Healthcare is in a period of accelerating change that requires continual innovation. Driven by economics, emerging care and business models aligned with personal values and well-being are signaling a major shift in how healthcare organizations will compete and operate in the years ahead [45]. The benefits of cloud in healthcare are a very broad topic; looking on how cloud technologies can improve and upgrade healthcare services is a representative example of the cloud paradigm shift. The most notable benefits of cloud in this case are costs streamlining, device and location independency, and proficient information management. Relating them to the healthcare, we can summarize a safer, faster, and more efficient healthcare system. Cloud-based billing and consumer-oriented management applications provide a better access to healthcare and data, especially in the remote and emerging areas. The possibility of expanding the use of electronic health records and exchanging information across and between providers are also significant benefits. Many regions in the US and other developed countries are establishing cloud health information exchanges, where information can be easily shared between hospitals, health systems, physicians, and clinics. Although data privacy, security and safety policies are still the recurring barriers for embracing cloud computing, the cloud healthcare will become a system which will globally connect information and facts into a shared, easy-to-access world.

According to a report [46], globally 32% of the healthcare facilities are already using cloud applications and close to 75% of the organizations – which are not using any cloud applications – are considering adopting it in the next three to five years.

4.2. Education

Cloud applications will enable the educational system to *leverage the efficiency across the nations* and to create a setup where students will be able to attend the classes irrespective of the geographical location. Many universities have already started to offer virtual tuitions to students located at distant places; as the number of cloud applications widens, an improved collaboration will be possible that will further enhance knowledge sharing, and people will be able to access the latest technologies at an affordable price.

Using the power of cloud computing, Cisco Networking Academy now connects a community of 20,000 ICT educators dedicated to preparing students to become skilled professionals [47].

A large effect of Cloud Computing can be seen in science. As pointed out in [48], in any engineering lab today, instead of clumsy equipment specific to the lab's specialty, one is more likely to find racks of computers since the complexity of today's scientific and engineering problems is far beyond the capabilities of traditional tools. Research is based on modeling and simulation that require massive amounts of computing power, and Cloud Computing provides ready access to it on a highly efficient pay-as-you-go basis.

Cloud Computing is advancing scientific progress in another way. While previously only the largest companies could afford their own massive computer clusters, immense processing performance is now within reach for any small research team or a group of individuals. In a sense, Cloud Computing democratizes computing power, giving researchers novel opportunities to "big science".

Typical advantages of Cloud Computing such as scalability and the possibility to create easy-to-use platforms are useful also for educational settings. Innovative teaching tools and reference materials allow educators to make the subject matter more interesting to the "visual generation" of their students.

4.3. Government Sector

Governments around the world are seeking to digitize their economies to connect all members of society through access to – and the sharing of – digital content via the Internet from anyplace at anytime to work, play, consume and learn. Government at all levels is looking for ways to improve services and justify budgets. One of the prominent aspects generally associated with Government bureaucracy is large paper trails. Currently there is a trend where the Government establishments are making a fast move towards utilizing the cloud technology for *safeguarding their networks and enabling faster transactions*. Through the cloud technology, Governments can streamline all the operations and thereby *save the taxpayer's money by reducing energy consumption and bringing about transparency and better collaboration*. As the cloud hosting providers put forward a perfect platform for managing the data along with a backup facility, the Government agencies can avoid any breaks in service in case of extreme weather conditions or network failures. The move to cloud technology will help the Government bodies with keeping the safety regulations in place while upgrading the Government agencies to the tech world where better services will be provided to the people.

Despite the steadfast progress in cloud adoption, cloud security remains a hot topic. Some surveys show upward to 70% of government employees has concerns around cloud security and compliance [49]. Cloud solutions must offer customers a peace of mind that citizens' data is safe in the cloud. Perceived security vulnerability is still the number one concern with the cloud and a major impediment to wider and faster cloud adoption in governments.

4.4. Hospitality and Tourism

Many large hotels have moved to cloud computing to get closer to customers. From reservation systems to menus, everything is available across the continents without any extra cost in infrastructure and individual training resources at every location. With cloud hosting services people will be able to simplify tasks like booking a room, apartment, restaurants and motels. With further improvisation in cloud technology, people will also be able to record these transactions directly to the company's payment systems. Everything would be served through the handheld devices in constant sync with the Cloud platforms.

4.5. Music and Broadcasting Media

With the appearance of Apple and Android technologies, people have started listening to music through the 3G networks as well. In the current scenario people can easily utilize any music service, select the songs they want and listen to them from anywhere in the world; all this is possible as a result of cloud computing services. There has been a constant innovative trend in the music industries and with the support of the cloud technology; it has become easier for the musicians to reach to their audience worldwide. Therefore when it comes to the music business, cloud technology is beneficial for both listeners (as they can listen to their favorite songs anywhere at any time) and for the musicians as well (as their compositions reach out to people through a fast and efficient medium).

The broadcast media market is discovering the business advantages that basing its communications on a cloud model can bring. Broadcast media is a late convert to cloud computing, but it is proving to be an enthusiastic one. The benefits are especially timely for an industry undergoing a transformation as it embraces the concept of 'TV Everywhere' at the same time as migration to IP networks for transmission. These two trends fit well together as broadcasting migrates from dedicated (and largely proprietary) infrastructures to IT-based platforms better suited to delivering video to a vast array of devices, rather than just conventional TV sets.

This, though, brings challenges: the devices come in all shapes and forms, which increases the complexity of delivering a format at sufficient quality and without consuming an unnecessary amount of bandwidth [50]. Various categories of operators are interested in cloud as a vehicle for reaching as many people as possible, but there are some conflicts of interest. Content owners holding the rights to broadcasts are anxious to avoid the cloud breaking existing agreements. Traditionally, rights to premium content such as movies and sport have been broken down into geographical silos often defined by country or even regions, as has happened in the US. This can inhibit cloud distribution of video content but it is also an opportunity – the cloud itself can become the 'place' where digital rights are negotiated and applied.

4.6. Energy and Utility

In addition to environmental benefits, the energy sector is fostered to adopt the cloud technology in order to reduce costs, enhance efficiency, and help address growing oil and power needs, such as increasing amounts of data, real time access to data, or integration and standardization of IT operations.

The benefits of adopting cloud in the utility and energy sector do not differ too much. Besides cost, flexibility, and speed, which translates into more agile and responsive services, the main benefit for the utility industry is the global entry of smart grid and advanced metering infrastructure into utility operating models.

IT is becoming an important part of the transformation of network operations as utility companies exploit new data sources in order to improve network efficiency. The need for large scale real-time computing, communication, transfer and storage of data generated by smart grid technologies is expected to be addressed by cloud computing services.

4.7. Accounting

Accounting firms deal with data day in and day out. The volume of numbers that go through an accounting office each day is unimaginable. Taking business to the cloud allows accountants to work from anywhere, at any time. It is a way to reduce costs, improve efficiency and make data more accessible. Most customers prefer communicating with their accountant via the Internet, and in many ways, the new cloud-based dashboards, reporting applications and unified communications systems that are now available only make this easier. By enabling better collaboration and communication among geographically diverse staff and clients, accounting firms' processes and workflows are vastly improved and the work gets done much faster – often with greatly reduced travel costs [51].

4.8. Manufacturing and Production

Through cloud computing the manufacturing industry will be able to avoid various technical and business issues that might occur while running their projects. Affordability is also ensured as the manufacturers will only have to pay for the resources utilized, they will not have to pay any additional expenses due to the fact of the non-requirement of private data center setup. Through cloud computing the manufacturers can also implement *large internet virtual server farms for facilitating better management of the business and manufacturing setup*. With the use of SaaS, Paas and IaaS, manufacturers will be able to establish *a virtual presence from any location around the world*, they will be able to connect plants to an IT infrastructure and they also find new business opportunities.

4.9. Travelling

The "consumerization" of technology is changing the way travelers interact, obtain information and purchase travel needs. They are becoming smarter: Increasingly informed, empowered and demanding. They are asking for differentiated experiences, and, indeed, if companies in this business do not take this to heart, they stand to lose share-of-wallet. As a result, new nimble business approaches are needed to sustain market share. Travelers need to be treated as a "segment of one," and experience positive moments of truth as they interact with travel and transportation providers at various stages of the travel ribbon. They need to be able to share their experiences with their social networks, make new arrangements in real time and add new services to their itineraries [52].

To support new business approaches and seamless travel experiences, a modern, flexible and scalable approach to applications and infrastructure must be adopted. The current distribution networks are not agile enough to address demands from technology empowered travelers.

In addition, changing business processes and the empowered traveler have driven transaction volumes and system loads to new levels never envisioned by the distribution companies.

Cloud computing offers new and flexible ways to provision resources — and through a new way to build and deploy contemporary new updated and modernized applications.

4.10. IT

Many software companies nowadays offer not only online distribution but also online use of software. Commoditization usually takes some time to develop in industries, but in some aspects of cloud it is happening rather quickly.

The cloud computing service model is a sound business model from both provider's and customer's perspectives. Providers invest in the necessary infrastructure and management, and in return receive a regular income stream from the investment by means of service subscriptions. Since at any given time substantial numbers of customers are inactive, the provider reaps the benefits of the economies of scale and can charge lower subscription fees. The customers in turn see convenience benefits from having data and services available from any location, from having data backups centrally managed, from the availability of increased capacity when needed, and from usage-based charging.

Recent IDC research shows that Worldwide revenue from public IT cloud services exceeded $21.5 billion in 2010 and will reach $72.9 billion in 2015, representing a compound annual growth rate of nearly 30% [53]. This rapid growth rate is over four times the projected growth for the worldwide IT market as a whole (6.7%). By 2015, one of every seven dollars spent on packaged software, server, and storage offerings will be through the public cloud model.

CONCLUSION

Cloud computing has reached maturity and many businesses are investing in it. The business benefits of cloud computing are extensive and are not limited to the IT department, but affect the entire enterprise.

Cloud cannot be sufficiently understood as a standalone phenomenon in the IT market, but rather as a core ingredient of a larger transformation of the IT industry - and many other industries using IT to transform themselves. Other ingredients enabled by cloud - and, in turn, accelerating cloud adoption - include the expanding "species" of mobile devices, the explosion of mobile apps, the growing availability of wireless broadband, and the explosion of big data tools.

Cloud Computing now has the opportunity to help us transform the world to a more sustainable, lower carbon and more resource-efficient future. Cloud cannot be sufficiently understood as a standalone phenomenon in the IT market, but rather as a core ingredient of a larger transformation of the IT industry - and many other industries using IT to transform themselves.

In this chapter we discuss how notable benefits of cloud computing model (reduced costs, economies of scale, flexibility, highly reliable services) can help different businesses and conclude that the further development of cloud computing will promote economic growth, increase productivity, and shift the type of jobs and skills required by industry.

What can we expect from Cloud Computing in 2013 and beyond? The past of cloud computing is bright, but the future of cloud computing is even brighter.

In the coming years any cloud computing firm that wants to survive in this industry must be able to provide services that are not only reliable, but also are available at ever increasingly high speeds. As the speed of internet connections increases, more and more software will start providing other services through cloud computing. There will be more and more companies opting for private cloud computing services, and the business of providing private cloud services will get a big boost in the future due to the high demand. Businesses are already acknowledging the need for mobile cloud storage; there will be applications that will give simple and fast access to applications and data as and when it will be required by smartphone users.

Technology experts expect they will 'live mostly in the cloud' in 2020 and not on the desktop; this will advance mobile connectivity through smartphones. Still, cloud computing has many difficulties to overcome, including concerns tied to the availability of broadband connection, the ability of diverse systems to work together, security, privacy, and quality of service. In the future, cloud security systems will be able to validate identities through a "centralized trust." Identity-based security is thought to be more secure than current forms of security. More people will begin to trust cloud computing when this happens. In addition to physical security, firewall and VPN technology will be improved to protect data transfer. New firewall policies, although not fully defined, will limit VPN traffic to specific IP addresses and ports. With upgraded firmware, breaches will be less likely to occur.

The development of future cloud infrastructures requires the collaboration of experts from various backgrounds related to cloud systems, from academia and industry equally. There are different research areas surrounded by cloud security, from official characteristics to novel methods; the research required is not only technological, but also in legal, economic, environmental and standardization areas. Among hot research topics are realistic issues related to data relocation in the cloud, business services based on semantics (Web 2.0), scalable programming (multicore), future networking, general service provisioning, storage management.

ACKNOWLEDGMENT

This work has been supported by the Serbian Ministry of Education and Science (project no. III44006).

REFERENCES

[1]   G. Raines, Cloud Computing and SOA, The MITRE Corporation, www.mitre.org, 2009.

[2]   The NIST definition of cloud computing, 2011, http://csrc.nist.gov/publications/ nistpubs/800-145/SP800-145.pdf

[3]   L. Tucker, "Introduction to Cloud Computing for Startups and Developers," Sun Microsystems, Inc., 2009.

[4]   A. Velte, T. Velte, R. Elsenpeter, "Cloud Computing: A Practical Approach", McGraw-Hill, 2009.

[5]   C. Gong, J. Liu, Q. Zhang, H. Chen, Z. Gong, The Characteristics of Cloud Computing, Proceedings of 39th International Conference on Parallel Processing, pp. 275-279, 2010.

[6]   "What Cloud Computing means for business, and how to capitalize on it", Deloitte, 2010.

[7]   User Survey Analysis: Using Cloud Services for Mission-Critical Applications, available online at http://www.gartner.com/id=2182216

[8]   Z. Morvay, D. Gvozdenac, "Applied industrial energy and environmental management", John Wiley and Sons, 2008.

[9]   "Business Agility and the True Economics of Cloud Computing", VMWare Whitepaper, 2011.

[10]   C. Weinhardt, A. Anandasivam, B. Blau, N. Borissov, T. Meinl, W. Michalk, and J. Stößer, "Cloud computing – a classification, business models, and research directions," *Business & Information Systems Engineering* (BISE), vol. 1, no. 5, pp. 391-399, 2009.

[11]   V. Chang, D. Bacigalupo, G. Wills, D. De Roure, A Categorisation of Cloud Computing Business Models, Proceedings of the 10th IEEE/ACM International Conference on Cluster, *Cloud and Grid Computing*, 2010, pp. 509-512.

[12]   Jericho Forum, "Cloud Cube Model: Selecting Cloud Formations for Secure Collaboration Version 1.0", Jericho Forum Specification, 2009.

[13]   Digital Agenda: New strategy to drive European business and government productivity via cloud computing, available online at http://europa.eu/rapid/press-release_IP-12-1025_en.htm

[14]   Deployment Methods Overview, available online at http://www.cloudconsulting.com/deployment-methods/

[15]   D. Plummer, "The Business Landscape of Cloud Computing", Gartner, 2012.

[16]   "The power of Cloud", *IBM Executive Report*, 2012.

[17]   "Common Risks of Using Business Apps in the Cloud", US-CERT, 2012.

[18]   P. Hofmann, D. Woods, Cloud Computing: The Limits of Public Clouds for Business Applications, *IEEE Internet Computing*, 2010, pp. 90-93.

[19]   NextIO Inc., Customer Case Study, available online at http://www.nextio.com/resources/case-studies/files/nextio-case-study-msp.pdf

[20]   S. Marston, Z. Li, S. Bandyopadhyay, A. Ghalsasi, Cloud Computing – The Business Perspective, Proceedings of the 44th Hawaii International Conference on System Sciences, 2011, pp. 1-11

[21]   "Cloud Adoption - The definitive guide to a business technology revolution", Fujitsu, 2011.

[22]   D. Petcu, Interoperability between Clouds at Several Layers, Future Internet Assembly, Aalborg, 2012.

[23]   B. C. Tak, B. Urgaonkar, A. Sivasubramaniam, Move or Not to Move: The Economics of Cloud Computing, available online at http://www.cse.psu.edu/research/publications/tech-reports/2011/cse-11-002.pdf, 2011.

[24]   J. Hurwitz, The Economics of the Cloud, available online at http://www.businessweek.com/authors/32430-judith-hurwitz

[25]   J. Feiman, D. W. Cearley, Economics of the Cloud: Business Value Assessments, Gartner RAS Core Research Note G00168554, available online at http://eval.symantec.

com/mktginfo/enterprise/other_resources/b-economics_of_the_cloud_bva_OR.en-us.pdf, 2009.

[26] Cloud computing set to create jobs and promote growth, available online at http://www2.lse.ac.uk/newsAndMedia/news/archives/2012/01/cloud.aspx

[27] M. Iansiti, G. L. Richards, "A study of economic impact of cloud computing", International Journal of Technology, Policy and Management, 12 (4), 2012.

[28] T. Leimbach et al., Cloud Computing - European Perspectives on impacts and potentials of Cloud Computing and Social Network Sites, available online at http://epub.oeaw.ac.at/ita/ita-projektberichte/e2-2a65-1.pdf, 2012.

[29] T. Alford, G. Morton, The Economics of Cloud Computing, available online at http://www.boozallen.com/media/file/Economics-of-Cloud-Computing.pdf, 2010.

[30] B. Brindley, Tech for a Brighter Future: The Humanitarian Cloud, available online at http://nethope.org/blog/2012/01/tech-for-a-brighter-future-cloud, 2012.

[31] S. Cohen, C. Li, J. Yang, C. Yu, Computational Journalism: A Call to Arms to Database Researchers, 5th Biennial Conference on Innovative Data Systems Research, 2011.

[32] B. Brumm, The Impact of Cloud Computing on IT Jobs, available online at http://www.computer.org/portal/web/computingnow/careers/content?g=53319&type=article&urlTitle=the-impact-of-cloud-computing-on-it-jobs, 2012.

[33] C. Weitz, Eyes on the sky: How cloud computing is shaping society, available online at http://globalblogs.deloitte.com/deloitteperspectives/2012/01/eyes-on-the-sky-how-cloud-computing-is-shaping-society.html, 2012.

[34] Cloud Computing the Greener Way, available online at http://www.thecloudcircle.com/article/feature-cloud-computing-greener-way

[35] Ericsson Whitepaper, available online at http://www.ericsson.com/res/docs/whitepapers/wp-50-billions.pdf

[36] How Dirty is your Data, GreenPeace International, available online at http://www.greenpeace.org/international/Global/international/publications/climate/2011/CoolIT/dirty-data-report-greenpeace.pdf

[37] International Energy Agency, http://www.iea.org

[38] The Benefits of Cloud Computing, Whitepaper, LocaLoop, 2013.

[39] Grids, Clouds and Virtualization, Springer, 2010.

[40] Best Practices Guide for Energy-Efficient Data Center Design, available online at http://www1.eere.energy.gov/femp/pdfs/eedatacenterbestpractices.pdf

[41] Minimising Data Centre Total Cost of Ownership Through Energy Efficiency Analysis, available online at http://www.cibse.org/content/cibsesymposium2012/Presentation016.pdf

[42] F. Owusu, C. Pattinson, The current state of understanding of the energy efficiency of cloud computing, Proceedings of IEEE 11th International Conference on Trust, Security and Privacy in Computing and Communications, pp. 1948-1953, 2012.

[43] Wyse Thin Computing and Virtualization Solutions, Wyse-Thin-Computing-Guide, Wyse Technology Inc.

[44] H. T. Dinh, C. Lee, D. Niyato, P. Wang, A Survey of Mobile Cloud Computing: Architecture, Applications, and Approaches, Wireless Communications and Mobile Computing, Wiley, 2013.

[45] IBM, Cloud Computing: Building a New Foundation for Healthcare, available online at
      http://www-05.ibm.com/de/healthcare/literature/cloud-new-foundation-for-hv.pdf
[46] Healthcare Cloud Computing (Clinical, EMR, SaaS, Private, Public, Hybrid) Market -
      Global Trends, Challenges, Opportunities & Forecasts (2012 – 2017), available online
      at   http://www.marketsandmarkets.com/Market-Reports/cloud-computing-healthcare-
      market-347.html
[47] Cloud   Computing   Delivers   Education   to   Millions,   available   online   at
      http://www.cisco.com/web/learning/netacad/WLC/pdf/NetAcad_Cloud_CS.pdf
[48] J. McEleney, The cloud's impact on society, available online at http://www.connect-
      world.com/~cwiml/index.php/magazine/global-ict/item/14040-the-cloud's-impact-on-
      society, 2011.
[49] Pega Cloud for Government: Security & Reliability for Government Agencies,
      Pegasystems Inc., available online at http://www.pega.com/sites/default/files/private/
      Pega-Cloud-for-Government-Security-And-Reliability-White-Paper-Feb2012.pdf,
      2012.
[50] P. Hunter, Cloud computing benefits for broadcast media industry, available online at
      http://eandt.theiet.org/magazine/2012/05/clouds-broadcast-benefits.cfm, 2012.
[51] J. Uglietta, Cloud Computing Benefits for Accounting Firms, available online at
      http://www.aisn.net/index.php/2012/08/cloud-computing-benefits-for-accounting-
      firms/, 2012.
[52] IBM, Cloud Computing for the Travel and Transportation Industry, 2012.
[53] Budget 2013, available online at http://www.ey.com/Publication/vwLUAssets/EY-
      Analysis-Budget_2013/$FILE/EY-Analysis-Budget_2013.pdf

In: Advances in Cloud Computing Research
Editor: Muthu Ramachandran

ISBN: 978-1-63117-192-5
© 2014 Nova Science Publishers, Inc.

Chapter 3

CONSULTING AS A SERVICE - DEMONSTRATED BY CLOUD COMPUTING CONSULTANCY PROJECTS IN GREATER CHINA

*Victor Chang**

School of Computing, Creative Technologies and
Engineering, Leeds Metropolitan University, Leeds, UK
Electronics and Computer Science,
University of Southampton, Southampton, UK

ABSTRACT

The objective of this paper is to highlight Cloud Computing projects with the mutual interests of both mainland China and Taiwan, which present the a strong case of Consulting as a Service (CaaS) as an innovative way for generating profits and delivering services for clients. This paper explains the IT and Cloud development in Greater China and presents three projects that Taiwanese have been involved in the design, implementation and research. The first project presents a case for Teradata and Shanghai Stock Exchange (SSE), where Taiwanese collaborators have been closely involved. The second project is about two sandstorm simulations in the Inner Mongolia of mainland China and investigates its impacts to the environment and health of the populations. The third project is the Universe Computing which responds to mainland China's call to develop space programme and to explore the unknown territory. Universe Computing includes simulations for satellite orbiting, galaxy formation and galaxy explosion. The author is an investigator for the second and third project and uses Cloud Computing Adoption Framework (CCAF) to design and deploy Software as a Service (SaaS) and Consulting as a Service (CaaS). Taiwanese research and development outputs have been influential to the IT development in Greater China. This is important to move away any differences and work together to establish more and better research and development results to create a mutual win-win and maintain a high GDP growth.

---

* Corresponding author: Victor Chang. School of Computing, Creative Technologies and Engineering, Leeds Metropolitan University, Leeds, UK. Electronics and Computer Science, University of Southampton, Southampton, UK. E-mail: V.I.Chang@leedsmet.ac.uk.

Keywords: Cloud Computing; Consulting as a Service; data services for Shanghai Stock Exchange (SSE); sandstorm simulations; Universe Computing; satellite orbiting, galaxy formation and galaxy explosion; Cloud Computing Adoption Framework (CCAF); Taiwanese high-technology research and development for the Greater China

1. INTRODUCTION

China became the world's second largest economy in 2010 and in the past ten years, its ranking moved all the way up surpassing a number of wealthy countries. Wang and Wheatley (2010) report that the outcome was due to hard work of the last three decades that turn successfully into economic growth. China, the Dragon in the East, have enjoyed a rapid growth in economic development with an average of 10% growth rate over the past thirty years (International Monetary Fund, 2011). The Economist (2011) predicts that in 2018, China will overtake the US in the GDP as the world's largest economy. In the survey conducted by the Economist (2011), their results show that China has surpassed America over half of twenty-one different indicators, including exports, fixed investment and manufacturing output. The rise of China is due to several factors and the effective development of information technology (IT) help to consolidate the economic growth, which is one of the 2012 national strategies set by the previous Chinese Prime Minister (CPM), Mr, Wen Jiabao (CPM national speech, 2012). Mr Wen Jiabao summarised that China's GDP reached 47.2 trillion yuan, an increase of 9.2% over the previous year; government revenue was 10.37 trillion yuan, an increase of 24.8%; and a total of 12.21 million new urban jobs were created. IT is the fifth national strategy identified by Mr. Wen Jiabao and IT has helped China to achieve a brilliant record for economic development. IT provides a solid and well-establish infrastructure, so that organisations can perform their work efficiently, and communications between different companies are improved to ensure business agility and continuity in place. IT also supports the development of transportation systems, electric and power systems, telecommunication systems and information systems (IS) for several countries including China (Lall, 1992; Amin, 2004; Xu et al., 2007, Qiu, 2009), which brings additional benefits such as improvement in the quality of life, the development of new products and services and the stimulant to the economic growth (McIntyre, 2001; Wilson and Corey, 2008; Bernardez, 2009; Qiu, 2009; CPM national speech, 2012).

IT also offers new business models that have added values to the economic growth (McIntyre, 2001; Adekola and Sergi, 2007; Torun and Cicekci; 2007). This includes Business to Business (B2B), Business to Customers (B2C), Consumer to Business (C2B) and Consumer to Consumer Model (C2C). The internet dot-com companies such as Sina and Sohu have hundred of millions of readers and bloggers reading and writing on daily basis (Koepp, 2012). The Sina microblog (or weibo) is the most popular Chinese blogging community with hundreds of millions of users online on regular basis (Baran, 2011). The Alibaba is a successful e-commerce platform to provide B2B, B2C, C2B and C2C services. QQ is another internet service that provides millions of Chinese users in China and abroad to communicate with their family, friends, colleagues, business partners and institutions. Baidu is another giant search engine company and has been among the most popular search engines in China.

Renren is another social-networking website for Chinese to stay in touch with their social and family contacts (Baran, 2011). China is also well-known as the world's manufacturer and distributor of different types of electronic products (Lüthje, 2004). This includes Apple products, which the research and development, product design, manufacturing and product testing are largely made in Taiwan and China. There are also remarkable achievements from IT companies. HTC, a Taiwanese company manufacturing Android-based mobile phones, are one of the best-selling mobile phones in the world. Another example is Lenovo and Acer which always compete between third and fourth largest computer manufacturers in the world. Lenovo purchased the IBM Desktop division to strengthen its position to offer a wide range of quality products and services. Acer is another Taiwanese-based IT company with a variety of products and services on offer, and it has done better in laptops but weaker in desktops than Lenovo.

There are well-known software companies and services in Greater China. One example is the security software industry which includes Trend Micro, a global software firm based in Taiwan. It has anti-virus to serve millions of global users around the world. Huawei is a network infrastructure company serving global users and offering consulting services to their client organisations (Inkpen and Ramaswamy, 2006). Gaming is another popular sector reporting to have billions of revenues. The establishment of internet infrastructure and services ensure a large percent of the population have access to the internet and can use internet for gaming and e-business. Popular games can attract millions of turnover per year and create generate revenues including start-up companies (Bhattacharya and Michael, 2008). Gaming has also extended to the mobile devices such as mobile phones and pads, so users can play games on their mobile devices. All these explain the role of IT is significant to China and is contributing to its GDP development (Qiu, 2009).

The objective of this paper is to highlight Cloud Computing projects with the mutual interests of both mainland China and Taiwan, and present all the projects as the case for Consulting as a Service (CaaS). Consulting services for Cloud Computing is not new. For example, consulting firms such as Accenture, PricewaterhouseCoopers, Deloitte and KPMG already have their Cloud consulting services for their clients. IT companies such as Google, Microsoft, IBM and Oracle offer different types of consulting services for a variety of sectors. Each consulting service has a different strength, and is suitable for different types of services and customers. For example, if a client requires a database-driven Cloud service, he is more likely to consult Oracle, or Google due to their reputation in software engineering. On the other hand, there are some local-based consulting firms such as in Greater China, which are less well-known globally, but they are very competent, experienced and quick to respond to the market needs. Those locally-based firms can establish a good reputation in the local and regional market in Greater China. This paper then describes consulting projects that those local-based firms have been involved. If any particular firm involved has concerns in revealing their identity, their names will not be mentioned, as the focus is on presenting Consulting as a Service as a useful strategy and implementation for delivering goods and services in Greater China. The structure of this paper is as follows. Section 2 explains Consulting as a Service (CaaS) and its elements. Three projects in regards to CaaS are presented in Section 3, 4 and 5 respectively. Section 3 presents a case for Teradata and Shanghai Stock Exchange (SSE), where Taiwanese collaborators have been closely involved. Section 4 describes a sandstorm simulation project that investigates the impacts to the Chinese citizen and the environment, which the author is lead investigator in his initiative.

Section 5 demonstrates a Universe Computing project to respond to China's space mission program that the author is an investigator in his initiative. Section 6 presents discussion topics in support with CaaS. Section 7 then sums up Conclusion and Future Work.

2. CONSULTING AS A SERVICE

This section presents Consulting as a Service (CaaS), and the three elements in association with the consulting model. The first element is the introduction of the framework to present the best practices. The second element is the summary of Taiwanese high-technology expertise.

2.1. Cloud Computing Adoption Framework Overview

There is an increased number of organisations which adopt Cloud Computing to consolidate resources, improves efficiency and reduce costs (Vouk, 2008; Chang et al., 2011 d). Organisational Cloud adoption has been confirmed to offer such benefits that Chang et al., (2011 b; 2011 c; 2011 d) report to have different types of return on investment (ROI) for SAP, Vodafone/Apple, National Health Service (NHS) UK and University of Southampton under the recommendation of Cloud Computing Adoption Framework (CCAF).

The use of CCAF is reported to provide added values for organisations that adopt Cloud, and resolve existing problems that those Cloud-adopting organisation needs to deal with in the process of using the Cloud. There are deliveries of services and projects presented as in Table 1.

Table 1. Deliveries of services and projects

Sectors or subjects	Summary of CCAF contributions	References
Finance	Demonstrate a platform to calculate more accurate computational and visualisations results for price and risk.	Chang et al., (2010 ; 2011 a; 2013 a; 2014 b)
Healthcare	Develop a platform to manage and archive Big Data, and allow scientists to exchange and sue data swiftly and effectively. Use the platform to simulate proteins, tumours, brain imaging and genes.	Chang et al., (2011 b; 2012 c; 2013 b); Chang (2013 e)
Education	Demonstrate Education as a Service (EaaS). Develop Cloud to save costs. Develop applications for learning.	Chang et al., (2012 a; 2013 b)
Natural Science	Develop a platform to simulate tsunami and sandstorm	Chang (2011 a; 2011 b)
Interdisciplinary	Provide a platform for service integration to calculate prices and risks in regard to taking each service.	Chang et al., (2011 d; 2012 b); Chang (2013 a)
	Provide a framework to disseminate good practices and recommendations	Chang et al., (2013 a; 2014 a)

All these successful deliveries of services support the case of CaaS, since each service has different requirements, designs and implementations. All lessons learned and recommendations are useful for stakeholders, organisations and individuals that plan to adopt and use Cloud Computing.

2.2. Contributions from Taiwanese Research and Development in the Development of High-Technology Sector in China

Taiwanese research and development have been internationally well-known in some key areas such as Chemistry, Microelectronics, high-technology and so on. Dr Yuan Tseh Lee is the Nobel Laureate in Chemistry in 1986 for his contributions concerning the dynamics of the dynamics of chemical elementary processes. He is currently the Director of Academia Sinica, the highest level of research and development institute in Taiwan. In addition, computer and microelectronics manufacturing by Taiwanese is well-established in the world market. A vast number of good-quality computer components (such as mother boards, graphics cards and monitors) and computer equipment are manufactured by Taiwanese firms based in China which reflect their high number of outputs from the research and development. Foxconn is a Taiwanese firm setting up factories in China and is the main manufacturer for global computer brands such as Dell and Apple. Apple iPhones and iPads are the most well-known products and they have been successful helping Apple to maintain offering the most popular products and to generate billions of revenues. There are current Cloud services in Taiwan across different sectors and Cloud Computing plays a more important role in the strategic IT development for both Taiwan and China (Chandrasekaran and Kapoor, 2011). The Council for Economic Planning and Development (2011) in Taiwan set three major objectives which can be summed up as follows:

Autonomous Supply:

- Develop a full fledged Cloud ecosystem of service providers
- Improvement of Internet infrastructure
- Encourage R and D to introduce value-added services

Demand Creation:

- Adoption in the public sector – Government-to-Consumer (G2C), Government-to-Business (G2B) and Government-to-Government (G2G) services
- Promotion of adoption of Cloud services by the private sector by increasing local awareness levels.
- Promoting export of Cloud services.

Integrated Governance:

- Steering Committee for Development of the Cloud Computing Industry to handle coordination and implementation of policy.
- Cloud Computing Industry Promotion Office to help domestic companies.

Another example for Taiwan-led services includes the Supply Chain Cloud to manage the process of manufacturing, transportation and business sales between different provinces in China and then between China and Taiwan to reduce costs and improve business agility (Chu, 2008; IBM 2011). Three projects described between Section 3 and 5 demonstrate Consulting as a Service (CaaS) as a result of Taiwanese contributions and development.

3. CLOUD COMPUTING DEVELOPMENT IN CHINA – SHANGHAI STOCK EXCHANGE (SSE)

Shanghai Stock Exchange (SSE) is a vital part of mainland Chinese economic development, since it serves millions of clients and has a combined market capitalisation of RMB 18 trillion (an estimate of £1.8 trillion) (City of London Economic Development, 2010). Shanghai is equally important as Hong Kong and Tokyo as the centre for finance, economic and business development in Asia. Technology adopted by SSE is highly relevant to help SSE fulfill its ambition as one of the most popular and established financial centers in the world. Millions of data are used for information and also produced by real-time transactions. Values for high-quality information and reliable transactions are essential for all types of investors. In addition, SSE needs to develop new services to cope with increasing demands over agility, reliability, confidentiality and efficiency. Thus, the challenge is to build terabytes of data which can be accessed and used in real-time. This ensures SSE to play as a strategic role and finance and maintains its leading position in Asia.

3.1. The Involvement with Teradata

Teradata is the contractor company for the SSE to develop terabytes of data, and started to build increasing amounts of data storage and real-time computing since 1990s. Teradata specialises in data warehousing, business intelligence, customer relationship management (CRM) and data integration. The author has an important Taiwanese collaborator, who is an ex-Vice President leading the software development and client support in the past twelve years. This section describes the contribution from Taiwanese-led team for SSE development since late 1990s. Their development has three key stages. The first stage began from 1990s to 2000 where the emphasis was to meet increasing demands of data usage and information processing. They built infrastructure, platform and software services to ensure data is accurate and up-to-date, and information can be retrieved and processed in real-time. This allows SSE to emerge as a prominent financial centre in Asia and the increasing stock market investment in China. The second key stage was between 2000 and 2007, where the emphasis was to improve existing infrastructures and ICT services and the overall quality of services. They also extended their data services into terabytes to allow the massive amount of information to be processed and displayed efficiently. They developed in-house data services to allow integrations of different requests and display of results.

Their third key stage began from 2007 to current period. Their emphasis is to ensure the better integrations of different services to allow their clients to perform a different type of tasks simultaneously.

The use of Cloud computing resources can ensure clients can query their data while making another service requests, and can also review their real-time stock market index and advice to make a better judgement of their investments. The multi-tasking service ability can provide business added values such as agility, since the processing time for each service can be reduced. It also offers improvement of efficiency, since multiple services can be handled simultaneously and to allow their clients with additional business advantages. This is crucial for financial services since the capability to offer accurate and up-to-date real-time is essential (ObjectStore, 2008; Chang et al., 2011 a).

3.2. Technology behind SSE and Teradata

SSE began to adopt Teradata technology, which offers the following advantages:

◆ The database has no limit to the number of users.
◆ It has a great scalability and supports up to 100TB per database
◆ It can optimise performance and allows up to a maximum of 64 nodes per database server.
◆ It has an excellent visualisation capability and provides integrations with different services.

Teradata Relationship Database Management System (RDBMS) has two major components: Parsing Engine (PE) and Access Module Processor (AMP). AMP can read data from the magnetic stripes of the disks and make data into readable formats and put the data back to PE. PE optimises the tasks for AMP, instructs AMP to perform tasks, and processes the data to send back to the database tables. The teradata architecture is influential to the database optimisation. The functional architecture for teradata has three layers, which include infrastructure as a service (IaaS), platform as a service (PaaS) and Software as a Service (SaaS). Their IaaS layer includes a large number of services, which include disk array, operating systems, teradata RDBMS, Data mining and Online Transaction Processing (OLTP).

All these features provide the fundamental requirements and functions for users. Their PaaS layer includes the following services: customer analysis, revenue analysis, product analysis, quality analysis, market analysis and marketing analysis. These PaaS services allow their clients to query the core functionalities and understand their business status based on feedback and results from their customers, revenues and market research. Their SaaS has two types of services. The first type of services is the advanced application services, which include loss of customer modelling, customer value modelling, customer confidence modelling, pricing modelling and product modelling. These functions are useful for the managers understand their strengths, weaknesses, opportunities and threats related to their businesses. The second type of services is the value-added SaaS services, which include fraud detection (Fraud 5.0), pre-product sales modelling (RPS 2.0), Customer Relationship Management (CRM 4.0), Performance Monitoring and Management (PM and M 3.0) and Collection 4.0. These additional services can ensure SSE clients to understand their business performances for different divisions. The use of Teradata ensures SSE can provide all types of information and data that clients demand in real-time (Teradata, 2006).

Consultancy and enterprise research contributions from Taiwanese-led team in the past twelve years are important to the database development to Teradata and SSE, since SSE requires a high-performing and accurate data for information exchange, processing and transactions. Their contributions also help their clients to have up-to-date data so that they can make a better decision about their investment.

4. SANDSTORM SIMULATION

China has experienced sandstorm over the decades and some provinces have suffered its destructive effects. The extent of such destructions has been increasingly severe due to climate change and the frequent human activities such as industrialisation and deforestation (Ci, 2001). The PRC Government has put in additional effort to reduce the level of destruction but the outcome does not have a significant difference (Wang and Chokkalingam, 2006). Sandstorm often occurs in spring, late summer and autumn in dessert, Inner Mongolia and neighboring provinces in the northeast and northwest of China (Ci, 2001; Liang, Eckstein and Liu, 2008). Sandstorm brings dryness, massive dust and poor visibility, which have related implications to health hazards including nausea, lung inflammation and so on (Health Effects Institute, 2004). In addition, sandstorm reduces the crop yielding and is a serious threat to the food sources to supply an approximate 1.3 billion population in China (Oxfam, 2009). Sandstorm simulations have great interests to PRC Government and scholars. Liu et al. (2007) have demonstrated their method of modelling and animating sandstorm based on their multiple-fluid model to simulate the motion of air, sand and dust particles. They explain how their 3D texture can work on Graphical Processing Unit (GPU) and also show screen-shots of several simulation results. They demonstrate how comparisons of different modelling outcomes between real and their simulation, and also between different levels of visibility. Zhang and Wang (2000) focus on their sandstorm simulations near Beijing area, and investigate its impacts based on their numerical model. They conclude their numerical model is useful to predict the movement and timing of the sandstorm formation near Beijing area. Sandstorm is not only an interest to Chinese scholars but also scholars from neighbouring countries such as Japan. Ministry of the Environment of Japan (2008) investigated the cause of sandstorms from Mongolia and China and its impacts to Japan. They showed their research methods and various numerical results of their investigations and summed up its impacts to Japan and proposed their monitoring system to track the sandstorm movement.

Sandstorm simulations and modelling are within interests of research communities in China and Japan, and different advanced techniques have been used. All these require years of training in order to investigate the impacts and understand the consequences caused by sandstorm. Advanced models are used to simulate sandstorm, including their formation, movement and levels of destructions. The use of Cloud applications and resources can open a new paradigm to the existing practices (Pandey, Karunamoorthy and Buyya, 2011). Chang (2011) explains how tsunami simulations can be achieved by using his Cloud applications to demonstrate all resources can be computed in the Cloud platform. Similarly, Cloud offers a platform to write, store, reuse and test code. Some software development done in the Japan tsunami project can be used for sandstorm investigation, although part of the code needs to be rewritten to convert them into easy-to-use commands.

In the Cloud, there are unified languages and tools to program software code for simulation. The easy-to-use commands can be used to demonstrate the sandstorm simulation which reduces the level of complexity to start with experiments and simulations. The CaaS project has developed his own private Cloud platform to run sandstorm simulations. The project lead and his team use Mathematica and MATLAB based platform for programming and simulations. The development team develops the commands to ensure one line of code can execute the software, which is equivalent to a few hundred lines of code. The development team runs their own Cloud resource to demonstrate sandstorm simulations and its impacts to the environments and health for residents.

Inner Mongolia and desserts in Mongolia are among places of origins in sandstorm formation and investigation on how and what leads to sandstorm can help scientists to find potential remedies. Figure 1 shows the sandstorm simulations in Inner Mongolia of China, where the sandstorm can be presented as waves of sand. The three dimensions of x, y and z-axis can demonstrate the scale of destruction, which is defined by the code. Technical details are not presented here due to the flavours of this journal.

The next scenario is to simulate the extreme scale of sandstorm after twenty years due to severe deforestation and human activities against environment sustainability. Figure 2 shows the sandstorm when its scale of destruction has increased several times. The reason for doing so is to exploit the potential maximum level of destruction to the environment and the surrounding provinces.

Results show that enforced protection on the environment and laws and investment in new technology are necessary to reduce the possibility of reaching this disaster scenario. Different scales of sandstorm simulations may help the scientists to understand the level of destruction when a sandstorm is formed and then investigates any methods to reduce its scale of destructions.

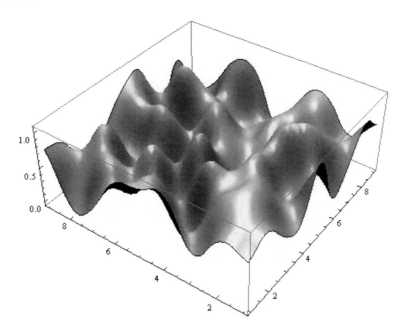

Figure 1. Sandstorm simulations in the Inner Mongolia.

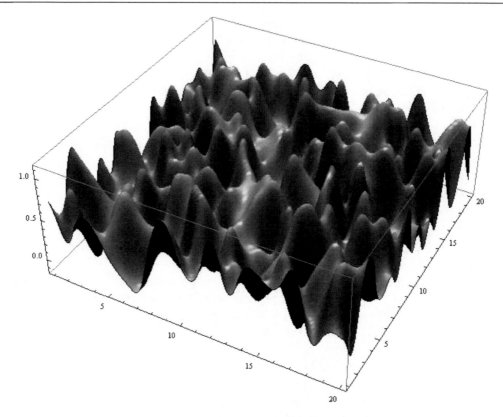

Figure 2. Sandstorm simulations in the Inner Mongolia 20 years later.

5. UNIVERSE COMPUTING

China has the interest and ambition to become one of the most developed countries in the space technology and exploration. China successfully launched their space programmes in 2003, 2005 and 2008 respectively and China became the third country in the world to send astronauts into the space. Space technology is one of the national Chinese strategies and they have successfully launched satellites, rockets, and space station (Fisher, 2011). In 2011, China launched "Tiangong 1", a space laboratory module and a testbed demonstrate the capabilities of running a space station centre. This largely exceeded expectations from international communities including NASA, which refused to help China to launch a space programme and building of a space station at the beginning. China has plans to explore the unknown territories, which include understanding the universe and making simulations related to the universe (Dicken and Ormrod, 2007; Chen 2011; Fisher 2011). Space exploration can widen our knowledge, which includes speed of light by Einstein, Newton's theory of gravitation and black hole theory by Stephen Hawkins. Space exploration helps mankind to investigate any possibilities for human habitation, as NASA has identified potential planets, or Super Earth such as Kepler-10b.

Cloud Computing offers a unique role in space technology, as it can reduce the level of complexity and presents different types of modelling and simulations to assist space mission. There are areas of interests such as satellite orbiting and galaxy formation and explosion.

The use of GPU and Cloud computing resources can model 3D and 4D of the galaxy to make analysis easier for scientists. The satellite orbiting simulation can help to offer accurate calculations and precisions related to speed, angle and direction of satellite movement in the space.

The author is the lead investigator in this Cloud initiative and has numerous good research outputs to disseminate. These include modelling and simulations for satellite orbiting, and galaxy formation and explosion in the use of advanced Cloud Computing techniques. Some examples are demonstrated as follows.

5.1. Satellite Orbiting Saturn

Figure 3 shows the satellite orbiting the Saturn. This is to simulate the scenario where the PRC launches a successful space mission and the satellite is exploring other planets in the Solar system. It would be a remarkable achievement for the PRC Government if their satellite can travel beyond the Mars.

Travelling to Saturn can symbolise their space mission success. The simulation is to model the way the satellite can perceive while orbiting the Saturn. The technology is based on Cloud Computing techniques which transform complex mathematical formulas into executing commands. This includes the orbiting movements and the vision that satellite can perceive. 3D visualisation offered by MATLAB and Mathematica can enhance the availability of satellite vision, which can be performed in real-time. Cloud Computing has reduced the level of complexity and there is less need to model intensive simulations based on orbiting movements.

Figure 3. Simulations of Chinese satellite orbits the Saturn.

5.2. Simulations of the Galaxy Formation

The ultimate ambition of space mission is to explore our own and other galaxies. The travel between the Earth and any galaxies may take thousands of light years. Current human technology has the limitation of achieving so because current technology is unable to produce anything that can travel as fast as the speed of light. Hence, it becomes apparent if an established platform can model and simulate the formation of the galaxy without investing further in satellite exploration outside our Solar system. Investigating the formation of the galaxy is useful to understand the life span of the universe and how the origin of life began. This can help establish any links with existing literature and space programs. Figure 4 shows the formation of a galaxy. Cloud Computing offers a platform to compute galaxy and the use of GPU technology can ensure a high quality of galaxy modelling can be computed. There are commands developed for the Cloud Computing platform which translate complex algorithms into commands. These commands can use GPU for advanced graphical modelling and then compute 3D simulation of the galaxy.

5.3. Simulations of the Galaxy Explosion

There are always different debates about the origin of life and the scientists led by Stephen Hawkings believe the Big Bang theory. However, how the universe was formed and how life began are still controversial, and there are scientists who believe in God to defend their faith and explain how science and creation can co-exist (Lehrman, 2008, Lennox, 2010). The intellectual challenge for this project is to model the explosion of the universe and the galaxy, so that simulations can be computed to understand how this happens and any useful observations when it happens. Cloud Computing offers a unique platform to compute complex models and can use the GPU to optimise the graphical processing capabilities.

Figure 4. Simulations of galaxy formation.

Special commands are developed to make the simulations as accurate and interactive as possible. When any key elements are changed, the graphical outputs will be dynamically changed.

See Figure 5 for the demonstration. This mini-project helps researchers to understand how, why and what makes the galaxy explosion. The explosion of the universe and galaxies can be presented at any stage and results can be extremely helpful to demonstrate the added value for astronomical research. Results of the research outcomes can be relevant to space science and high performance computing communities in Greater China and the United Kingdom.

Cloud Computing offers a platform and resource to open up possibilities to compute advanced modelling, which was expensive and difficult to achieve in the past. There is no need to buy, organise and manage thousands of computers for high-demand processing of client-server requests and applications. The use of Cloud Computing can ensure similar type of experiments and modelling can be achieved in a smaller scale.

The next scenario is to simulate the extreme scale of sandstorm after twenty years due to severe deforestation and human activities against environment sustainability. Figure 2 shows the sandstorm when its scale of destruction has increased several times. The reason for doing so is to exploit the potential maximum level of destruction to the environment and the surrounding provinces.

Results show that enforced protection on the environment and laws and investment in new technology are necessary to reduce the possibility of reaching this disaster scenario. Different scales of sandstorm simulations may help the scientists to understand the level of destruction when a sandstorm is formed and then investigates any methods to reduce its scale of destructions.

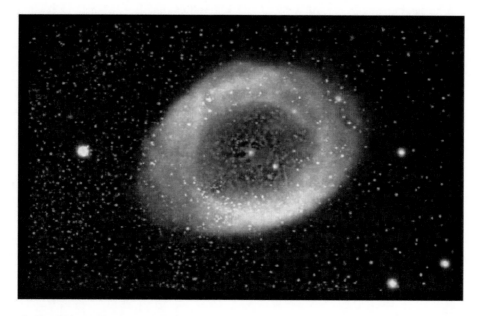

Figure 5. Simulations of galaxy explosion.

6. Discussions

There are two topics for discussions. The first topic is about the use of a recommended framework to design and deploy these services, and the second topic is the added values from these three projects from Taiwanese contributions.

6.1. The Role of Cloud Computing Adoption Framework (CCAF)

There is an increased number of organisations adopts Cloud Computing to consolidate resources, improves efficiency and reduce costs (Vouk, 2008; Chang et al., 2011 d). Organisational Cloud adoption has been confirmed to offer such benefits that Chang et al., (2011 b; 2011 c; 2011 d) report to have different types of return on investment (ROI) for SAP, Vodafone/Apple, National Health Service (NHS) UK and University of Southampton under the recommendation of Cloud Computing Adoption Framework (CCAF). CCAF is a dynamic framework to help organisations to achieve good design, deployment and services for organisational Cloud adoption. It has several case studies to demonstrate the benefits and added values for organizational Cloud adoption. CCAF has three key areas and the one relates to this paper is Portability, which defines the migration of services from desktops to Clouds and between Clouds. There are two types of Portability – the first type is the migration of the existing services and the second type is the design and deployment of a completely new service. The last two projects in this paper have been designed and completed in the recommendation of CCAF. The SSE data services belong to the first type of portability and their services have been migrated a while ago. Both sandstorm simulations and Universe Computing belong to the second type of the portability that are completely designed and deployed from the very beginning of the software life cycle by the author. Comparing with two types of portability, new Cloud development has the advantages over migration of existing services as follows:

1   There is no need to design new functions and update existing functions for Cloud portability: Applications are designed and built from the beginning of the software life cycle and functions are consistent throughout the software life cycle. There is no need to introduce new functions or update existing functions as a result of change in software requirements due to portability.
2   There is a greater consistency in the software as a service: The new services are designed, built and tested on the Cloud throughout the software engineering and IT management life cycle. There is a greater consistency and synchronisation, and there is no need to perform tasks at different locations of the system and then move the results over like some Cloud software do. This is helpful in the case when the user requirements evolve from time to time, since there is no need to write additional software to meet new user demands.

CCAF is instrumental in designing and building different types of software for different sectors. Chang et al. (2011 a) have demonstrated financial portability with IBM US and Commonwealth Bank of Australia (CBA), and they have used Least Square Method (LSM) of the Monte Carlo Simulation and Black Scholes Model (BSM) to calculate the best pricing and risk values from the results of up to 100,000 simulations. Results have been helpful to financial services and a few such as CBA have considered adoption. Academia Sinica has also adopted financial portability similar to approach recommended by CCAF and they have disseminated their publication to Taiwanese research and banking community (Peng et al., 2012). Chang (2011) also presents his Cloud portability in tsunami and seismic simulations to investigate the tsunami impacts to Japan in 2011 in the United Nations (UN) Information Society Forum. Results have been helpful to the UN authority and Japan delegates. This research is relevant to Taiwan due to the similarity in geographical and ecological factors that both Taiwan and Japan are located at the earthquake and typhoon zones.

6.2. The Added Values from These Three Projects As a Result of Taiwanese Contributions

Taiwanese research and development outputs have been influential to the IT development in Greater China. The phenomenon contributions include microelectronics and computer manufacturing industry that contributes to the GDP growth and job creation in China. Advanced technology products and services described in this paper have highlighted its strategic importance to long-term IT development. Data services for SSE are significant to the economy in China. The sandstorm simulation is highly relevant to investigate its impacts to our weather, environments and the health of the populations. The implications and outcomes from sandstorm simulations are not only useful for scientific research but also are relevant to the national strategy of the People's Republic of China (PRC) government to reduce impacts caused by natural disasters. The Universe Computing is a testbed for simulations in regard to the PRC's plan of its space programme and the exploration of the Universe. Cloud Computing offers a platform to simulate satellite orbiting other planets such as Saturn. Formation and explosion of galaxies help scientists to understand the origins of the life and how the galaxies can interact. These simulations and modelling with advanced technology and techniques are useful for our IT development and creation of new knowledge.

6.3. Consulting As a Service (CaaS) – Successful Lessons to Be Reproduced in European Projects

Reproducibility is an important aspect in Science to ensure that the steps and processes involved in the design and deployment of Cloud services can be reproduced at another environment to get similar results. Reproducibility can ensure the lessons learned and recommendations can be available to Cloud-adopting organisations, including the European projects. There are similarities between European projects and these consulting firms described as follows. Firstly, these projects are research and development focused, with the similar objectives to explore the unknown, provide recommendations and solutions and improve the conditions of current practices. Secondly, these consulting projects can generate incomes in the long-term. The first project in regard to SSE can have a direct impact to the economy in China.

The second project helps the Chinese population calculate the extent of damage caused by the sandstorm, and can provide a higher accuracy to do sufficient preventive measures in order to save costs as a result of over destructions. The third project can provide a testbed to simulate an unknown territory. Exploring the unknown with a higher accuracy rate can save the space authority costs of running its operational activities. The use of CaaS can provide strong cases for funded European projects.

CONCLUSION AND FUTURE WORK

The objective of this paper is to present Consulting as a Service (CaaS) and use Cloud Computing consulting projects with the mutual interests of both mainland China and Taiwan as an example. This paper supports contributions offered by Cloud Computing to the IT development in Greater China and presents three projects that Taiwanese have been involved in the design, implementation and research. The first project presents a case for Teradata and Shanghai Stock Exchange (SSE), where Taiwanese collaborators have been closely involved. SSE requires a high-performing and accurate data for information exchange, processing and transactions. CaaS contributions help their clients have up-to-date data to improve business agility, so that client companies can make better decisions about their investment. The second project to support CaaS is the sandstorm simulations in mainland China, which investigates its impacts to the environment and health of the populations. Sandstorm brings dryness, massive dust and poor visibility, which have related implications to health hazards. Cloud Computing offers a platform to understand the extent of destruction and to find any remedies for improvements. Two scenarios of sandstorm simulations in Inner Mongolia of China are presented. The first simulation symbolises the current status of sandstorm formation and the scale of destruction. The second simulation shows the extreme scale of sandstorm after twenty years due to severe deforestation and human activities against environment sustainability. Results show that enforced protection on the environment and laws and investment in new technology are necessary to reduce the possibility of reaching this disaster scenario. Space simulations by Cloud Computing offer opportunities to understand more about the unknown in space, and the one of the PRC Chinese strategies and they have successfully launched satellites, rockets, and space station.

The third project is the Universe Computing which responds to mainland China's call to develop simulation testbeds in space programme and to explore the unknown territory. Cloud Computing offers a unique platform for space simulations, as it can reduce the level of complexity and presents different types of modelling and simulations to assist space mission. The use of GPU and Cloud computing resources can model 3D and 4D of the galaxy to make analysis easier for scientists. There are three mini projects under Universe Computing. The first mini-project is to simulate the way the satellite can perceive while orbiting the Saturn. The objective is to calculate the orbiting movement while surrounding other planets such as Saturn and the view that satellite can perceive. The second mini-project is a simulation of galaxy formation modelled by Cloud Computing. Investigating the formation of the galaxy is useful to understand the life span of the universe and how the origin of life began. The third mini-project is the explosion of the universe and the galaxy. Simulations make full use of GPU for dynamic graphical processing.

The explosion of the universe and galaxies can be presented at any stage and can be extremely helpful to demonstrate the added value to astronomical research. Results of the research outcomes can be relevant to the space science community in Greater China and the European Union including Britain. The use of CCAF is instrumental for the sandstorm simulation and Universe Computing projects. CCAF is useful for Cloud computing development and portability, and ensures there is a greater consistency in software functionality and a better match to user requirements.

Taiwanese research and development outputs have been influential to the IT development in Greater China. This is important to move away any differences and work together to establish more and better research and development results. Taiwanese firms such as HTC, Acer, Foxconn, Eva Air, Want-want and so on have gained economic revenues through 1992-consensus. This strategy is not only on politics and economic development but should also be extended to research and development, as there are not many Taiwanese-led high-technology research projects focusing on Greater China's interests. These include Cloud Computing, which offers a platform to improve efficiency, reduce costs, consolidate resources, provide added values and contribute to research with national interests and commercial values. More advanced research in sandstorm simulation and Universe Computing will continue, and collaboration with elite scientists and well-known institutions are welcome to further establish research records and quality of results. The win-win outcome will be a phenomenon similar to mainland China's rapid GDP growth when more collaboration, funding, research investment and support are available to ensure the world-class research outputs can be produced and disseminated in Greater China.

ACKNOWLEDGMENTS

We thank that Mr Simon Yang, the ex-Vice President of the Teradata, for his information, assistance and collaboration. Some information is not available to the public, so that there is no any diagram to show the architecture and deployment scenario related to Teradata and Shanghai Stock Exchange.

REFERENCES

Adekola, A. and Sergi, B. S. (2007), *Global Business Management: A Cross-Cultural Perspective,* Ashgate Publishing, ISBN: 978-0-7546-7112 1, Copyright.

Amin, M. (2004), Balancing Market Priorities with Security, *IEEE power and energy magazine,* July/August edition.

Baran, R. (2011), Social Networking in China and the United States: Opportunities for New Marketing Strategy and Customer Relationship Management, *AFBE Journal*, Volume 4, No. 3, December.

Bernardez, M. (2009), The power of entrepreneurial ecosystems: extracting booms from busts, Working paper, *Expert2Business*, 2009.

Bhattacharya, A. K., Michael, D. M. (2008), How Local Companies Keep Multinationals at Bay, *Harvard Business Review*, March.

Chandrasekaran, A., Kapoor, M. (2011), State of Cloud Computing in the Public Sector – A Strategic analysis of the business case and overview of initiatives across Asia Pacific, Frost and Sullivan Consulting Market Insight.

Chang, V. (2011 a), A thorough investigation of Cloud Computing: Sustainability Modelling and Enterprise Portability for Industry and Academia. At: *"Set for Britain" 2011*, The House of Commons, The Parliament, UK.

Chang, V. (2011 b), Cloud Computing: Tsunami and seismic simulations to study impacts to Japan. At: *United Nations World Summit Information Society*, Geneva, Switzerland, 16 - 20 May 2011 (Chang, 2011 b).

Chang, V. (2013 a), Business integration as a service: computational risk analysis for small and medium enterprises adopting SAP, *International Journal of Next-Generation Computing*, 4, (3).

Chang, V. (2013 b), Brain Segmentation – A Case study of Biomedical Cloud Computing for Education and Research. In: *Learning Technologies Workshop*, Higher Education Academy (HEA), University of Greenwich, June.

Chang, V. (2013 c), Cloud Computing for brain segmentation technology. In: *IEEE Cloud Com 2013*, 02 - 05 Dec., Bristol, UK.

Chang, V. (2013 d), Cloud Bioinformatics in a private cloud deployment. In: *Advancing Medical Practice through Technology: Applications for Healthcare Delivery, Management, and Quality*, IGI Global.

Chang, V. (2013 e), Business Integration as a Service: The Case Study of the University of Southampton. In: *Trends in E-Business, E-Services, and E-Commerce: Impact of Technology on Goods, Services, and Business Transactions.*, IGI Global.

Chang, V. and Wills, G. (2013 c) A University of Greenwich Case Study of Cloud Computing – Education as a Service. In: *E-Logistics and E-Supply Chain Management: Applications for Evolving Business*, IGI Global.

Chang, V., De Roure, D., Wills, G., Walters, R. (2011 b), T., Organisational Sustainability Modelling for Return on Investment: Case Studies presented by a National Health Service (NHS) Trust UK, *Journal of Computing and Information Technology*, 19 (3). ISSN Print ISSN 1330-1136 | Online ISSN 1846-3908.

Chang, V., De Roure, D., Wills, G., Walters, R. (2011 c), Case Studies and Organisational Sustainability Modelling presented by Cloud Computing Business Framework, *International Journal of Web Services Research*. ISSN 1545-7362.

Chang, V., Li, C. S., De Roure, D., Wills, G., Walters, R., Chee, C. (2011 a), The Financial Clouds Review, *International Journal of Cloud Applications and Computing*, 1 (2), pp. 41-63. ISSN 2156-1834, eISSN 2156-1826.

Chang, V., Walters, R. J., Wills, G. (2012 b), Business Integration as a Service, *International Journal of Cloud Applications and Computing*, 2, (1), 16-40.

Chang, V., Walters, R. J., Wills, G. (2012), Cloud Storage in a private cloud deployment: Lessons for Data Intensive research. In: *The second international conference on Cloud Computing and Service Sciences (CLOSER 2012)*, April, Porto, Portugal.

Chang, V., Walters, R. J., Wills, G. (2013 a), The development that leads to the Cloud Computing Business Framework, *International Journal of Information Management*, 33 (3), June.

Chang, V., Walters, R. J., Wills, G. (2013 b), Cloud Storage and Bioinformatics in a private cloud deployment: Lessons for Data Intensive research. In: *Cloud Computing and Service Science*, Springer Lecture Notes Series, Springer Book.

Chang, V., Walters, R. J., Wills, G. (2014 a), Review of Cloud Computing and existing Frameworks for adoption, *Advances in Cloud Computing Research*, Nova Publishers.

Chang, V., Walters, R. J., Wills, G. (2014 b), Financial Clouds and modelling offered by Cloud Computing Adoption Frameworks, *Advances in Cloud Computing Research*, Nova Publishers.

Chang, V., Wills, G., De Roure, D., Chee, C. (2010), Investigating the Cloud Computing Business Framework - modelling and benchmarking of financial assets and job submissions in clouds, In: *UK e-Science All Hands Meeting 2010 "Research Clouds: Hype or Reality?, Workshop, 13 - 16 Sep.*, Cardiff, UK.

Chang, V., Wills, G., Walters, R. (2011 d), Towards Business Integration as a Service 2.0 (BIaaS 2.0), In: *IEEE International Conference on e-Business Engineering*, The 3rd International Workshop on Cloud Services - Platform Accelerating e-Business, 19-21 October, Beijing, China.

Chang, V., Wills, G., Walters, R., Currie, W. (2012 a), Towards a structured Cloud ROI: The University of Southampton cost-saving and user satisfaction case studies, In: *Sustainable ICTs and Management Systems for Green Computing*, IGI Global, page 179-200.

Chen, H. (2011), *Large Research Infrastructures Development in China: A Roadmap to 2050*, Book, ISBN 978-642-19367-5, Springer.

Chinese Prime Minister's national speech (2012), available on Chinese government portal (http://english.gov.cn), March.

Chu, A. (2008), *Doing business in a changing China, PwC white paper*, Issue 13 reprint, China-US Business Services.

Ci, L. (2001), *Disasters of Strong Sandstorms over large areas and the spread of land desertification in China*, Chapter Ten, Book Chapter, China's Experience with Calamitous Sand-dust Storms.

City of London Economic Development (2010), The Shanghai International Board: Challenges and Opportunities, *Government Report prepared for the City of London Corporation by Trusted Sources*, June.

Council for Economic Planning and Development (2011), *Cloud Computing – Taiwan's Next Trillion Industry, strategic paper and government official announcement*, Taiwan.

Dickens, P., Ormrod, J. (2007), *Towards a sociology of the universe*, ISBN 0-2-3-94150-0, printed by Rouledge.

Fisher, R. (2011), *China's Space Plane Program, Research Article*, International Assessment and Strategy Center, July.

Health Effects Institute (2004), *Health Effects of Outdoor Air Pollution in Developing Countries of Asia: A Literature Review, Special Report*, April.

IBM white paper (2011), A Chinese municipal government delivers service in the cloud: IBM WebSphere CloudBurst and IBM Rational help reduce data center overhead, white paper, December.

Inkpen, A., Ramaswamy, K. (2006), *Global Strategy: Creating and Sustaining Advantage Across Borders*, Oxford University Press, ISBN: 978-0-19-516720-7, Copyright.

International Monetary Fund (IMF) report (2011), World Economic Outlook Database, IMF Edition, September.

Koepp, R. W. (2012), *Betting on China*, John Wiley and Sons, ISBN 978-1-118-08716-9, Singapore, copyright.

Lall, S. (1992), Technological Capabilities and Industrialization, *World Development*, Volume 20, Number 2, page 165-186.

Lehrman, S. (2008), The Christian Man's Evolution: How Darwinism and Faith Can Coexist, article, *Scientific American*, November 2008.

Lehrman, S. (2008), The Christian Man's Evolution: How Darwinism and Faith Can Coexist, article, *Scientific American*, November.

Lennox, J. (2010), As a scientist I'm certain Stephen Hawking is wrong. You can't explain the universe without God, article, *Mail Online*, September.

Liang, E, Eckstein, D., Liu, H. (2008), Climate-growth relationships of relict Pinus tabulaeformis at the northern limit of its natural distribution in northern China, *Journal of Vegetation Science* 19: 393-406, March.

Liu, S., Wang, Z., Gong, Z., Huang, L., Peng, Q. (2007), Physically based animation of sandstorm, Computer Animation and Virtual Worlds, *Comp. Anim. Virtual Worlds*; 18: 259–269.

Lüthje, B. (2004), *Global Production Networks and Industrial Upgrading in China: The Case of Electronics Contract Manufacturing, Working paper, No. 74*, East-West Working Center, Honolulu, Hawaii.

Ministry of the Environment Japan (2008), *Dust and Sandstorm, scientific article*.

ObjectStore White Paper (2008), Real-Time Data Caching for Enterprise Applications.

Oxfam Briefing Paper (2009), Suffering the Science: Climate change, people and poverty, Oxfam International, July.

Pandey, S., Karunamoorthy, D., Buyya, R. (2011), *Workflow Engine for Clouds, Chapter 12, Cloud Computing: Principles and Paradigms,* ISBN-13: 978-0470887998, Wiley Press, February.

Peng, H. T., Chang, C. F., Liao, S. L., Liao, M. Y., Lai, F., Ho, J. M. (2012), The Development of a Real-time Valuation Service of Financial Derivatives, *IEEE Computational Intelligence for Financial Engineering and Economics*, March 29-30, New York City, US.

Qiu, J. L. (2009), *Working-Class Network Society, Communication Technology and the Information Have-Less in Urban China*, ISBN: 978-0-262-17006-2, The MIT Press.

Teradata (2006), *Introduction to Teradata Warehouse, User Guide*, September.

The Economist (2011), The dating game: We invite you to predict when China will overtake America, special edition, December 27th.

Torun, H., Cicekci, C. (2007), *Innovation: Is the Engine or the Economic Growth?, Working Paper*, Ege University, Turkey, April.

Vouk, M. A. (2008), Cloud Computing – Issues, Research and Implementations, *Journal of Computing and Information Technology - CIT 16*, page 235–246, Volume 4.

Wang, A., Wheatley, A. (2010), China overtakes Japan as No. 2 economy: FX chief, special column article, *Reuters*, June.

Wang, C. F., Chokkalingam, U. (2006), *National Overview*, Chapter 2, Book Chapter, Learning lessons from China's forest rehabilitation efforts.

Wilson, M., Corey, K. E. (2008), Global Positioning: Strategic Planning for Urban Competitiveness, *Working Paper, Urban Policy Research Series*, Michigan State University.

Xu, G. X., Liu, J. H., Tao, Z. H., and Li, X. C. (2007), The Research and Development of the Highway's Electronic Toll Collection System, World Academy of Science, *Engineering and Technology*, Issue 31, July.

Zhang, X. L., Wang, Y. C. (2001), Weather analysis and numerical simulation of sandstorm in Beijing area, *Gansu Meteorology Journal*, Beijing Institute of Meteorological Science, Beijing, China.

In: Advances in Cloud Computing Research   ISBN: 978-1-63117-192-5
Editor: Muthu Ramachandran   © 2014 Nova Science Publishers, Inc.

Chapter 4

CONTINUOUS DELIVERY IN THE CLOUD: AN ECONOMIC EVALUATION USING SYSTEM DYNAMICS

Olumide Akerele and Muthu Ramachandran*
School of Computing, Creative Technologies, and Engineering,
Faculty of Arts, Environment and Technology,
Leeds Metropolitan University, Leeds, UK

ABSTRACT

The continuous delivery paradigm has been recently introduced to help facilitate the speedy deployment of working software into production and shifting software delivery exercise from a major event culture to an effortless activity. Recent advancements have made it possible to practice continuous delivery in the cloud. However, many practitioners are still skeptical about the economic profitability of practicing continuous delivery in the cloud.

This work investigates the economic profitability of carrying out continuous delivery in the cloud and compares it with on-premise continuous delivery adoption using system dynamics. Results show that the continuous delivery in the cloud environment over a six year period has a Net Present Value (NPV) over twice that of the on-premise continuous delivery.

Keywords: Continuous Delivery, Dynamic Continuous Delivery, Agile Software Development, Cloud Services

---

* Email: o.akerele@leedsmet.ac.uk.

INTRODUCTION

What is Continuous Delivery?

Software delivery suffers as a result of many post-development issues: Configuration management problems, lack of testing in a clone of the production environment and insufficient collaboration between the development teams and the deployment team (operations) are the major problems that cause software rejection at this stage (Humble and Farley, 2010). An example is the complete failure of the software in the production environment due to assumptions built into previous test environments - which are different from the specifications of the production environment. The end result: delivery failure. These problems are the rationale for the need of the expedient continuous deployment of software features into a sandbox, staging or production environment and ensuring the system behaves as required before being classified as "accepted stories" or "release candidates". This practice is called Continuous Delivery (Humble and Farley, 2010). One of the main goals of continuous delivery is to achieve build-in quality and customer satisfaction (Agile manifesto).

Continuous Delivery facilitates the effortless deployment working software to the customer environment by using a pull-approach. As such, customers have "production ready" software and are always deployable into their production environment on request without hassle. This ensures that software releases are only hindered by business decisions and not IT constraints. Continuous delivery is distinct to the post development journey of the software to the actual deployment of the software. Hence, is bound by activities within the integration of working /functionality to the successful deployment of the working software.

This chapter aims to solve the problem of unexpected software project delivery patterns, non-systematic approaches to continuous delivery principles, and to fine tune dynamic system models towards cloud services. In this context, we have contributed to producing an innovative model known as dynamic continuous delivery model which incorporates dynamic system modelling and simulation with continuous delivery principles for cloud service delivery.

This chapter investigates the economic profitability of carrying out continuous delivery in the cloud and compares it with on-premise continuous delivery adoption using system dynamics. The earlier results are encouraging and show that the continuous delivery in the cloud environment over a six year period has a Net Present Value (NPV) over twice that of the on-premise continuous delivery.

DYNAMIC CONTINUOUS DELIVERY

The *delivery pipeline* encapsulates a series of four stages depending on the extent of testing required by the application. We investigate a generic 4-tier deployment pipeline in our research which could be further modified to fit each varying project requirements: Commit stage, Automated Acceptance Testing (AAT), Manual Testing and Release to Production. Therefore we have proposed a model for continuous delivery known as Dynamic Continuous Delivery (DCD as shown in Figure 1) which incorporates dynamic modelling, story driven development, and delivery pipeline & delivery principle. The corresponding deliverables of each stage are represented in boxes as shown in Figure 1.

The notion of dynamic modelling refers to behaviour-driven development (BDD) is an integral aspect of Test-Driven Development (TDD) as the key part of Agile manifesto. We discuss BDD using dynamic system development model and simulation for Agile projects is also proposed in this chapter. The idea of a delivery pipeline refers to move away from traditional delivery series of (new features, integration, testing & release) into parallel thinking of adding new features/changes into continuous delivery with continuous availability of the system in operational mode. Therefore, achieving the Agile principles of software delivery such as (Humble and Farley, 2010):

1   *Create a Repeatable, Reliable Process for Releasing Software*. This makes delivery process as simple as possible thus achieving the Agile principle of Simplicity. The repeatability and reliability derive from two principles:
2   *Automate almost everything*, and keep everything you need to build, deploy, test, and release your application in version control
3   *Keep Everything in Version Control*
4   *If It Hurts, Do It More Frequently, and Bring the Pain Forward*
5   *Build Quality In*
6   *Done Means Released*. This refers 100% satisfied with all user stories proposed in our dynamic delivery model
7   Everybody Is Responsible for the Delivery Process
8   Continuous Improvement. Follow Deming cycle of plan, do, study, act (PDSA) or similar approach of continuous improvement and delivery.

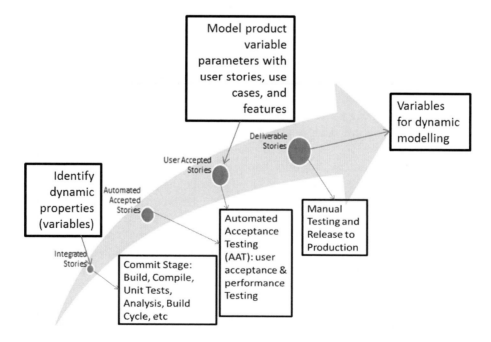

Figure 1 Dynamic Continuous Delivery (DCD) Model.

In addition to our dynamic continuous model activities, there are fundamental & main steps that should be covered as part of the CD process:

1   Build – compile, unit test, version, package
2   Quality – metrics, documentation
3   Test – acceptance-, regression- and performance tests
4   Provision environments – deployment to test- and staging environment
5   Production – green/blue deployment to production

We urge readers to look at reference by Humble and Farley (2010) for detailed discussion on this topic.

CLOUD COMPUTING

Cloud computing has been a coveted buzzword in the computing industry and has been trending since year 2005. Cloud computing is the technology behind the provision of software applications, data storage, computation and data access by service providers to their customers (businesses or individuals) – making use of the internet as the deployment medium. This leads to the lack of necessity for acquiring traditional infrastructure that would otherwise be needed for on-premise computing operations. The cloud service provider is typically located remotely and the customer is charged proportionally to the amount of service or infrastructure usage.

Cloud computing has emerged to provide a more cost effective solution to businesses and services while making use of inexpensive computing solutions which combines pervasive, internet, and virtualisation technologies. Cloud computing has spread to catch up with another technological evolution as we have witnessed internet technology which has revolutionised communication and information super highway. Cloud computing is emerging rapidly and software as a service paradigm has increasing its demand for more services. However, this new trend needs to be more systematic with respect to software engineering and its related process. For example, current challenges that are faced with cyber security and application security flaws, lessons learned and best practices can be adopted. Similarly, as the demand for cloud services increases and so increased importance sought for security and privacy. The business of cloud technology can only be sustained if we can maintain balance between demand for services in-line with improved cloud security and privacy.

Cloud service providers such as Microsoft, Google, Sales force.com, Amazon, GoGrid are able to leverage cloud technology with pay-per-use business model with on-demand elasticity by which resources can be expended or shortened based on service requirements. They often try to co-locate their servers in order to save cost. There every effort by several other enterprises to establish their cloud efforts to build their own cloud (private clouds) on their premises but can't afford to compromise security of their applications and data which is their major hurdle in their new effort. Most important of all, they need to develop a legitimate and controlled way of establishing service-level-agreements with their clients and to embed these rules to be built-in with services.

Standardisation has been active in software development and information technology to ensure systematic use of process, methods, and to that of client's requirements. Standards include on Quality, Quality of Services (QoS), Usability, and Process such as ISO, CMMI, and others to ensure product and service quality are adhered. The emergence and adherence of standardization such as Information Technology Infrastructure Library (ITIL), ISO/IEC 27001/27002, and Open Virtualization Format are critical in establishing expected cloud sustainability and trust in this new technological service business. Hence, it is highly recommend OVF standard as vendor and platform independent, open, secure, portable, efficient and extensible format for the packaging and distribution of software to be run in virtual machines (software stack that incorporates the target applications, libraries, services, configuration, relevant data, and operating system).

Software development has been tremendously boosted since the introduction of cloud computing (Bykov et al., 2012). Apparently, every individual development phase and activity in the software projects can now be executed in the cloud; this includes coding, testing, deployment and maintenance of software projects. In other words, Cloud computing = autonomic computing (self management) + client-server model of distributed computing + grid computing (virtualisation + distributed + parallel computing) + the power of a main frame computing (Enterprise resource planning (ERP) & management + transaction processing) + Utility computing (packaging of computing resources (resources + meter/rates) + peer-to-peer networking architecture (a distributed architecture without need for a central co-ordination). Cloud computing has emerged to offer services and resources cost effectively. The main characteristics of a cloud are to offer services that are dynamically scalable and to provide virtualised resources.

Services are the basic principle behind the emergence of cloud computing. Cloud computing has now been considered as a good business and enterprise model for the future of computing sectors. There are three main services can be offered by any cloud architecture and technology that can support such as *Software as a Service (SaaS)* is a concept of providing software applications as a service on demand over the internet which means it can be run anywhere anytime and to pay per use rather than to buy, *Platform as a Service (PaaS)* is a concept of providing a complete service level application development environment as a service over the internet right from requirements to the complete life cycle, and *Infrastructure as a Service (IaaS)* is concept of providing the whole IT infrastructures such as storage, virtual environment, servers, platforms, and applications.

Our earlier work on cloud computing developed a number of best practice design guidelines for components based design that supports componentising cloud applications, explicitly Ramachandran (2008); Ramachandran, (2011); Ramachandran, (2011); Ramachandran, (2012); Ramachandran, (2013a); Ramachandran, (2013b) .

We have also proposed a process model based on CBSE, which is specifically customised for developing cloud applications. We have also developed a software security engineering process for developing cloud services with build-in security. A case study on Amazon cloud EC2 has been designed based on software component model for cloud computing.

The challenge for cloud services developers as well as cloud providers are to manage and delivery services that are sustainable. Therefore, the Agile development paradigm along with continuous delivery principle applied to cloud service delivery will enhance and sustain cloud computing business.

CONTINUOUS DELIVERY (CD) MEETS THE CLOUD

The cloud through the concept of virtualization has made it possible for customers to scale up and down the amount of resources required. Customers do not need capital investment to acquire the hardware and software to complete development, testing and deployment activities. Customers want to pay for their usage and reduce the redundancy of the infrastructure they will be requiring to perform many of these continuous delivery tasks. Also, the operations cost necessary for the maintenance of the infrastructure and management of on-site systems are quite daunting.

CD has been inhibited by the requirement to have vast capital investment on infrastructures, hardware and software to help in the continuous deployment of good quality software. Advancements in cloud technologies have made it not a possibility to carry out the entire CD process - starting from automated running of integration builds to the deployment activities in the cloud using SaaS and IaaS offerings. Even outside the CD boundaries, cloud IDEs such as *Cloud9* and *Nitrous.IO* have been developed to aid in writing production code without developers having to install any software or purchase any license before they can get started with coding. They offer a desktop IDE like impression and are designed for literally all programming languages. It is now possible to carry out these activities - including all the testing tasks - all from a browser. An area of viable potential research is the impact of the agile practices on the CD process (Akerele et al., 2013a) The main aim of the cloud movement is to shift the Capital Expense (Capex) of organizations to Operational expense (Opex) (Akerele et al., 2013b).

Cloud Development Platform

Nowadays, various IDE's are provided by PaaS vendors to create a typical development environment and make the developers feel no different than they feel when they develop in a normal desktop IDE application. The major problem though is the most PaaS platforms function in their own DSL which increases the barrier of exit. This is referred to as *vendor lock-in*. Examples of such platform are *heroku, force.com* and the *Google App Engine.*

Cloud Source Control System

It is now possible to have remote access to the various versions of software and effectively visualize and manage them. Commits to the mainline can be made remotely for the use of the team irrespective of their locations. Remote access is granted to patches, pull request workflow, branches and so on of software. The privilege to have access to all this without cloud technology involves high enterprise investment in hardware and also on system administrators. A typical example of a cloud source control system is the *Github, BeanStalk* and *BitBucket.*

Cloud Continuous Integration Server

A continuous integration serer is vital in continuous delivery of software to effectively manage the integration of source code into the mainline. Some teams dedicate an entire system as the CI server while others depend on expensive licenses from CI server vendors to help monitor their integrations. Not only are these expensive, the configuration of these systems may also take a lot of time and resources which may deter many teams from continuous integration practice.

Recently, tools such as *CircleCI* and *CloudBees* have been designed to be accessible in the cloud and help to effectively manage builds in a system. They detect any changes to the code base and trigger the build tests and notify the team of the feedback from the build after completion.

Cloud Automated Acceptance Testing

Cloud testing is the practice of carrying out the testing phase and activities of the development process in the cloud; hence, preventing the need for the vast capital expenditure on acquiring infrastructure, licenses and set-up on customer site. The most popular applicability of cloud testing has been in performance and load testing where there is need to generate multi-user traffic from various locations – which would ideally need numerous high configuration servers for the traffic simulation. For example, a project needing to carry out load testing by hitting the test server with 30,000 users simultaneously; this will require a decent amount of infrastructure among other costs which may be quite daunting.

Testing in the cloud has been an area of interest in the recent years particularly in load and performance testing (Akerele at al., 2012). Automated acceptance testing has also now been extended to the cloud with the aid of tools like *Saucelabs* which make it possible to pay per use for their platform usage. This platform has also been extended to mobile usage, and to make it easy to test mobile applications. They completely obliterate the need for any infrastructure and allow easy running of selenium and JavaScript unit tests. Just like the normal automated acceptance test platforms, they give a comprehensive feedback with metadata of the test results.

Cloud Deployment

Infrastructure such as servers and storage all cloud based have made deployment in the cloud realizable. A typical example of this is the *Amazon AWS* which provides *Amazon S3* for virtual storage and *EC2* for virtual servers designed for deployment purposes. This is a typical example of IaaS platform . Amazon AWS enable users to have access to on-demand instances with the benefit for fees payment in proportion to the compute capacity used. This exempts the user from investing heavily on the planning, buying and maintenance of hardware . This is a typical example of the CapEx conversion to OpEx as these fixed costs are converted to small variable costs.

SYSTEM DYNAMICS MODELLING OF THE PROFITABILITY OF CLOUD BASED CONTINUOUS DELIVERY

As businesses ponder whether to migrate their continuous delivery process to the cloud, it is still unclear whether it is actually economically profitable to do so. Using System Dynamics (SD), a simplistic and generic model to be designed to compare the cost effectiveness of continuous delivery in the cloud and on-premise to guide management of potential adopters of cloud based continuous delivery.

Methodology

Due to the nature of this work, it will be impossible to have such leeway to alter the project variables of an actual project using an empirical approach. Empirical studies do not possess this sort of flexibility. Even when attempted to be used for such research work, the cost and excessive time of execution is a major deterrent to any research group.

Simulations help to overcome the shortcomings of empirical analysis: cost, flexibility and time consumption (Abdel-Hamid & Madnick, 1991). It provides the computerized prototype of an actual system run over time (iteratively) to improve project understanding and knowledge base of project stakeholders.

SD is the modelling and simulation platform used for this work. SD models are used to visualize the complexity of a system in feedback loops to study how the system behaves over a specified period of time (Madachy, 2008). The SD platform enables the user to run simulations and monitor the evolvement of a system over a defined period of time- without any prior knowledge of coding.

When the simulation model is correctly parameterized, System dynamics modelling of various decision scenarios has been shown to be helpful in predicting project cost, effort, quality and schedule trends (Abdel-Hamid & Madnick, 1991). Variables exhibiting dynamic behaviour and inter-relationships in the model are represented by the dynamic feedback loops- and are linked through a set of interacting equations.

A system dynamic model becomes useful in software management when managers want to evaluate the possible cost and schedule consequences of their decisions. The system dynamics model allows repeated experimentation to gain understanding and make predictions about the implications of managerial actions and policies (Abdel-Hamid & Madnick, 1991).

SD models are used to visualize the complexity of a system in feedback loops to study how the system behaves over a specified period of time (K. Ogata, 2003).

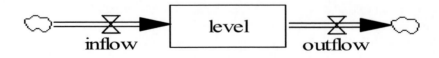

Figure 2. System Dynamic Components.

Legend- Level: Entity that builds or diminishes over a specified period of time; **Inflow/Outflow:** Rate of change in level.

To achieve the goal of this work, we design the model to calculate the Net Present Value (NPV) of both deployment environments i.e., cloud based environment and the on-premise environment. The NPV is defined as the:

$$NPV = PV - FV/(1 + r)^t \text{ (Damodaran \& Aswath, 2012)}$$

Where PV = present value, FV = future value, r = discounted rate and t = number of years.

When the NPV is positive, it indicates profitability in the investment while a negative value indicates a project will not recoup its capital investment. A value of "0" implies the business just manages to break even. Hence, the higher the value of the NPV for various investment options, the more desirable it is from the perspective of a potential investor. In this context, the Present Vale, PV, is the sum total of the capital investment at the start of the project while the future value, FV, is the value of the future earnings minus the future ongoing costs.

Model Variables and Parameters

Continuous Delivery is a new and upcoming paradigm with many companies at the introductory stage of its practice. Practitioners of continuous delivery in the cloud are even less due to the skeptism of its cost effectiveness. This makes it quite difficult to get real data from a company that has successfully migrated to the cloud to use for the calibration of the model. As a result, fictional but realistic variable parameters are used to simulate this model. Most of the costing parameters are sourced from websites of software and cloud vendors.

In this study, it is assumed that free or open source tools used in either deployment environments are not adopted. Model parameters are italicized.

On-Site Deployment Variables

Total Initial Investment On-Premise Deployment
This is the cost of the infrastructure required such as the hardware, application and database servers and storage. Based on the average specifications used in the cloud requirements estimate, we assume an average of $40,000. The extra cost for floor space required is ignored.

Labour for set up: $10000

Ongoing on-site Deployment Cost

This includes the on-going yearly average costs for: Software licenses: $20,000 (Total yearly software licensing such as Operating System, Database (MySQL- $5000 enterprise edition). Also includes any licenses necessary for all the necessary automated testing in the delivery pipeline.)

Ongoing labour cost for maintenance: This includes the ongoing labour cost for database and operating system maintenance service.

Power: This is the cost of supplying power for the infrastructure such as servers and so on.

hardware lifespan: 5yrs

hardware replacement cost: $40000

labour for infrastructure maintenance: $8,000/month i.e., $96,000/year

power : $8000/month i.e., $96000/year

Rate of on-premise FV accumulation: (expected revenue-ongoing onsite deployment cost)/((1+discounted rate))^Time

Future Value for On-premise deployment: Rate of on-premise FV accumulation expected revenue: 300,000 pa

NPV for on-premise deployment: FV for on-premise deployment- total initial investment on-premise deployment

Discount rate: 8%

Cloud Deployment Variables

Total Initial Investment in Cloud Deployment: DSL learning cost+one-off cloud broker fees

Ongoing Cloud Deployment Cost.

labour for cloud service maintenance: Estimated to be about one-fourth that required by onsite deployment : $24,000.

*Average IaaS (*Infrastructure -as-a Service*) fees*: EC2 costing, a cloud server offering by Amazon, depends on the OS, capacity of the server required as well as the duration of usage . Assuming a mid-range specification of server costing, pricing is $1.81/hour [http://aws.amazon.com/ec2/?navclick=true#pricing]. approx $1300/month i.e., $15,600pa. *S3*, a cloud storage offering by Amazon helps to store and retrieve data from the cloud. The pricing depends on the size of storage required. Average of $0.065 per GB and we can estimate a average sage of 500TB. *S3* cost is estimated to : 0.065 x 500 = 32,500pa. Total IaaS fees estimate/annum = $48,100

Average PaaS (Platform-as-a-Server) fees: Estimated fees based on 10 users and specifications. $1,200/month i.e., $14,400/year

Average SaaS fees: Estimated fees based on 10 users and specifications : $5,200/year

Average Software Lifespan: 6-10yrs (Lientz & Swanson, 1980)

Total Initial Investment on Cloud Deployment: DSL learning cost+one-off cloud broker fees.

*DSL(*Domain Specific Language*) learning Curve*: s-shaped (Abdel-Hamid & Madnick, 1991)

DSL Learning Cost: This is the resource spent on training developers on new language. This is estimated to be $ 50,000.

One-off cloud broker fees: This is the estimated consultancy fees of an expert sought to advice on best platform choices that best align with the goal of the organization and help in the organization's migration : $5,000

Rate of Cloud FV accumulation: (expected revenue-ongoing cloud deployment cost)/((1+discounted rate))^Time

FV for Cloud Deployment: Rate of Cloud FV accumulation

NPV for cloud based migration: FV for cloud deployment-total initial investment cloud deployment

The full diagram of the model is presented in the Figure 3.

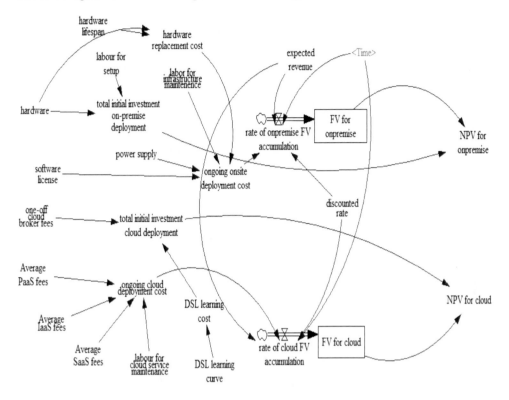

Figure 3. SD Model for the Economic Evaluation of both Environments.

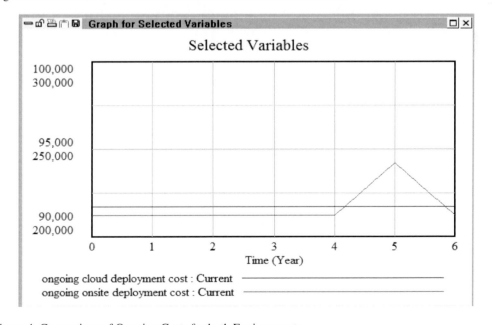

Figure 4. Comparison of Ongoing Costs for both Environments.

MODEL RESULTS

After the calibration and parameterization of the model, the simulation procedure is carried out for a period of 6 years by setting the maximum time of the simulation platform to 6 years, considering the fact that a software has an average lifespan of between 6-10 years (Lientz & Swanson, 1980). This has been illustrated Figure 4.

Table 1. Tabular results for Future Values of Cloud and On-Premise Deployments

Time (Year)	Selected	FV for cloud	FV for onpremise
0	Variables	0	0
1	Runs:	208300	88000
2	Current	402973	170243
3		584910	247106
4		754945	318940
5		913856	386075
6		1.06237e+006	427428

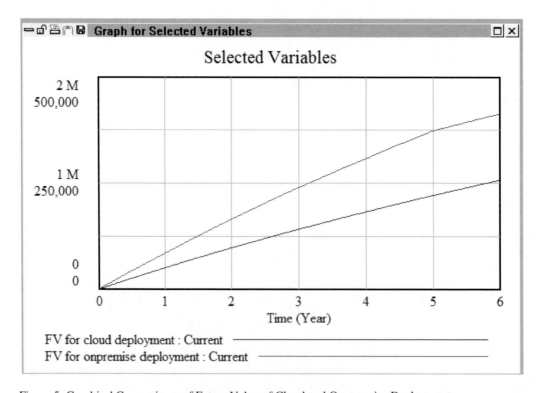

Figure 5. Graphical Comparisons of Future Value of Cloud and On-premise Deployments.

Table 2. Tabular results for NPV for both Environments

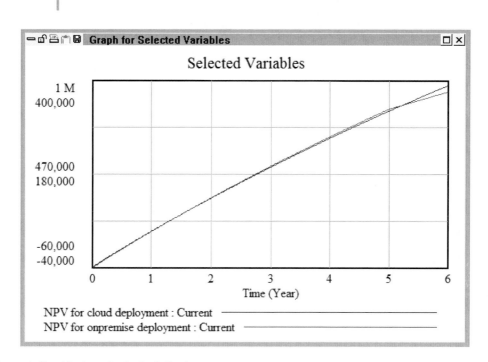

Table Time Down			
Time (Year)	Selected	FV for cloud	FV for onpremise
0	Variables	0	0
1	Runs:	208300	88000
2	Current	402973	170243
3		584910	247106
4		754945	318940
5		913856	386075
6		1.06237e+006	427428

Figure 6. Graphical results for both Environments.

Discussion

Figure 4 clearly shows the ongoing costs of both environments. The value of the *ongoing costs for onsite deployment* rises in the 5th year due to the need for the organization to invest in new hardware due to the end of the lifespan of the hardware being used. The ongoing cost for cloud deployment is much lower than that of the onsite deployment and remains constant over the 6-year period.

Figure 5 shows that the future values for both instances and clearly shows that the cloud deployment option is much more profitable than onsite deployment over the six year period.

Over the six year period, the cloud option remains at least twice more financially profitable compared to the onsite deployment option.

Figure 6 shows the NPV comparisons, the most important metric in the model in the determination of the profitability of booth instances over the 6 year period. The onsite NPV starts off being higher than that of the cloud but it becomes obvious that after the first year, the NPV for the cloud environment exceeds that of the onsite scenario and this margin gathers pace and widens over the 6 year period.

The shape of the NPV for onsite deployment towards the 6th year makes it interesting to investigate what happens if it is assumed the lifespan of the software is prolonged and the software lasts much longer than the 6 year period. As an experiment, the behaviour of both environments is simulated over a 50 year period- where it is assumed the software keeps getting improved with new features but still keeps it core functionalities.

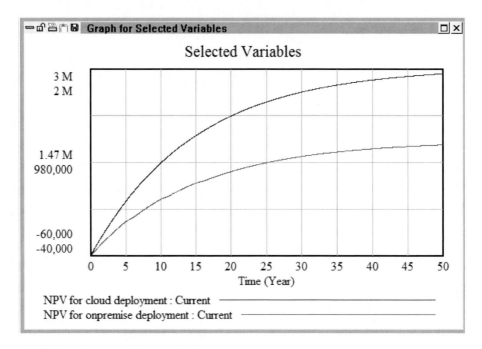

Figure 7. NPV results over a 50year period.

The results shows an exponential graph for both instances in which the NPV starts dropping off after the 25th year for the on-premise scenario and in the 35th year for the cloud deployment scenario. This indicates that the cloud deployment option is likely to remain viable for a longer period of time over the on-premise scenario.

REFERENCES

Humble, J. & Farley, D., 2011. *Continuous delivery: reliable software releases through build, test, and deployment automation*, Upper Saddle River, NJ [u.a.]: Addison-Wesley.

Bykov, S. et al., 2011. Orleans: Cloud Computing for Everyone. In Proceedings of the 2Nd ACM Symposium on Cloud Computing. SOCC '11. New York, NY, USA: ACM, pp.

16:1–16:14. Available at: *http://doi.acm.org/10.1145/2038916.2038932* [Accessed December 11, 2013].

Akerele, O., Ramachandran, M. & Dixon, M., 2013. *System Dynamics Modeling of Agile Continuous Delivery Process*. In Agile Conference (AGILE), 2013. Agile Conference (AGILE), 2013. pp. 60–63.

Akerele, O., Ramachandran, M. & Dixon, M., 2013. Testing in the Cloud: Strategies, Risks and Benefits. In Z. Mahmood & S. Saeed, eds. Software Engineering Frameworks for the Cloud Computing Paradigm. Computer Communications and Networks. Springer London, pp. 165–185. Available at: *http://link.springer.com/chapter/10.1007/978-1-4471-5031-2_8 [Accessed December 11, 2013]*.

Abdel-Hamid, T. & Madnick, S.E., 1991. *Software Project Dynamics: An Integrated Approach*, Upper Saddle River, NJ, USA: Prentice-Hall, Inc.

Madachy, R.J., 2008. Software process dynamics, Piscataway, NJ.; Chichester: Wiley-*IEEE*/; John Wiley, distributor].

Ogata, K., 2004. *System dynamics*, Upper Saddle River, NJ: Pearson/Prentice Hall.

Damodaran, A., 2012. *Investment valuation: tools and techniques for determining the value of any asset,* Hoboken, N.J.: Wiley.

Ramachandran, M (2008) *Software components: guidelines and applications*, Nova Publishers, NY.

Ramachandran, M (2011) Software components for cloud computing architectures and applications, Springer, Mahmmood, Z and Hill, R (eds.).*www.springer.com/computer/communication+networks/book/978-1-4471-2235-7*

Ramachandran, M (2011) Software Security Engineering: Design and Applications, Nova Science Publishers, New York, USA, 2011.ISBN: 978-1-61470-128-6, *https://www.novapublishers.com/catalog/product_info.php?products_id=26331*

Ramachandran, M (2012) Service Component Architecture for Building Cloud Services, Published: August 20th, 2012, Service Technology Magazine Issue LXV, *http://www.servicetechmag.com/I65/0812-4*

Ramachandran, M (2013) Software security engineering for cloud computing services, *Encyclopaedia of Information* Technology, IGI Global.

Ramachandran, M (2013) Business Requirements Engineering for Developing Cloud Computing Services, Springer, Software Engineering Frameworks for Cloud Computing Paradigm, Mahmmood, Z and Saeed, S (eds.), *http://www.springer.com/computer/communication+networks/book/978-1-4471-5030-5*

Lientz, B.P. and Swanson, E.B (1980) *Software Maintenance Management, A Study Of The Maintenance Of Computer Application Software* In 487 Data Processing Organizations. Addison-Wesley, Reading MA, 1980. ISBN 0-201-04205-3

In: Advances in Cloud Computing Research　　　　ISBN: 978-1-63117-192-5
Editor: Muthu Ramachandran　　　　　　　　　© 2014 Nova Science Publishers, Inc.

Chapter 5

FINANCIAL CLOUDS AND MODELLING OFFERED BY CLOUD COMPUTING ADOPTION FRAMEWORK

Victor Chang[1,2], Robert John Walters[2] and Gary Wills[2]*
[1]School of Computing, Creative Technologies and Engineering,
Leeds Metropolitan University, Leeds, UK
[2]Electronics and Computer Science, University of Southampton, Southampton, UK

ABSTRACT

Cloud Computing Adoption Framework (CCAF) is a framework for designing and implementation of Could Computing solutions. This paper focuses on how CCAF can help to address portability in Cloud Computing implementations in Finance domain. Portability involves migrating entire applications from desktops to clouds and between different Clouds in a way which is transparent to users so they may continue to work as if still using their familiar systems. Reviews for several financial models are studied, where Monte Carlo Methods (MCM) and Black Scholes Model (BSM) are chosen to demonstrate portability between desktops and clouds. A special technique in MCM, Variance-Gamma Process, is used for error corrections while performing analysis of good quality. Coding algorithm for MCM and BSM written in MATLAB are explained. Simulations for MCM and BSM are performed on different types of Clouds. Benchmark and experimental results are presented and discussed, together with implications for banking and ways to track risks in order to improve accuracy. We have used a conceptual Financial Cloud platform to explain how this fits into the CCAF, as well as Financial Software as a Service (FSaaS). Our objective is to demonstrate portability, speed, accuracy and reliability of applications in the clouds, while demonstrating portability for CCAF and FSaaS.

Keywords: Financial Clouds; Cloud Computing Adoption Framework (CCAF); Monte Carlo Methods; Monte Carlo Simulations; Black Scholes Model; Financial Software as a Service (FSaaS); Variance-Gamma Processes (VPG); MATLAB SaaS applications on Clouds; programming methods for Cloud Computing; enterprise portability for Clouds

---

* V.I.Chang@leedsmet.ac.uk.

1. INTRODUCTION

Finding solutions to the Global economic downturn triggered by the finance sector is an interdisciplinary research problem which requires that experts from different sectors work altogether. There are different interpretations for the cause of the problem. Firstly, Lord Turner, Chair of the Financial Service Authority (FSA), is quoted as follows: "The problem, he said, was that the banks' mathematical models assumed a 'normal' or 'Gaussian' distribution of events, represented by the bell curve, which dangerously underestimated the risk of something going seriously wrong." (Financial Times, June 2009). Secondly, there were reports of a lack of regulations on financial practices. Currently remedies are being proposed by several governments to improve on this (Financial Times, 2010; City A.M, 2010). Thirdly, there was the "Madness of Mortgage Lenders" as identified in a study conducted by Hamnett (2009) whereby uncontrolled lending to those who could not afford to repay led to a housing bubble and subsequent collapse. Irresponsible mortgage lending was a key factor in the collapse of Lehman Brothers which seemed to trigger the global financial crisis. All the above in combination contributed to creating the conditions that led to the global downturn.

All the above suggested possibilities contribute to complexity that caused global downturn. The global economic downturn triggered by finance sector is an interdisciplinary research question that the use of Cloud resources offers innovative approaches for risk analysis, and knowledge sharing in a community-oriented and professional platform (Feiman and Cearley, 2009). Cloud resources can be used to improve accuracy of risk analysis, financial modelling and knowledge sharing in an open and professional platform (Buyya et al., 2009; Chang et al., 2010 a; 2010 c; 2011 b; 2011 c; 2011 d; 2013 a). There are demonstrations presented by authors to confirm the added values of Cloud adoption, and sectors including healthcare, finance and education receive added value including improvement in efficiency, collaboration, revenue, cost-savings and service rating in healthcare, finance and education sectors as a result of Cloud adoption (Chang et al., 2011 d; 2012 a; 2012 b; 2012 c; 2013 a; 2013 b; 2013 c; Chang 2013 a; 2013 b; 2013 c). The extended rationale for providing added values for finance is as follows: Clouds provide a common platform on which to run different modelling and simulations based on Gaussian and non-Gaussian models. The Clouds then offer distributed high-performing resources for experts in different areas within and outside financial services to study and review the modelling together, including models using Monte Carlo Methods and Black Scholes Model. The Clouds allow regulations to be taken with ease while establishing and strengthening security and policy within the Clouds resources.

There are different types of clouds in the market such as Health clouds, Energy clouds, Security clouds and Telecommunications clouds, with exceptions for Finance clouds. It is apparent from the relative lack of existing literature on the subject that there has been little academic research into Financial Clouds (FC). Based on literatures and interviews (Chang et al.,2010 a; 2010 c; 2011 a), we have identified several reasons for this. Firstly, a majority of financial practices are closed-source, since this relates to the way they make profits and business opportunities, and sharing this type of information will be undesirable within a business context (Bryan T, 2009). Secondly, human decision makers can overrule any computing analysis for risks and even introduce excessive risk taking that can result in adverse effects as illustrated between 2008 and 2009 (Flouris and Ylimaz, 2010). Thirdly, despite advanced technologies being introduced, many financial practices still use desktop-oriented tools such as Excel and VBA together with desktop based statistical software such as SAS. A few use Grid technologies, and of among them, not all will use Clouds (Chen, Chee, Huang, Jin, Tseng, Wang and Wong, 2010, by interviews). Fourthly, finance projects are mostly investigated by business schools which have few active involvements with Grid and Cloud communities (with one notable exception in Austria, and the new interdisciplinary centres in Oxford, UCL, KCL and Warwick, although it is the industrial vendors who are leading in this area).

1. LITERATURE REVIEW

There are three sub-sections in Literature Review, and each is presented as follows.

2.1. Organisational Challenges of Cloud Adoption

There are existing Cloud Computing problems experienced in the current organisational adoption of Cloud (Chang et al., 2010 a; 2011 a; 2013 b; Chang 2013). Firstly, all cloud business models and frameworks proposed by other leading researchers are either qualitative (Briscoe and Marinos, 2009; Chou, 2009; Weinhardt et al., 2009; Schubert, Jeffery and Neidecker-Lutz, 2010) or quantitative (Brandic et al., 2009; Buyya et al., 2009; Armbrust et al., 2009). Each framework is self-contained, and not related to others' work. There are few frameworks or models which demonstrate linking both quantitative and qualitative aspects but when they do, the work is still at an early stage.

Secondly, there is no accurate method for analysing risk and return other than the stock market. A limitation with current practices in the stock market is that it is subject to accuracy and reliability issues (Chang et al., 2011 b; 2011 c; 2011 c). There are researchers focusing on types of business model for which cloud business can be successful (Chou, 2009; Weinhardt et al., 2009) but these business model classifications need more cases to support them and more data modelling to validate them for sustainability. Ideally, a structured framework is required to review risk and return analysis and sustainability in systematic ways.

Thirdly, communications between different types of clouds from different vendors are often difficult to implement. Work-arounds require writing additional layers of APIs, an interface or a portal. This highlights interesting research questions such as portability; allowing existing applications on desktop or other computing environments to work on Cloud, or moving enterprise applications and services (not just files or VM) to the Cloud Computing environments. Enterprise portability of some applications from desktop to cloud can be challenging (Beaty et al., 2009; Armbrust et al., 2009). The scope of enterprise portability refers to moving enterprise applications and services, and not just files or VM over clouds.

2.2. Cloud Services

Services provided by Cloud Computing implementations may be divided into a number of classes as follows:

- Software as a Service (SaaS). The term "Software as a Service" (SaaS) was first used by Saleforce.com in 1999 when they saw the vision of merging Web Services (WS) and Service Oriented Architecture (SOA). Referred to as Service or Application Clouds, these offer implementations of specific business functions and business processes that are provided with cloud capabilities. They provide applications and/or services using a cloud infrastructure or platform, rather than providing cloud features themselves. SaaS is a popular type of cloud service and provides added value on top of WS and SOA (Foster et al., 2008; Briscoe and Marinos, 2009; Buyya et al., 2009). This paper addresses financial SaaS on Clouds and provides solutions for enterprise portability.
- Platform as a Service (PaaS): provides computational resources via a platform upon which applications and services can be developed and hosted. PaaS typically makes use of dedicated APIs to control the behaviour of a server hosting engine that executes and replicates the execution according to user requests (e.g., access rate).
- Infrastructure as a Service (IaaS) is divided into Compute Clouds and Resource Clouds. Compute Clouds provide users access to computational resources such as CPUs, hypervisors and utilities. Resource Clouds contain managed and scalable resources as services to users – they provide enhanced virtualisation capabilities.

2.3. Financial Models

Gaussian-based mathematical models have been frequently used in financial modelling (Birge and Massart, 2001). As pointed out by the FSA, many banks' mathematical models assumed normal (Gaussian) distribution as an expected outcome, and might underestimate the risk for something going wrong. According to Hutchinson (2010), "The Gaussian model is too optimistic about market stability, because it uses an unrealistically high number for the key variable, the exponential rate of decay, known to its friends as alpha". To address this, other non-Gaussian financial models need to be investigated and demonstrated for how financial SaaS can be successfully calculated and executed on Clouds where Section 4 and 5 present more details. Based on the various studies (Feiman and Cearley, 2009; Hull 2009), one model for pricing and one model for risk analysis should be selected respectively. A number of methods for calculating prices include Monte Carlo Methods (MCM), Capital Asset Pricing Models and Binomial Model. MCM is often used in stochastic and probabilistic financial models, and provides data for investors' decision-making (Hull, 2009) and is our choice for MCM for pricing. On the other hand, methods such as Fourier series, stochastic volatility and Black Scholes Model (BSM) are more appropriate for volatility. As a main stream option, BSM is selected for risk analysis in this paper as BSM has finite difference equations to approximate derivatives.

2.3.1. Monte Carlo Methods in Theory

Monte Carlo Simulation (MCS), originated from mathematical Monte Carlo Methods, which is a computational technique used to calculate risk analysis and the probability of an event or investment to happen. MCS is based on probability distributions, so that uncertain variables can be described and simulated with controlled variables (Hull 2009; Waters 2008). Originated from Physics, Brownian Motions follow underlying random variables can influence the Black-Scholes models, where the stock price becomes

$$dS = \mu S\, dt + \sigma S\, dW_t.$$

(1)

where W is Brownian—the dW term here stands in for any and all sources of uncertainty in the price history of the stock. The time intervals are divided into M units of length δt from time 0 to T in a sampling path, and the Brownian motion over the interval dt are approximated by a single normal variable of mean 0 and variance δt, and leading to

$$S(k\delta t) = S(0)\exp\left(\sum_{i=1}^{k}\left[\left(\mu - \frac{\sigma^2}{2}\right)\delta t + \sigma\varepsilon_i\sqrt{\delta t}\right]\right)$$

(2)

for each k between 1 and M, and each is a draw from a standard normal distribution. If a derivative H pays the average value of S between 0 and T then a sample path ω corresponds to a set and hence,

$$H(\omega) = \frac{1}{M+1}\sum_{k=0}^{M} S(k\delta t).$$

(3)

The Monte Carlo value of this derivative is obtained by generating N lots of M normal variables, creating N sample paths and so N values of H, and then taking the average. The error has order convergence in standard deviation based on the central limit theorem.

2.3.2. Monte Carlo Methods for Variance-Gamma Processes

Reibero and Webber (2002) demonstrate improved calculation techniques based on Monte Carlo Methods (MCM) on top of the Variance-Gamma (VG) Process, which has been a subject of studies by researchers (Carr et al., 2002; Reibero, Webber, 2002). They explain stratified sampling method and how to stratify VG bridge. They have benchmarked the methods with European options (a finance model). However, Reibero and Webber do not provide any details of hardware and software environments used for benchmarking, and there is no information for their coding algorithm. To demonstrate Variance-Gamma, we have opted for Asian options with 10,000 MCM simulations. They perform this experiment using a desktop environment, two private clouds and one Amazon EC2 public cloud as the proof of concept and benchmarking. Details are described in Section 4. The purpose of demonstration is not about the finance model; either European or Asian, but it is about presenting a systematic and logical proof of concepts. In another paper published by Reibero and Webber (2004), they explain that there is simulation bias in MCM for financial options including VG process.

2.3. Black Scholes Model (BSM)

The BSM is commonly used for financial markets and derivatives calculations. It is also an extension from Brownian motion. The BSM formula calculates call and put prices of European options (a financial model) (Hull, 2009). The value of a call option for the BSM is

$$C(S,t) = SN(d_1) - Ke^{-r(T-t)}N(d_2)$$
(4)

where and $d_2 = d_1 - \sigma\sqrt{T-t}.$

The price for the put option is

$$P(S,t) = Ke^{-r(T-t)}-S+(SN(d_1)-Ke^{-r(T-t)}N(d_2)) = Ke^{-r(T-t)}-S+C(S,t).$$ (5)

For both formulas (Hull, 2009),

- N(•) is the cumulative distribution function of the standard normal distribution
- T - t is the time to maturity
- S is the spot price of the underlying asset
- K is the strike price
- r is the risk free rate
- σ is the volatility in the log-returns of the underlying

2. MOTIVATION FOR THE CLOUD COMPUTING ADOPTION FRAMEWORK (CCAF)

We propose the Cloud Computing Adoption Framework (CCAF) to address the technical and business challenges of Cloud Computing, particularly the three business problems described earlier. CCAF aims to help organisations achieve good Cloud design, deployment and services. The CCAF is an enhancement to the work of Weinhardt and others (Weinhardt et al.,2009) in which they fit technical solutions and Business Models into their Cloud Business Model Framework (CBMF). CCAF offers quantitative methods for measuring Risk and return analysis, and detailed descriptions and good practices for Cloud portability and migration. Compared with CCAF, CBMF does not offer quantitative techniques for measuring Risk and return analysis, nor does it provide detailed descriptions for Cloud portability and migration.

Foster et al. (2008) explain that Grids and Clouds are in common in terms of solutions and research questions that both Grids and Clouds are dealing with. Sobel et al. (2009) argue that Grid and Cloud are different; in particular in the way Web 2.0 is involved in Clouds right from the beginning and also that whilst Web 2.0 may be considered to be a subset of Clouds, this is not necessarily so for Grids. In contrast, Weinhardt et al. (2009) assert that the difference between Grids and Clouds is in their business models, where Clouds provide new business opportunities. This is supported by the observation that since 2007, there is an increasing number of organisations offering many different Cloud solutions and services.

The CCAF has the following advantages:

- Classification of business models to offer Cloud-adopting organisations right strategies and business cases.
- It offers a robust method to analyse risk and return of Cloud adoption accurately and systematically.
- It can deal with enterprise portability to ensure existing services from desktop or other computing systems can work in the Cloud, and allow Cloud communications between different clouds offered by different vendors.
- IT provides linkage and relationship between different cloud research methodologies, and between IaaS, PaaS, SaaS and Business Models.

CCAF can also accommodate a series of conceptual methodologies which it can apply and fit into Cloud Architecture and Business Models. For this paper, the objective is to focus on challenge of enterprise portability between desktops and clouds, and between different clouds.

3.1. Our Work for Research Questions within the CCAF

A good framework should be able to accommodate multiple methods or solutions to work in different contexts and consolidate all towards the goal of the framework (Sander WH et al., 2004; Jiang T J et al., 2006). In an ideal situation, a framework would address research questions and provide methodology proving supporting the validity. Referring to Section 2.1, there are three business challenges to deal with for CCAF. Based on the descriptions in Section 2.3 and Section 3, our work for these research questions can be summed up as: (i) Classification; (ii) Organisational Sustainability, (iii) Portability and (iv) Linkage:

- Classification: This refers to the upper-most layer in the CCAF where the top-down strategic direction is provided to guide organisations into the right track of operating their cloud projects and businesses. Currently the Cloud Cube Model (CCM) has been used for classification of eight Cloud Business Models (Chang et al., 2010 a). Bottom-up approaches require methods of validation such as experiments, modelling and simulation. A summary of such outcomes can be used for classification for good practices, and is not focus in this paper.
- Organisational Sustainability: This includes modelling to review and evaluate cloud business projects, past and present and also enables forecasting for cloud businesses in the future. Sustainability modelling is suitable for all IaaS, PaaS and SaaS.

- Portability: This refers to enterprise portability, which involves migrating entire application services from desktops to clouds and between different clouds. For financial services and organisations that are not yet using clouds, portability involves a lot of investment. Thus is an organisational challenge (Chang et al., 2010 c; 2011 a). Portability deals with IaaS, PaaS and SaaS. Examples in Education, Health and Finance will be demonstrated. Financial SaaS (FSaaS) Portability is the focus for this paper. See Figure 1 on page 11.

- Linkage: There are two aspects to linkage. The first aspect is to determine when a service should be upgraded to the next level, and to identify direct relations between different services. The second aspect is to integrate different services in a central platform, allowing different services, roles and functionalities to work together in a linkage oriented framework where the outcome of one service can be input to another, without the need to translate from one domain or language to another.

Classification provides strategic directions and guidelines for business adopting the appropriate business models. Both (Organisational) Sustainability and Portability apply to different sectors and domains using Cloud Computing, and all lessons learned are summed up. Linkage allows integration of different services and roles.

3.2. The Updated CCAF Architecture

Four research areas in the CCAF are discussed and presented in Section 3.1. The CCAF helps organisations to achieve good Cloud design, deployment and services, and having the architecture is useful for summing up useful components and recommendations for organisations undertaking Cloud migration and development. The updated CCAF Architecture is presented in Figure 1. Chang et al. (2011 b) present Business Integration as a Service (BIaaS) in the CCAF, which is ready for each layer of service and is able to integrate with other services, activities and projects by other departments (for large organisations), other organisations and other businesses in other domains. Chang et al. (2010 b) demonstrates the Hexagon Model to measure risk and return of Cloud adoption without the need to reveal confidential data, and is useful to review any Cloud project or organisation at any time. The Hexagon Model can be used to bridge the gap between qualitative and quantitative methods for case studies, which are used to demonstrate positive impacts that collaborators have gained from adopting the CCAF. The benefits of adopting CCAF, particularly in the area of Portability, can be applied to any domain including Finance, Healthcare and Education. In the Financial Cloud domain, Commonwealth Bank Australia and IBM US (Chang et al., 2010 c; 2011 a) has worked with the University of Southampton in improving the prototype of Financial Clouds and services. Referring to Figure 1, OSM stands for Organisational Sustainability Modelling to analyse risk and return of system adoption such as Cloud Computing, and portability of Cloud Computing to finance applications is the focus for this paper.

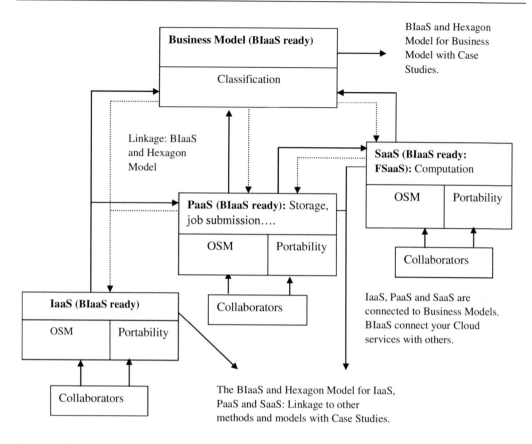

Figure 1. The updated CCAF Architecture.

3.3. The CCAF: Portability for Financial Software as a Service (FSaaS)

In relation to finance, portability is highly relevant. This is because a large number of financial applications are written for a desktop environment. Although there are financial applications for Grid, not all of them are portable onto Clouds. Portability often requires rewrites in software design and the provision of an API suitable for Clouds. Apart from portability, factors such as accuracy, speed, reliability and security of financial models migrating from desktop to clouds must be considered. The second problem related to finance is there are few financial clouds, as described in opening section. Salesforce offers on-demand CRM, but it is not directly related to financial modelling. Enterprise portability from desktops to clouds, and between different clouds, is useful for businesses and financial services, as they cannot afford to spend considerable time and money fully migrating entire applications, API libraries and resources from their existing ones to clouds (Chang, et al., 2011 a). Portability must be made as easy as possible. However, there are more advantages in moving all applications and resources to clouds. These added values include the following benefits:

- The community cloud – this encourages groups of financial services to form an alliance to analyse complex problems.
- Risk reduction – the financial computing results can be compared and studied together to reduce risks. This includes running additional, less conventional models (non-Gaussians) to explore causes of errors and uncertainties. Excessive risk taking can be minimised with the aid of stricter regulations.

The Financial Software as a Service (FSaaS) is the proposal for dealing with finance-specific problems. The FSaaS is designed to improve the accuracy and quality of both pricing and risk analysis. This is essential because incorrect analysis or excessive risk taking might cause adverse impacts such as financial loss or severe damage in credibility or even another credit crunch. The research demonstration is on SaaS, which means it can calculate best prices or risks based on different values in volatility, maturity, risk free rate and so forth on cloud applications. Different models for FSaaS are presented and explained in Section 2.3 onwards. Monte Carlo Methods (MCM) and Black Scholes Models (BSM) are the core models used in the FSaaS.

4. FSaaS Portability with Monte Carlo Methods (MCM) and Black Scholes Model (BSM)

This section describes how Financial SaaS portability on clouds can be achieved. This mainly involves Monte Carlo Methods (MCM) and Black Scholes Model (BSM). Before describing how they work and how validation and experiments are done we need to describe existing practice in Finance. Visual Basic for Applications (VBA) is very commonly used in Finance applications, which include a wide range of software and tools. In contrast, HPC languages such as C++, Visual C++ and MATLAB are less commonly used. The drawback of migrating desktop applications such as VBA to Clouds mainly is because of security with the following reasons:

- VBA Macro is commonly used to support advanced techniques, but VBA Macro is a common way for writing and sending viruses (Sovereign, 2005).
- Additional security applications or tools need to be in placed to enforce security, but these tools or applications need additional work if integrations with other technologies are required.

Comparisons between VBA and HPC languages such as MATLAB are presented in Table 1.

Chang et al. (2011 a) demonstrate the use of risk analysis and financial modelling on Clouds based on MATLAB and Mathematica, which offer benefits such as performance, accuracy and integration with security. This includes the selection of Linear Square Method (LSM) that can compute 100,000 simulations in one go, which takes between 4 to 25 seconds depending on the number of time steps. It can also work with IBM Fined-Grained Security Model, and it can provide a safer environment for FSaaS on Clouds.

Table 1. Comparisons between VBA and HPC languages such as MATLAB

Portability comparisons	VBA	MATLAB
Performance	It can execute fast calculations in Microsoft environments only. Better performance is available on Office 2007 and above.	It works on different platforms. It can be used in HPC environments. Applications can run on its open source equivalent.
Security	It is a concern, and needs enforced security and policy. Some vendors such as Google disable Macro, and advanced financial analysis on Cloud cannot work without it.	It has a better status than VBA although some work is in progress. MATLAB is working on its own improvement with security. It allows integrations with other security applications or tools.
Risk modelling	There is a limit for risk modelling, and it cannot go beyond 100,000 simulations in one go in our experiments.	It can go 100,000 simulations in one go provided with the right model and coding algorithms are provided.
Costs and impacts	Licence fees can be expensive. Open Office can be used to reduce costs, but challenge becomes interoperability with MS VBA Macro.	It is expensive if all Clouds adopt MATLAB licences, but the use of its open source equivalence (Octave) can much reduce costs.

4.1. Selection of MATLAB with Emphasis on Error Corrections

Error corrections in financial modelling are important since when errors are identified, rectifications need to be in place and automatically corrected (Zimmermann, Neuneier and Grothmann, 2006). The rationale behind is, a slight discrepancy in financial analysis may cause adverse impacts such as financial loss. Chang et al. (2011 a) use LSM that offers better performance and accurate analysis. It is helpful if another model can be used for error corrections, and computational results from both models can be jointly used for decision-making. Chang et al. (2010 c) select Variance-Gamma Processes (VGP) for risk analysis and early version of error correction techniques. VGP is a technique used in MCM. The use of VGP offers two advantages as follows:

- It simulates the pricing and risk analysis, which include the expected and out of range data;
- It removes out of range of data, and computes simulations again, and presents the improved simulations.

In order to demonstrate the use of VGP, the core code algorithm is presented in this Section.

4.2. Monte Carlo in MATLAB – Calculating the Best Buy/Sell Prices

Mathematical models such as MCM are used in Risk Management area, where they are used to simulate the risk of exposures to various types of operational risks. Monte Carlo Simulations (MCS) in Commonwealth Bank Australia are written in Fortran and C#. Running such simulations may take several hours or over a day (Chang et al., 2010 c; 2011 a). The results may be needed by the bank for the quarterly reporting period. MCM is suitable to calculate best prices for buy and sell, and provides data for investors' decision-making (Waters, 2008). MATLAB is used due to its ease of use with relatively good speed. While the volatility is known and provided, prices for buy and sale can be calculated. Part of the code (fareastmc.m) to is used to present formulas in MCM and demonstrate coding algorithm presented in Table 2.

Table 2. Coding algorithm in Monte Carlo in MATLAB for best buy/sell prices

```
dt=T/(NSteps-1);
vsqrdt=sigma*dt^0.5;
drift=(r-(sigma^2)/2)*dt;
x=randn(NSimulations,NSteps);
Smat=zeros(NSimulations,NSteps);
Smat(:,1)=S;
for i=2:NSteps;
Smat(:,i)=Smat(:,i-1).*exp(drift+vsqrdt*x(:,i));
end
```

The following demonstrates running the code and the calculated prices. Call prices are for buy and put prices are for sale. The program calculates the lower limit, ideal value and the upper limit for each buy and sale category.

> **fareastmc**
                [LowerLimit MCPrice UpperLimit]
Call Prices: [4.196694 4.248468 4.300242]
Put Prices: [7.610519 7.666090 7.721662]

4.3. Coding Algorithm for Variance-Gamma Processes

Codes are written to demonstrate the VG process in the MCM. The following shows the initial part of the code, where key figures such as maturity, volatility and risk free rate are given in Table 3.

Table 3. The first part of coding algorithm for Variance-Gamma Processes

```
S=100; %underlying price;
K=101; %strike;
T=0.5; %maturity;
sigma=0.12136; %volatility for VG model;
r=0.1; %risk free rate;
VG_nu=.3; %nu for VG model;
VG_theta=-0.1436; %theta of VG model;
nsimulations=10000; % no. of MC simulations;
k=4; %2^k: the no. of resets, Asian option;
nsimulations=(floor(nsimulations^.5))^2;
tmpdim=nsimulations^0.5;
omega=(1/VG_nu)*( log(1-VG_theta*VG_nu-sigma*sigma*VG_nu/2));
```

In MATLAB, there is a function, gamrnd, to calculate variance gamma model, presented in Table 4.

Table 4. The second part of coding algorithm for Variance-Gamma Processes

```
thmean=T;
thvar=VG_nu*T;
theta=thmean/thvar;
alpha=thmean*theta;
G(:,n+1)=gamrnd(alpha,theta,nsimulations,1);
subplot(5,1,1);
subplot(2,2,1);
hist(G(:,n+1),100);
title('original gamma vars');
```

The third part of the code is to calculate stratified gamma sampling presented in Table 5. This includes replicate and tile array (repmat function) and returns the inverse of the gamma cumulative distribution function (cdf) (gaminv function).

The fourth part of code in Table 6 is to calculate random variable from the normal distribution.

Table 5. The third part of coding algorithm showing stratified gamma sampling

```
vvec=rand(nsimulations,1);
midxvec=1:tmpdim;
midxvec=midxvec';
midxvec=repmat(midxvec,tmpdim,1);
uvec=(midxvec-1+vvec)/tmpdim;
uvec2=gaminv(uvec,alpha,theta);
subplot(2,2,2);
hist(uvec2,100);
title('stratified gamma vars');
```

Table 6. The fourth part of coding algorithm

```
X(:,n+1)=normrnd(VG_theta*G(:,n+1),sigma*sigma*G(:,n+1));
subplot(2,2,3);
hist(X(:,n+1),100);
title('original normal vars');
```

This fifth part of code in Table 7 is to calculate stratifying random variables from normal distribution. This includes replicate and tile array (repmat function), reshape the array (reshape function) and computes the inverse of the normal norminv cdf (norminv function).

Table 7. The fifth part of the coding algorithm

```
G(:,n+1)=uvec2;
midxvec=1:tmpdim;
midxvec=repmat(midxvec,tmpdim,1);
midxvec=reshape(midxvec,tmpdim*tmpdim,1);
vvec=rand(nsimulations,1);
uvec=(midxvec-1+vvec)/tmpdim;
X(:,n+1)=norminv(uvec,VG_theta*G(:,n+1),sigma*sigma*G(:,n+1));
subplot(2,2,4);
hist(X(:,n+1),100);
title('stratified normal vars');
```

Additional formulations in Table 8 are added to calculate the best calling price based on MCM.

Table 8. The sixth part of the coding algorithm

```
Tvec=0:1/(2^k):1;
Tvec=T*Tvec;
Tmat=repmat(Tvec,nsimulations,1);
Smat=exp( log(S)+r*Tmat+omega*Tmat+X );
Avgvec=mean(Smat(:,2:2^k+1),2);
payoffvec=max(Avgvec-K,0);
mc_callprice=exp(-r*T)*mean(payoffvec);
return;
```

4.4. The Outcome of Executing Variance-Gamma Processes

The outcome of executing Variance-Gamma Processes is presented in Figure 2. The top half shows differences between original and stratifying gamma random variables and the lower half shows the original and stratifying random variables from normal distribution. The stratifying model eliminates infrequent variables and also concentrates on more frequently-seen results. In that way, it is more accurate than the original modelling by MCM.

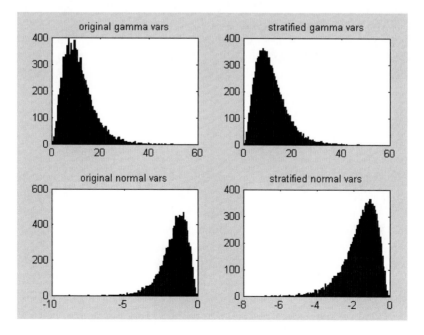

Figure 2. The Variance-Gamma Process modelling based on MCM.

The code calculates the best buying price is 0.0225. Stratified normal randomisation calculates a negative value, because theta starts as negative. The code can facilitate similar tests for different variances for volatility, maturity and risk free rate. So if either of volatility, maturity or risk free rate changes, the best values for call prices can be calculated. The outcome is a bell curve that is a normal (Gaussian) distribution. Even so, stratified sampling has corrected errors and can recalculate the best range of prices. Removal of errors is important for quality assurance of FSaaS and financial services.

4.5. Experiment and Benchmark in the Cloud Environments

Codes written for Variance-Gamma Processes in Section 4.2 have been used for experimenting and benchmarking in the Clouds. 5000, 10,000 and 15,000 simulations of Monte Carlo Methods (MCM) are performed and the time taken at each of a desktop, private clouds and Amazon EC2 public clouds are recorded and averaged with three attempts. Hardware specifications for desktop, public cloud and private clouds are described as follows.

The desktop has 2.67 GHz Intel Xeon Quad Core and 4 GB of memory (800 MHz) with installed. Two Amazon EC2 public clouds are used. The first virtual server is a 64-bit Ubuntu 8.04 with large resource instance of dual core CPU, with 2.33 GHz speed and 7.5GB of memory. The second virtual server is Ubuntu 7.04 with small resource of 1 CPU with 2.33 GHz speed and 1.5 GB of memory. There are two private clouds set up. The first private cloud is hosted on a Windows virtual server, which is created by a VMware Server on top of a rack server, and its network is in a network translated and secure domain. The virtual server has 2 cores of 2.67 GHz and 4GB of memory at 800 MHz. The second private cloud is a 64-bit Windows server installed on a rack, with 2.8GHz Quad Core Xeon, 16 GB of memory. All these five settings have installed Octave 3.2.4, an open source compiler equivalent to MATLAB. Octave takes more time than MATLAB in code compilation; however, selection of Octave offers zero cost comparing to high MATLAB licence fees. Only Desktop and two private clouds have MATLAB 2007 installed. The experiment began for running the MATLAB code (in Section 4.2) on desktop, private cloud and public cloud and started one at a time.

4.6. The Benchmark Results

Table 9 summarises the timing benchmark result while running the modelling of assets (MoA) code (in Section 4.2) in five different hardware infrastructures. It took longer time to run simulations in the public cloud with small instances, which is not recorded in Table 9. This is due to their low CPU and memory requirements resulting in longer completion time.

Refer to Table 8 for timing comparisons. Private cloud (rack server) has the best hardware requirements and running codes on 64-bit system improves the time completion. Since MoA code runs directly on the desktop instead on top of virtualised environment, this explains why the time taken in running MCM simulations on the desktop is slightly shorter than on the private cloud (virtual server). Public cloud (large instance) takes slightly more time than private cloud (virtual server) and desktop, probably because of network downtime speed, where private clouds have the advantage.

Table 9. Timing benchmark to run MoA code on Octave 3.2.4

Number of simulations and time taken (sec)	5,000	10,000	15,000
Desktop	11.08	11.92	12.71
Public cloud (large instance)	11.95	12.30	13.15
Private cloud (virtual server)	11.31	12.13	12.90
Private cloud (rack server)	9.63	10.51	11.48

Figure 3 refers to benchmark results if using MATLAB 2007, which compile faster than Octave, are only available on desktop, private cloud (virtual server) and private cloud (rack server) hosted on Windows. The same code runs faster on MATLAB 2007, but it comes with higher prices.

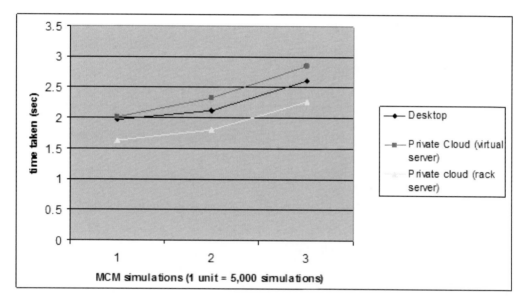

Figure 3. Timing benchmark comparison for MATLAB 2007.

Desktop and two private clouds have Windows and MATLAB 2007 installed. The same experiment is repeated on these three settings, and time taken is recorded. Figure 3 shows timing benchmark, where private cloud (rack server) completes the simulations the quickest.

4.7. Black Scholes Model (BSM) Coding Algorithm

We first focus on call price and define *function [price, delta, gamma, vega, theta] = BlackScholesPrice(CallPutFlag,S,X,T,r,v)*. Black Scholes use time series to calculate. This code algorithm can be divided into two parts. The first part of coding algorithm is shown in Table 10.

Table 10. The first part of Black Scholes coding algorithm

```
d1 = (log(S / X) + (b + v ^ 2 / 2) * T) / (v * T^0.5);
d2 = d1 - v * T^0.5; % T is the time to maturity
        price=0;
    if CallPutFlag == "c" ,
    price = S * normal_cdf(d1) - X * exp(-r * T) * normal_cdf(d2); % normal_cdf is a
    cumulative distribution to compute
if noutparams>1,
    delta=exp((b-r)*T)*normal_cdf(d1);
    theta_tmp1= -( S*exp((b-r)*T)*normal_pdf(d1)*v )/(2*T^0.5);
    theta_tmp2= -(b-r)*S*exp((b-r)*T)*normal_cdf(d1);
    theta_tmp3= -r*X*exp(-r*T)*normal_cdf(d2);
    theta=theta_tmp1+theta_tmp2+theta_tmp3;
endif
```

Table 11. The second part of coding algorithm

```
else % The following shows coding for the put price
price = X * exp(-r * T) * normal_cdf(-d2) - S * normal_cdf(-d1); % X is the strike price
if noutparams>1,
  delta=exp((b-r)*T)*(normal_cdf(d1)-1);
  theta_tmp1= -( S*exp((b-r)*T)*normal_pdf(d1)*v )/(2*T^0.5);
  theta_tmp2= (b-r)*S*exp((b-r)*T)*normal_cdf(-d1);
  theta_tmp3= r*X*exp(-r*T)*normal_cdf(-d2);
  theta=theta_tmp1+theta_tmp2+theta_tmp3;
    endif
end
if noutparams>1,
  gamma=(normal_pdf(d1)*exp((b-r)*T)) / (S*v*T^0.5);
  vega=S * exp((b-r)*T)*normal_pdf(d1)*T^0.5;
endif
```

Finite-difference methods are numerical methods for approximating the solutions to differential equations using finite difference equations to approximate derivatives (Waters, 2008; Hull, 2009). A file fdcall.m is written to calculate call price based on this method. Table 12 shows its key values for calculations.

Table 12. The key values in Finite-difference methods

```
S=100; %Spot price
K=100; %Strike
UB=115; %upper boundary
r=0.15; %risk free rate
T=.5; %maturity
sigma=0.2; %volatility
D=0.05; %dividend yield
assetsteps=150; %Explicit time steps
```

The following demonstrate the key components and its values:

• strike price: the price targeted for sale.
• upper boundary: the highest possible range a price or risk can reach
• risk free rate: interest an investor would expect from an absolutely risk-free investment over a period of time.
• maturity: the loan is due to be repaid on a fixed date.
• volatility: used to quantify the risk of assets.
• dividend yield: the return on investment for an asset.
• asset steps: a specific BSM method called explicit time steps. The more steps, the more accurate the analysis.

While running this code, it calculates call option price.
> *fdcall*
option_price = 1.0675

4.8. Asset Steps Benchmark on the Clouds

Our code allows editing explicit scheme time steps, where 1,500 is the maximum. 500, 1,000 and 1,500 steps are taken and the same test described in Section 4.2 is performed for Black Scholes. Time taken was recorded.

This code only focuses on calculation and therefore runs faster than the MoA code in Section 4.2. Calculation is more accurate and gets call price as 1.0704 while asset steps increase up to its maximum of 1,500 steps. Public cloud (small instance) takes the longest time to complete, and is not included for comparison. Figure 4 below shows the benchmark in other four settings.

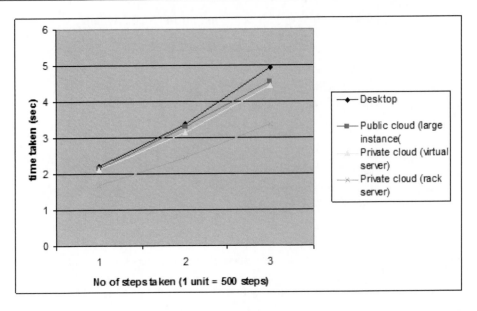

Figure 4. Timing benchmark comparison for Octave 3.2.4.

5. DISCUSSIONS

There are five areas for discussions, which include added values provided by portability of financial clouds and FSaaS presented as follows.

5.1. Variance in Volatility, Maturity and Risk Free Rate

Calculating the impacts of violatility, maturity and risk free rate is helpful to risk management. Our code in Section 4.2 and 4.8 can calculate these three aspects with these observations. Firstly, the higher the volatility is, the lower the call price, so that risk can be minimised. Secondly, the more the maturity becomes, the higher the call price, which improves higher returns on assets before the end of life in a bond or a security. Thirdly, the higher the risk free rate, the higher the call price, as high risk free rate has reduced risk and boosts on investors' confidence level. Both Monte Carlo Methods and Black Scholes models are able to calculate these three aspects.

5.2. Accuracy

Monte Carlo Simulations are suitable to analyse pricing and provide reliable calculations up to several decimal numbers. In addition, the use of Variance-Gamma Processes reduces and corrects errors, and thus improves the quality of calculation. New and existing ways to improve error corrections are under further investigation while achieving enterprise SaaS portability onto Clouds.

5.3. Implication for Banking

There are implications for banking. Firstly, security is a main concern of the banking industry where some security issues still experience evolving challenges. This is in particular when Cloud vendors tend to mitigate this risk technically by segregating different parts of the Clouds but still need to convince clients about the locality of their data. Secondly, financial regulators are imposing tighter risk management controls. Thus, financial institutions are involved in running more analytical simulations to calculate risks to the client organisations. This may present a greater need for the use of the Cloud computation and resources. Thirdly, Cloud portability can imply letting clients to install their own libraries. Users who run MATLAB on the Cloud may only need the MATLAB application script or executable and to install the MATLAB Runtime once on the Clouds. For financial simulations written in Fortran or C++, users may also need Mathematical libraries to be installed in the Clouds.

5.4. A Conceptual Financial Cloud Platform

Figure 5 shows a conceptual architecture based on Operational Risk Exchange (www.orx.org), which currently includes 53 banks from 18 countries for sharing the operational risk data, and demonstrated how financial clouds could be implemented successfully for aggregating and sharing operational risk data. This cloud platform offers calculation for risk modelling, fraud detection, pricing analysis and any critical analysis with warning over risk-taking. It reports back to participating banks and bankers about their calculations, and provides useful feedback for their potential investment.

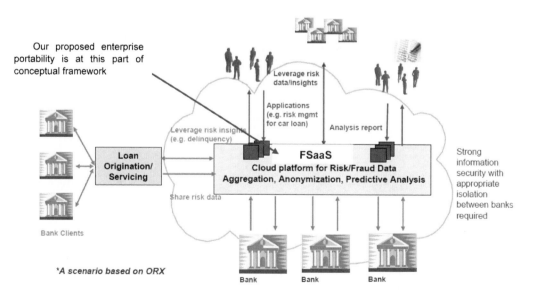

Figure 5. A conceptual financial cloud platform [using orx.org as an example] and contributions from Southampton in relations to this platform.

Risk data computed by different models such as MCM, BSM and other models can be simulated and shared within the secure platform that offers anonymisation and data encryption. It also allows bank clients to double check with mortgage lending interests and calculations whether they are fit for purpose. This platform also works closely with regulations and risk control, thus risks are managed and monitored in the Financial Cloud platform. Our FSaaS is one part of the platform (the red arrow) to demonstrate accuracy, performance and enterprise portability over Clouds, and is not only in conceptual but is implemented.

5.5. Enterprise Portability to the Clouds

Enterprise portability involves moving the entire application services from desktops to clouds and between different clouds, and users need not worry about complexity and use as if on their familiar systems. This paper demonstrates financial clouds that modelling and simulations can take place on the Clouds, where users can connect and compute. This has the following advantages:

- Performance and speed: Calculations can be completed in a short time.
- Accuracy: The improved models based on Variance-Gamma Processes provide a more accurate range of prices comparing to traditional computation in normal distribution.
- Usability – users need not worry about complexity. This includes using iPhone or other user-friendly resources to compute. However, this is not the focus of this journal.

However, the drawback for portability is that additional APIs need to be written (Chang et al., 2010 c; 2011 a). Clouds must facilitate an easy way to install and configure user required libraries, without the need to write additional APIs like several practices do. If writing APIs is required for portability, an alternative is to make APIs as easy and user-friendly as like Facebook and iPhone do. In our demonstration, there is no need to write additional APIs to execute financial clouds. In addition, virtualisation on Cloud is made easier since portability helps in virtualisation management and migration processes.

5.6. Variance-Gamma Processes (VPG) versus Least Square Methods (LSM)

Chang et al. (2011 a) demonstrates the use of Least Square Methods (LSM) used for all FSaaS and LSM provides better performance, which includes the capability to offer running 100,000 simulations in one go that take between 4 to 25 seconds depending on the complexity involved. Variance-Gamma Processes (VPG) in this paper can offer up to 20,000 simulations in one go (15,000 simulations in one go in our experiments) and it takes slightly a longer time than LSM. However, the benefits of adopting VPG are for quality assurance as it focuses more on error reduction and removal of out of range data analysis. This is important for some financial services that rely much more on stress testing and quality of their computational results. LSM offers accuracy, and the difference between two methods are, LSM reports out of range data but need not remove them. VPG in our paper involves in the removal of out of range data analysis, which is suitable for quality assurance.

5.7. Future Directions

Our framework can work with finance industry to provide better accessibility, collaboration, efficiency and performance. The next target is to enforce governance for both IT and policy, as the economic downturn is also partly due to the lack of controlled governance. Our framework can provide recommendation and lesson learned for the finance industry. Additionally, Business Integration as a Service (BIaaS) is a pioneering approach to allow different services collaborating and working as a single service (Chang et al., 2011 d; 2012 b; Chang 2013 a). The use of BIaaS can compute two types of services, such as one for cost-saving and one for risk-analysis, to ensure that the financial industry can receive greater added values than current practices.

CONCLUSION AND FUTURE WORK

MCM and BSM are used to demonstrate how portability, speed, accuracy and reliability can be achieved while demonstrating enterprise portability for financial applications onto Clouds. This well fits-in the third objective in the CCAF to allow portability on top of, secure, fast, accurate and reliable clouds. Financial SaaS provides a useful example to provide pricing and risk analysis while maintaining a high level of reliability and security. Our research purpose is to port and test financial applications to run on the Clouds, and ensure enterprise level of portability is workable, thus users can work on Clouds as if they work on their desktops or familiar environments. Five areas of discussions are presented to support our cases and demonstration.

Benchmark is regarded as time execution to complete calculations after portability is achieved. Timing is essential since less time with accuracy is expected in using Financial SaaS on Clouds. HPC languages such as C++ are planned to be used for the next stage. There are plans to jointly investigate Financial SaaS and its enterprise portability over clouds with Commonwealth Bank Australia and IBM US. Proof of concepts for FSaaS has been demonstrated to show the added values that CCAF and FSaaS can offer. Future collaboration includes writing and improving FSaaS based on another model, Linear Square Method, and to provide accurate and speedy pricing and risk modelling on Clouds. We hope to deliver a more improved prototypes, proof of concepts, advanced simulations and visualisation.

ACKNOWLEDGMENT

We thank those professionals that we interviewed to provide valuable feedback and recommendation. We thank Dr Chung-Sheng Li, the Director of Commercial Systems, IBM T.J. Watson Research Center, USA, for his advice in financial computation for Cloud

Computing. We thank Howard Lee, a Researcher from Deakin University, Australia, for his advice on advanced MATLAB programming.

REFERENCES

Abdallah, M.A., Lei, Z.M., Li, X., Greenwold N., Nakajima, S.T., Jauniaux, E., Rao, C.V. (2004), Human Fetal nongonadal tissues contain human chorionic gonadotropin/ luteinizing hormone receptors. *J. Clin. Endocrinol. Metab.* 89, 952-956.

Aplin, J.D., (1991), Implantation, trophoblast differentiation and hemochorial placentation , Mechanistic evidence *in vivo* and *in vitro*. *J. Cell. Sci.* 99 , 681-692.

Aplin, J.D., Haigh, T., Jones, C.J., Church, H.J., Vićovac, L., (1999), Development of cytotrophoblast columns from explanted first-trimester human placental villi, role of fibronectin and integrin alpha5beta1. *Biol. Reprod.* 60, 828-38.

Armbrust, M., Fox, A., Griffith, R., Joseph, A. D., Katz R H, Kownwinski, A., Lee, G., Patterson, D., Rabkin, A., Stoica, I., Zaharia, M. (2009), *Above the Clouds: A Berkeley View of Cloud computing.* Technical Report Number UCB/EECS-2009-28, UC Berkeley, February.

Beaty, K., Kochut, A. and Shaikh, H. (2009), Desktop to Cloud Transformation Planning, *IEEE International Symposium on Parallel and Distributed Processing",* May 23-May 29, Rome, Italy.

Birge, L. and Massart, P. (2001), Gaussian model selection, *Journal of the European Mathematical Society,* Vol. 3, No. 3, page 203-268, April.

Brandic, I., Music, D., Leitner, P. and Dustdar, S. (2009), VieSLAF Framework: Enabling Adaptive and Versatile SLA-Management., *the 6th International Workshop on Grid Economics and Business Models 2009 (Gecon09),* 25- 28 August, Delft, The Netherlands.

Briscoe, G. and Marinos, A. (2009), *Digital ecosystems in the clouds: towards community cloud computing, the 3rd IEEE International Conference on Digital Ecosystems and Technologies,* June 1-3, New York, USA.

Bryant, T.(2009), *Mutuality 2.0, Working Paper,* Leeds Metropolitan University and selected paper for Guardian, July.

Buyya, R., Yeo, C. S., Venugopal, S., Broberg, J. and Brandic, I. (2009), Cloud computing and emerging IT platforms: Vision, hype, and reality for delivering computing as the 5th utility, *Journal of Future Generation Computer Systems,* Volume 25, Issue 6, June, Pages 559-616.

Carr, P., Geman, H., Madan, D., and Yor, M. (2002), The fine structure of asset returns: An empirical investigation, *Journal of Business,* 75 (2), 305-332.

Chang, V., Wills, G. and De Roure, D. (2010 a), Towards Financial Cloud Framework: Modelling and Benchmarking of Financial Assets in Public and Private Clouds, *IEEE Cloud 2010, the third International Conference on Cloud Computing,* 5-10 July, Miami, Florida, USA.

Chang, V., Wills, G. and De Roure, D. (2010b), A Review of Cloud Business Models and Sustainability. In: *IEEE Cloud 2010, the third International Conference on Cloud Computing,* 5-10 July, Miami, Florida, USA. pp. 43-50.

Chang, V., Wills, G., De Roure, D. and Chee, C. (2010 c), *Investigating the Cloud Computing Business Framework - Modelling and Benchmarking of Financial Assets and job submissions in Clouds,* the UK e-Science All Hands Meeting 2010, Research Clouds: Hype or Reality Workshop, 13-16th September, Cardiff, UK.

Chang, V., Li, C. S., De Roure, D., Wills, G., Walters, R. and Chee, C. (2011 a) The Financial Clouds Review. *International Journal of Cloud Applications and Computing, 1* (2). pp. 41-63. ISSN 2156-1834, eISSN 2156-1826.

Chang, V., De Roure, D., Walters, R. J. and Wills, G. (2011 b), Organisational Sustainability Modelling for Return on Investment: Case Studies presented by a National Health Service (NHS) Trust UK. *Journal of Computing and Information Technology, 19,* (3).

Chang, V., De Roure, D., Wills, G. and Walters, R. (2011 c), Case Studies and Organisational Sustainability Modelling presented by Cloud Computing Business Framework, *International Journal of Web Services Research, 8,* (3), 26-53.

Chang, V., Wills, G. and Walters, R. J. (2011 d), Towards Business Integration as a Service 2.0. In, IEEE International Conference on e-Business Engineering, *The 3rd International Workshop on Cloud Services - Platform Accelerating e-Business,* Beijing, China, 19 - 21 Oct.

Chang, V., Wills, G., Walters, R. and Currie, W. (2012 a), Towards a structured Cloud ROI: The University of Southampton cost-saving and user satisfaction case studies. In *Sustainable ICTs and Management Systems for Green Computing, IGI Global,* page 179-200.

Chang, V., Walters, R. J. and Wills, G. (201 b), Business Integration as a Service, *International Journal of Cloud Applications and Computing, 2,* (1), 16-40.

Chang, V., Walters, R. J. and Wills, G. (2012 c), Cloud Storage in a private cloud deployment: Lessons for Data Intensive research, (Best student paper). In *The second international conference on Cloud Computing and Service Sciences* (CLOSER 2012), April, Porto, Portugal.

Chang, V., Walters, R. J. and Wills, G. (2013 a), *The development that leads to the Cloud Computing Business Framework, International Journal of Information Management, 33* (3), June 2013.

Chang, V., Walters, R.J. and Wills, G. (2013 b), Cloud Storage and Bioinformatics in a private cloud deployment: Lessons for Data Intensive research, In *Cloud Computing and Service Science,* Springer Lecture Notes Series, Springer Book.

Chang, V. and Wills, G. (2013 c) A University of Greenwich Case Study of Cloud Computing – Education as a Service. In, *E-Logistics and E-Supply Chain Management: Applications for Evolving Business,* IGI Global.

Chang, V. (2013 a), Business integration as a service: computational risk analysis for small and medium enterprises adopting SAP, *International Journal of Next-Generation Computing, 4,* (3).

Chang, V. (2013 b), Brain Segmentation – A Case study of Biomedical Cloud Computing for Education and Research. In *Learning Technologies Workshop, Higher Education Academy (HEA),* University of Greenwich, June.

Chang, V. (2013 c) Cloud Computing for brain segmentation technology. In, *IEEE CloudCom* 2013, 02 - 05 Dec, Bristol, UK.

Chen, X., Chee, C., Huang, E., Jin, L., Tseng, R., Wang, C. and Wong, C. (2009*), banking professionals, were asked in details for what software they use for financial work,* by interviews.

Chou, T. (2009), *Seven Clear Business Models,* Active Book Press.

City A.M, *Ongoing and several special editions about regulation of financial practices,* 2010.

Etro, F. (2009), The Economic Impact of Cloud Computing on Business Creation, Employment and Output in Europe, *Journal of Review of Business and Economics,* May.

Financial Times (2009), *Interview with Lord Turner,* Chair of Financial Services Authority, June.

Financial Times (2010), *Special editions about regulation of financial practices.*

Feiman, J. and Cearley D W (209), Economics of the Cloud: Business Value Assessments, *Gartner RAS Core Research White Paper,* September.

Flouris, T. and Yilmaz, A. K. (2010), The Risk Management Framework to Strategic Human Resource Management, *International Research Journal of Finance and Economics.*

Foster, I., Zhao, Y., Raicu, I. and Lu, S. Y. (2008), Cloud Computing and Grid Computing 360-Degree Compared, *IEEE Grid Computing Environments (GCE08),* 12-16 Nov, Austin, Texas, USA.

Hamnett, C. (2009), The Madness of Mortgage Lenders: Housing finance and the financial crisis, *Working Paper,* King's College London UK.

Hull, J. C. (2009), *Options, Futures, and Other Derivatives,* Seventh Edition, Pearson, Prentice Hall.

Hutchinson, M. (2010), *A Finer Formula for Assessing Risk, Special column,* Business Section, New York Times, May.

Jiang, T.J., Liu, D., Liu, K.M., Yang, W.Z., Tan, P.T., Hsieh, M.J., Chang, T.H. and Hsu, W.L. (2006), OpenVanilla – A Non-Intrusive Plug-In Framework of Text Services, ACM *Journal, Computing Research Repository,* 2006.

Li, C. S. (2010), *Cloud Computing in an Outcome Centric World,* keynote in IEEE Cloud 2010 conference, July 5-10, Miami, Florida, USA.

Rebeiro, C. and Webber, N. (2002), Valuing Path Dependent Options in the Variance-Gamma Model by Monte Carlo with a Gamma Bridge*, Working Paper,* No.02-04, Warwick Business School, September.

Ribeiro, C. and Webber, N. (2004), Valuing path-dependent options in the variance-gamma model by Monte Carlo with a gamma bridge, *The Journal of Computational Finance 7* (2):81–100.

Sanders, W. H., Courtney, T., Deavours, D., Daly, D., Derisavi, S. and Lam, V. (2004), Multi-Formalism and Multi-Solution-Method Modelling Frameworks: The Mobius Approach. In *Proceedings of the Symposium on Performance Evaluation.*

Schubert, H., Jeffery, K. and Neidecker-Lutz, B. (2010), The Future for Cloud Computing: Opportunities for European Cloud Computing Beyond 2010, *Expert Group report,* public version 1.0, January.

Sobel, W., Subramanyam, S., Sucharitakul, A., Nguyen, J., Wong, H., Klepchukov, A., Patil, S., Fox, A. and Patterson, D. (2008), Cloudstone: Multi-Platform, Multi-Language Benchmark and Measurement Tools for Web 2.0 In *Proceeding of Cloud Computing and its Applications* (CCA 2008), 22-23 October, Chicago, USA.

Sovereign, B. (2005), Microsoft Office XP/2003 Executable Content Security Risks and Countermeasures, *The US Government Working Paper,* National Security Agency, May.

Waters, D. (2008), *Quantitative Methods for Business,* Fourth Edition, Prentice Hall, Financial Times.

Weinhardt, C., Anandasivam, A., Blau, B. and StoBer, J. (2009), Cloud Computing – A Classification, Business Models, and Research Directions, *Journal of Business and Information Systems Engineering.*

Weinhardt, C., Anandasivam, A., Blau, B. and StoBer J (2009), Business Models in the Service World, *IEEE Computer Society selected paper,* March/April, 1520-9202/09.

Zimmermann, H. G., Neuneier, R. and Grothmann, R. (2006), Active Portfolio-Management based on Error Correction Neural Networks, *Working Paper,* Siemens AG.

In: Advances in Cloud Computing Research
Editor: Muthu Ramachandran

ISBN: 978-1-63117-192-5
© 2014 Nova Science Publishers, Inc.

Chapter 6

REVIEW OF CLOUD COMPUTING AND EXISTING FRAMEWORKS FOR CLOUD ADOPTION

Victor Chang[1,2,], Robert John Walters[2] and Gary Wills[2]*
[1]School of Computing, Creative Technologies and Engineering,
Leeds Metropolitan University, Leeds, UK
[2]Electronics and Computer Science,
University of Southampton, Southampton, UK

ABSTRACT

This paper presents a selected review for Cloud Computing and explains the benefits and risks of adopting Cloud Computing in a business environment. Although all the risks identified may be associated with two major Cloud adoption challenges, a framework is required to support organisations as they begin to use Cloud and minimise risks of Cloud adoption. Eleven Cloud Computing frameworks are investigated and a comparison of their strengths and limitations is made; the result of the comparison is that none of them is able to deal with all the Cloud adoption challenges thoroughly and a new, comprehensive framework is required if organisations are to overcome these challenges. This ideal framework would ensure that benefits of Cloud adoption are maximised whilst minimising the risks of Cloud adoption.

Keywords: Cloud Computing; Review of Cloud Computing Frameworks; Resolving Cloud adoption challenges

1. INTRODUCTION

Cloud Computing has transformed the way many organisations work and offers added value for operation management and service computing.

---
* Email: V.I.Chang@leedsmet.ac.uk.

Researchers have demonstrated the positive impacts Cloud can offer for business engineering and service level management (Ambrust et al., 2009; Brandic et al., 2009; Buyya et al., 2009). Ambrust et al. (2009) identified cost reduction in IT services from using Cloud Computing. They also presented their Cloud Computing economics and ten major challenges for Cloud Computing. They emphasise a shift of risk from maintaining data centres and the capital costs of running them to the loss of data while managing Clouds in a demand-based model. Buyya et al. (2009) assert that Cloud Computing offers billing-based Service Level Agreements (SLA) which can be used for operational management offering cost savings and streamlining business activities and processes. In addition, Cloud Computing offers a variety of other benefits including agility, resource consolidation, business opportunities and green IT (Foster et al; 2008; Weinhardt et al., 2009 a; 2009 b; Schubert, Jeffery and Neidecker-Lutz, 2010; Kagermann et al., 2011; Khajeh-Hosseini et al., 2010 a; 2010 b; Chang et al., 2010 a; 2010 b; 2011 b; 2011 c; 2013 a).

There is an increasing number of organisations offering Cloud Computing products and services in industry. Salesforce.com is a pioneer in Cloud Computing and offers their Customer Relation Management (CRM) applications to a large number of their users. Amazon is the market leader in Public Cloud Computing and offers Elastic Compute Cloud (EC2) for computing capacity and Simple Storage Service (S3) for storage capacity. Microsoft provides Windows Azure services for developers to store their code and develop new applications for their clients or companies. IBM and Oracle (following their acquisition of Sun Microsystems) both offer products and services ranging from hardware to application services. In addition, there are many more Small and Medium Enterprises (SMEs), who can offer different types of business models and perspective (Marston, et al., 2010), developing and selling Cloud Computing services and products.

Computing Clouds are commonly classified into Public Clouds, Private Clouds and Hybrid Clouds (Ahronovitz et al., 2010; Boss et al., 2007; Marston et al., 2011). Their definitions are summarised below:

- Public Cloud – Cloud services offered in public domains such as Amazon EC2 and S3. This approach is for organisations wishing to save costs and time without obligations on deployment and maintenance. For organisations without Cloud Computing deployment, this is the quickest way to start using Cloud Computing although there can be concerns for data security in public domains including data loss and conflicts, legal and ethical issues.
- Private Cloud – Bespoke cloud services deployed within the organisation, thus data and accessibility are only for internal users. This approach is suitable for organisations focusing on privacy and data security, or to change or simplify the way people work. The downside is that some implementations are complicated, time-consuming or costly to complete.
- Hybrid Cloud – An integrated approach which uses part Public and part Private Cloud to deliver a solution. This approach is suitable for organisations wishing to reduce costs whilst maintaining privacy and data security. Integrating the different architectures is not easy and implementations tend to develop into either Public Cloud or Private Cloud due to additional time and complexity in maintenance.

- Community Cloud – Ahronovitz et al. (2009) from National Institute of Standard and Technology (NIST) propose a fourth type of Cloud; the Community Cloud. They say, "A community cloud is managed and used by a group of organisations that have shared interests, such as specific security requirements or a common mission." It can take years to build a working community for sharing and mutual learning. However, the added values and benefits for the Academic Community could be worth far more than the time and effort spent. Briscoe and Marinos (2009) propose that the concept of the Community Cloud draws from Cloud Computing, Digital Ecosystems and Green Computing, with these five major characteristics: Openness; Community; Graceful Failures; Convenience and Control; and Environmental Sustainability.

Cloud adoption is dependent on the type of Clouds and the intended use for the deployment. For small organisations that aim to save cost and test their software products before release, using public clouds is a good option (Khajeh-Hosseini et al., 2010 a; 2010 b). For organisations that have sensitive data and have data ownership and privacy concern, hosting private clouds is more suitable. Chang et al. (2011 a; 2013 a; 2013 b) demonstrate the use of private clouds designed and adopted in finance and healthcare sectors. Hybrid clouds may be used for large-scale simulations and experiments, since they allow scientists at different sites to work and collaborate with one another (Ahronovitz et al., 2010; Khajeh-Hosseini et al., 2010 a; 2010 b).

The majority of Cloud literature defines a Cloud Computing Framework as a Service Oriented Architecture (SOA) (Foster et al; 2008; IBM, 2008; Dillion et al., 2010; Chang et al., 2010 a; 2010 b; 2013 a; Schubert, Jeffery and Neidecker-Lutz, 2010) offering one of three types of service:

- Infrastructure as a Service (IaaS) is divided into Compute Clouds and Resource Clouds. Compute Clouds provide access to computational resources such as CPUs, hypervisors and utilities. Resource Clouds provide managed and scalable resources as services to users – in other words, they provide enhanced virtualisation capabilities.
- Platform as a Service (PaaS) provides computational resources via a platform upon which applications and services can be developed and hosted. PaaS typically makes use of dedicated APIs to control the behaviour of a server hosting engine that executes and replicates the execution according to user requests.
- Software as a Service (SaaS) offers implementations of specific business functions and business processes that are provided with a Cloud (also referred to as Service or Application Clouds). Therefore they provide applications and/or services using a cloud infrastructure or platform, rather than providing cloud features themselves.

Lin et al. (2009) provide an overview of industrial solutions for Cloud Computing, and summarise the list of challenges for the enterprise. They state that adoption benefits of cost and flexibility are enterprise-ready, but security, performance and interoperability need significant improvement. There are two issues to be resolved for each of security, performance and interoperability.

The remainder of this article is structured as follows. Section 2 presents motivation for organisations adopt Cloud Computing and Section 3 describes technical review for Cloud Computing. Section 4 explains Cloud business models and Section 5 lists risk factors and categorises them into Cloud adoption challenges from stakeholders' points of views, which leads to Section 6 that a framework for Cloud Computing is necessary. Section 7 evaluates a shortlist of eleven frameworks for Cloud Computing and concludes that none of them addresses all Cloud adoption challenges fully so that a new framework is required. Sections 7 and 8 explain our proposal for the framework. Section 8 discusses two topics related to the proposed framework and Section 9 sums up Conclusion and Future Work.

2. WHAT DRIVES ORGANISATIONS ADOPTING CLOUD COMPUTING?

There are several explanations for the rise of Cloud Computing. Firstly, many technologies in Grid Computing and Web 2.0 are mature enough and able to simplify the complex process while maintaining high performance capability and web-interfaced environments. The fusion between Grid and Web 2.0 allows ease of use for business processes and technical resolutions (Hunter, Little and Schroeter, 2008). Secondly, the economic downturn makes many organisations want to consolidate their data centre deployment. Reduction in servers, server maintenance and staffing costs by virtualisation make this attractive (Gillen, Grieser and Perry, 2008). Electricity and operational costs can be saved as shown by the CA Technologies case (Dunn, 2010) which highlighted savings of US $6.5 million for labour costs; and US $2.4 millions of operational costs in 5 years through the closure of 19 server sites.

The type of Cloud an organisation adopts will depend on the organisation's needs and the volumes, types of services and data the organisation plans to have and use. Cost-saving offered by Cloud Computing is a key benefit acknowledged by academia (Buyya et al., 2009; 2010 b; Celik; Holliday and Hurst; 2009; Khajeh-Hosseini et al., 2010 a; Schubert, Jeffery and Neidecker-Lutz 2010) and industrialists (Creeger, 2009; Dunn 2010; Oracle, 2009 a; 2009 b; 2010). It is one of the reasons for its popularity and organisational adoption in the economic downturn.

Achieving long-term organisational sustainability is an important success factor for organisations particularly in an economic downturn. Chang, Mills and Newhouse, (2007) present case studies of organisations which achieve more than ten years of organisational sustainability and conclude that their success factors include cost-saving methodology. Creeger (2009) and Dunn (2010) demonstrate their cost-saving methodology and conclude that it helps their organisations to do well in an economic downturn. This explains why cost-saving is a common organizational goal of technology adoption.

From the academic point of view, Buyya et al. (2009) introduced Service Level Agreement (SLA) led cost-saving models and explained how to calculate savings in detail. Buyya et al. (2010 a) also demonstrate applications and services developed for Cloud Computing, and these services are helpful for start-up firms generate additional revenues. Further to their work, Buyya et al. (2010 b) introduced a Return on Investment (ROI) power model which can calculate power cost-saving and present it using 3D visualisation. Celik,

Holliday and Hurst (2009) introduce their Broadcast Clouds technique which allows communications and cost-savings.

They use simulations to support their proposal. Khajeh-Hosseini et al. (2010 a; 2010b) use qualitative research methods to explain how industry can save costs. They present case studies of two companies and demonstrate cost-saving in infrastructure costs, and support and maintenance costs. Schubert, Jeffery and Neidecker-Lutz (2010) present an overview and opportunities including cost-saving as an added value offered by Cloud Computing.

In industry, CA Technologies (a global IT firm) use Cloud Computing for cost-saving including: US $6.5 million for labour costs; and US $2.4 millions of operational costs in 5 years; and closure of 19 server sites. This allows CA Technologies to consolidate their infrastructure and remove maintenance costs such as staffing and resource expenses (Dunn, 2010). In addition, Oracle who faced a similar challenge after acquiring Sun Microsystems, consolidated their infrastructure and resources using Cloud Computing. After spending a six month transition period, Oracle is able to share and use a similar level of IT resources and data centres to before acquisition, instead of doubling its size. This is largely due to virtualisation. Many of their servers and services are in clusters of virtual machine (VM) farms, facilitating effective management from architects and management (Oracle 2009 a, 2009 b, 2010).

2.1. Benefits and Characteristics of Cloud Computing Adoption

There are several discussions about the benefits of adopting Cloud Computing, amongst which Schubert, Jeffery and Neidecker-Lutz (2010) provide the most relevant in this context. They divide benefits into non-functional, economic and technical aspects. However, some of their descriptions are duplicates of existing points. Their review (Schubert, Jeffery and Neidecker-Lutz, 2010) can be summarised as follows:

Non-functional:

- Elasticity: This provides users flexibility in selecting the amount and size of data supported by an application or the number of concurrent users. Elasticity is closely related to agility and adaptability, which include real-time reaction to changes in the number of requests and size of requested resources, as well as handling swift changes to demands and services. Agility and adaptability are considered as a subset of elasticity, which allows the dynamic integration and extraction of physical resources from the infrastructure, and can enable rapid scaling up and down of resources.
- Quality of Service (QoS): QoS is the capability to guarantee services. Factors such as response time, throughput and so on must be guaranteed to ensure the quality guarantees of cloud users are met.
- Reliability: Reliability offers the capability to ensure constant operation of system without disruption including no loss of data, and is normally achieved via redundant resource utilisation. It has close relations with availability except reliability focuses on prevention of loss.
- Availability: Availability is the ability to introduce redundancy for services and data so failures can be masked transparently. This can be enhanced by replication of data

and services to distribute them across different resources for load-balancing, and thus it can be regarded as the origin of scalability for clouds.

Economic:

- Pay per use: This allows pay-as-you-go style of operation for the amount of resources and period used, without the need to pay for additional contractual costs, and without the need to buy and maintain servers. This provides great flexibility for SME and researchers to pay only for resources they use and saves costs for server maintenance.
- Cost reduction: This allows organisations to save money from IT operations, since it provides an outsourcing model and the opportunity to scale down IT expenditure. In place of capital expenditure to build infrastructure, organisations need only focus on operational expenditure. For large organisations with internal infrastructure, it can reduce cost for infrastructure maintenance and acquisition by consolidating, reallocating and optimising available resources.
- Return of investment (ROI): This allows SME to sell their services quickly and easily without delays caused by acquiring and building the infrastructure. Moreover, CC may offer organisations direct (eg., more customers) and indirect (benefits from advertisements) ROI. It also allows organisations to offer outsourcing business models and services.
- Going Green: Using less resources and infrastructure reduces carbon footprint and emissions.

Technological:

- Virtualisation: This is a core characteristic of CC, and the use of Virtual Machines (VM) and VM Consoles enable enhanced flexibility through routing, aggregation and translation. This offers additional advantages, including (i) ease of use; (ii) infrastructure independency; (iii) flexibility and adaptability; and (iv) location independence.
- Multi-tenancy: This is another core characteristic of CC that allows the same resources to be shared by multiple users, and shared resources such as data and applications to be made available in multiple isolated instances.
- Data and Storage Management: Data consistency must be maintained over a wide distribution of replicated resources, and systems must be mindful of latencies for data location and workload. Data management also needs consistency guarantees.
- APIs, metering and tools – APIs provide common programming models for developers to improve on scalability and autonomic capabilities. Tools are end-products to support development, migration and usage of cloud services. A metering service is essential for elastic pricing, charging and billing.
- Security, Privacy and Compliance – this is a crucial part and essential for all cloud systems and services.

2.2. Surveys for Cloud Computing Adoption

There are different factors for organisations to adopt or consider adoption. Khajeh-Hosseini et al. (2011 a) assert that organisational adoption for Cloud computing is an emerging challenge due to factors such as cost, deployment and organisational change. They also explain that understanding the benefits and drawbacks is not straight forward because the suitability of the cloud for different systems is unknown; cost calculations are complicated; the adoption results in a considerable amount of organisational change that will affect the way employees work and corporate governance issues are not well understood. However, there are benefits of adopting Cloud such as consolidation of resources, green IT, cost-saving and new business opportunities which make adoption attractive (Buyya et al., 2009; 2010 b; Celik; Holliday and Hurst; 2009; Khajeh-Hosseini et al., 2010 a; Schubert, Jeffery and Neidecker-Lutz 2010; Creeger, 2009; Dunn 2010; Oracle, 2009 a; 2009 b, 2010).

Khajeh-Hosseini et al. (2010 a) also conduct a large number of interviews with stakeholders who decide in favour of organisational Cloud adoption. They perform stakeholder analysis and summarise benefits and risks arriving at top ranking factors as follows.

Benefits:

- Improve satisfaction of work
- Opportunity to develop new skills
- Opportunity for organisational growth
- Opportunity to offer new products/services
- Improved status
- Opportunity to manage income and outgoings

Risks:

- Lack of supporting resources
- Lack of understanding of the Cloud
- Departmental downsizing
- Uncertainty with new technology
- Deterioration of customer care and service quality
- Increased dependence on third parties
- Decrease of satisfying work

Khajeh-Hosseini et al. explain their rationale for each top-ranked factor. Interestingly, the top ranked-factors for benefits are different from the researchers' views which include factors such as availability, agility, scalability and elasticity (Armbrust et al., 2009; Buyya et al., 2009). Those top ranked factors for benefits indicate the outcome of adopting Cloud from the perspective of organisations. Employees can learn new skills. They will enjoy their work more if they find those skills are useful and interesting. This is particularly true for technical developers. If their work can be completed while maintaining the quality of their service, they can have better satisfaction of work. In addition, Cloud computing can offer the organisations new products and services, which then offer opportunity for organisational growth with potentially more customers, cost-saving and revenues involved. On the other hand, the top-ranked risks factors suggest that organisations are concerned about lack of supporting resources and understanding of the Cloud. Stakeholders are uncertain whether Cloud adoption can provide the long-term benefits they look for. The risk-level increases when there is a temporary upsizing in the IT department or a surge in demands for services. Those factors need to be clarified and explained intelligently by a framework and model that can provide guidance to the organisation as to whether they should adopt Cloud computing or use another alternative.

According to Dillion et al. (2011), IDC conducted a survey in 2008 (sample size = 244) to investigate what type of IT systems or applications migrated to Cloud. Their results indicate as follows: IT Management applications (26.2%), Collaborative applications (25.4%); Personal Applications (25%); Business Applications (23.4%); Application Development and Deployment (16.8%); Server Capacity (15.6%) and Storage Capacity (15.5%). Those results show that some organisations which have migrated to the Cloud have several different types of applications and also suggest organisations deploy more SaaS than IaaS to Cloud because core activities are kept in house with additional software outsourced to Cloud.

IT outsourcing is an alternative to Cloud migration and adoption and there are researchers investigating the implications of IT outsourcing. Dibbern et al. (2004) studied the impacts of outsourcing and found that although it was beneficial to the organisation at the beginning, outsourcing projects performed unsatisfactorily after going through several rounds of contracts. This led some organisations to take previously outsourced IT systems and services back in house as a result of unsatisfactory service levels, change in strategic direction or cost-saving failure (Overby, 2003). Some organisations use Cloud as an alternative to outsourcing their resources. However, Khajeh-Hosseini et al. (2011 a) explain there is a key difference between Cloud Computing and IT outsourcing: Self-service, scalability and pay-as-you-go model give clients more flexibility and control than traditional IT outsourcing.

2.3. Personalisation for Cloud Computing

Personalisation has become a popular area since the rise of World Wide Web and has been a topic of interest in e-Learning since early 2000 where the focus is to make learning courses flexible and tailored for individual needs. This concept is applicable to Cloud Computing. Gillett (2009) presents his model of Personal Cloud for Research (PCR) and demonstrates how it works on the basis of convenience, accessibility and security. Gillett defines PCR as "digital devices and services will combine to create the personal cloud, an integrated resource for organising, preserving, sharing, and orchestrating personal information and media." Another approach to illustrate PCR is by Application Programming Interface (API). Lesem (2012) explains that Personal Cloud can be demonstrated by using Cloud Storage APIs to access and utilise Cloud Storage, which should have capabilities for file functions, advanced functions, provisioning APIs, billing APIs and management APIs. Lesem also presents a service provider, Mezeo API overview, which includes file services, metadata services, sharing and collaboration and finally billing management and provisioning. Tian et al. (2011) provide a reference model for their Personal Cloud Computing, including their methodologies and architecture. They demonstrate how different technologies can work for mobile thin clients to act as a personal cloud.

Personalisation is related to Social Networks. There are research outputs to demonstrate Social Networks for Clouds and the benefits of the hybrid approach. Mohaisen et al. (2012) demonstrate the use of Social Networks for building distributed computing services and assert the benefits of Social Networks and personalisation working well in the blended environment between Social Networks and Clouds. Chard et al. (2012) present the use of Facebook applications on Amazon Web Services (AWS) and perform a number of experiments in different scenarios. Their implementations assert that personalisation and software customisation can be achieved in parallel in Cloud Computing.

Understanding these benefits helps organisations with Cloud adoption, whether they go for public, private or hybrid Cloud because it helps them to reduce operational costs, improve efficiency, streamline the processes and mitigate operational risks to vendors (Briscoe and Marinos, 2009; Martson et al., 2010; Schubert, Jeffery and Neidecker-Lutz, 2010). Chang et al., (2012) demonstrate the cost-saving is achieved and the improvement in user satisfaction in Cloud adoption by the University of Southampton.

3. TECHNICAL REVIEW FOR CLOUD COMPUTING

Chen et al. (2010) define Cloud Computing as a tower architecture where the virtualisation layer sits directly on top of hardware resources and sustains high-level cloud services. It goes onto the IaaS, PaaS and SaaS layers. The IaaS layer provides an infrastructural abstraction for self-provisioning, controlling and management of virtualised resources. In PaaS, consumers may leverage the development platform to design, develop, build, and deploy cloud applications. The SaaS layer is the top of the cloud architectural tower and delivers specific applications as a service to end users. There is a self-managing cloud system for dynamic capacity planning which is underpinned by monitoring and accounting services. Capacity planning hides complex infrastructural management tasks from users by automatically scaling in and out virtualised resource instances in order to enforce established SLA commitments. Security applies at each of the service delivery layers to ensure authenticated and authorised cloud services and features include identity management, access control, single sign-on and auditing. Chen et al. (2010) also identify CC for research challenges and classify this as Research Clouds. They have presented six user cases as below:

- Cloud Sourcing: Researchers using cloud capabilities (compute, storage, platform) provided by public Cloud Service Providers (CSPs) to develop, test or run research applications.
- Cloud Bursting: HEIs own research computing services while bursting and offloading to public cloud services due to fluctuating demands. Cloud bursting is commonly used to improve demand management.
- Private clouds: HEIs own research cloud computing services shared inside an institution only.
- Hybrid clouds: Cases involving both private cloud and public cloud.

- Community clouds: Multiple private clouds with shared requirements and interfaces. This includes federations of multiple private clouds.
- Cloud tool/services provisioning: Provisioning of self-management facilities, programming abstraction tools, debugging tools, and other platform services to public and/or private clouds.

Use cases are useful to support technical Cloud projects and support the validity of Cloud technical review.

Rozsnyai et al. (2007) propose an Event Cloud, where they use XML and AJAX technologies to implement a Cloud Search platform and they explain how their Cloud Architecture works. Their Event Cloud also provides ranking of search outcomes. Hammond et al. (2010) provide an overview of Cloud Computing for research and classify Political, Social, Economic, Societal, Technological and Legal issues to be resolved while adopting Cloud Computing. They have presented research use cases in storage, Monte Carlo simulations, bioinformatics and SLA.

There are additional technical reviews for Cloud Computing, which are essential for organisations to adopt Cloud. These technical reviews present current literature and state-of-art solutions for Cloud implementations, which allow stakeholders and management need to know limitations and challenges as a result of Cloud adoption.

3.1. Security for Cloud Computing

Security is always a popular topic and there are the following areas of specialisations for Clouds: identity management, access control, single sign-on and auditing (Chen et al., 2010; Martino and Bertino, 2009). In Chen et al., (2010) context, auditing means intrusion and detection mechanisms as well as policy-related security. The Hwang et al. (2009) proposal for cloud security relates to intrusion and detection despite having identity management enforced. Yee and Korba (2008) identify that personalising a security policy to a particular customer is needed. Therefore, Yee and Korba (2008) propose a flexible security personalisation approach that aims to allow an Internet or Web service provider and customer to negotiate an agreed-upon personalised security policy. They also present two application examples of security policy personalisation. The proposal from Paci et al. (2008) is for access control where they explain and demonstrate their Access-Control Framework for WS-BPEL, so that WS-BPEL not only has high performance but also maintains a high level of security for Web Services and interoperability. Kangasharju et al., (2008) investigate mobile WS security and focus on XML security with binary XML.

Security is a concern for some organisations to adopt Cloud, since privacy and data ownership are amongst key factors for organisations that decide not to move to Cloud Computing. Chang et al. (2011 a) introduce "IBM Fined Grained Security Framework" (IFGSF) developed by the IBM Research Division in the implementation of Cloud security. There are three layers of security mechanisms in place to protect the data and access. The first layer of defence is Access Control and firewalls, which only allow restricted members to access. The second layer consists of Intrusion Detection System (IDS) and Prevent System (IPS), which detect attack, intrusion and penetration, and also provide up-to-date technologies to prevent attack such as Denial of Service (DoS), anti-spoofing, port scanning, known vulnerabilities, pattern-based attacks, parameter tampering, cross site scripting, SQL injection and cookie poisoning. The third layer is the isolation management: It enforces top down policy based security management; integrity management – which monitors and provides early warning as soon as the behaviour of the fine-grained entity starts to behave abnormally. It offers both weak and strong isolations. Weak isolation focuses more on monitoring and captures end-to-end provenance. Strong isolation can fully isolate malicious hosts and cut all attacking connections to ensure that existing services are not affected by the attacks or unauthorised intrusion.

3.2. Portability for Cloud Computing

Ambrust et al. (2009) state Cloud portability is one of the challenges in Cloud deployment. Ahmed (2010) identifies data risk mitigation to Cloud as an adoption challenge where the portability is important in ensuring data risk mitigation to Cloud over different Clouds. Ahronovitz et al. (2010) identify applications portability as a challenge and classify it as a Cloud bursting, a desirable characteristic for Cloud Computing. Friedman and West (2010) focus on privacy and security of Cloud Computing as a focus in Cloud risk mitigation to Cloud which they explain as adoption challenges. They make these recommendations:

- Transparency: This allows users to understand the security precautions taken by a particular provider and have enough information to make an informed choice between two alternatives about their risk exposure.
- Competition: Cloud infrastructure is a competitive marketplace in which the service provider must improve the extent of security functionality and services. Providers must be large enough to leverage economies of security investment, information sharing and usable interfaces.
- Legal Clarifications: The first issue is the privacy rights of all users should be protected. The second issue is that the law must reflect how Cloud-based data and systems will become a new target for online criminals.

3.3. Business Integration

In their pioneering paper on business integration (BI) for Cloud Computing, Service Oriented Architecture (SOA) is a common approach. Chrisdutas (2008) presents SOA Java business integration (JBI), and he explains the operation of JBI including each individual component and the interactions between different JBI containers. This work is based on SOA architecture which either focuses on JBI or semantic approaches. The first 'pure' Cloud approach is designed by Papazoglou and van den Heuvel (2011), who present two models related to BI. The first is a cloud delivery model in which they explain interactions between virtualised applications, clients and a stack comprising IaaS, PaaS and SaaS suitable for Business Process as a Service (BPaaS). Their second model, the blueprint model, is proposed to allow BPaaS or SaaS applications to run dynamically on virtualised clouds to enable service virtualisation. There are three components to the model: (i) blueprint definition language (BDL); (ii) blueprint constraint language (BCL) and (iii) blueprint manipulation language (BML). They also explain an architectural scenario showing how blueprint support for the cloud service life cycle can work. However, their approach is at the system design level without details of implementation, testing or use cases. Moran et al. (2011) present Rule Interchange Format (RIF), RIF Mapping, RIF-expressed rules and a use case. They explain how semantic based integration can be achieved on IaaS level. However, their notion of BI is not the same as ours for the following reasons. Firstly, their integration is based on data exchange between different VMs to update the RIF status in the Cloud. Secondly, it is not clear whether their use case only works for IaaS, although they seem to imply this approach may work on PaaS and SaaS level in future work.

Understanding how to integrate different Cloud services is important, since this is also a Cloud adoption challenge, where Buyya et al. (2010 a) propose a Federated Clouds to provide work-around and solutions for service integrations. Integrations between different services can offer benefits including improvement in efficiency and collaboration while bringing down the costs of deployment and maintenance. Chang et al. (2012 b) present the concepts of Business Integration as a Service (BIaaS), which includes the architecture, implementation and discussions. There are two case studies involved. Firstly, the University of Southampton has adopted BIaaS to allow different departments to work on business analytics projects, which can compute both of cost-saving and risk modelling calculations in one go without using two different services. Secondly, the Vodafone case study allows the computations of profitability and risk modelling to be performed simultaneously. This allows the investors and stakeholders to understand the pricing and risks associated with their investment at any time.

4. CLOUD COMPUTING FOR BUSINESS USE

Cloud adoption requires organisations to link computing and business. Business Computing is an area to achieve this as it provides insights into how challenges can be resolved in the business context with improvements in efficiency, profitability and customer satisfaction (IBM SOA, 2008). Business Computing is closely related to the Cloud, since Cloud Computing offers business opportunities and incentives (Schubert, Jeffery and Neidecker-Lutz, 2010). The use of Business Computing is influential in the types of Cloud adoption and business model an organisation deploys. For Cloud businesses to perform well with long-term organisational sustainability, having the right business models is essential (Chou, 2009; Weinhart et al., 2009). There are eight Cloud business models classified by Chang et al., (2010 a; 2010 b; 2013 a), who explain the background, literature and rationale of Cloud business models categorisation and benefits of using multiple business models. This information is highly relevant to stakeholders who need to decide the best strategies for operating their Cloud business model and computing.

Several papers have explained IaaS, PaaS and SaaS as the cloud business model (Buyya et al., 2009; Chen, Wills, Gilbert, Bacigalupo, 2010; Armbrust et al., 2009; Weinhardt et al., 2009; Schubert, Jeffery and Neidecker-Lutz, 2010). Despite being focussed differently, all of these may be classified as "Service Provider and Service Orientation" models, regardless of whether they are IaaS, PaaS, or SaaS service providers, or their focus is on billing, SLA or

CRM, since this is a mainstream model that still has areas of unexploited opportunities. CC can also offer substantial savings by reducing costs whilst maintaining high levels of efficiency (Oracle 2009; Schubert, Jeffery and Neidecker-Lutz, 2010). Oracle (2009) and Vmware (2010) both propose using "In-House Private Clouds" to maximise use of internal resources to obtain added value offered by CC while keeping costs low. This allows organisations to build their own to satisfy IT demands and maintain low-costs including private cloud development (Claburn 2009), and is a new model from a micro economic point of view (Hull, 2009). Successful business models are not restricted to particular sectors or areas of specialisation and can be applicable for businesses including Cloud Computing businesses. Table 1 below gives a summary of criteria and supporting papers.

Table 1. Papers for Criteria of Business Model Classification

Criteria of Business Model Classification	Papers
Service Provider and Service Orientation	Buyya et al., (2009) Chen, Wills, Gilbert and Bacigalupo (2010) Patterson, Armbrust et al., (2009) Weinhardt et al., (2009 a; 2009 b) Schubert, Jeffery and Neidecker-Lutz (2010)
Support and Services Contracts	Lazonick (2005); Etro (2009)
In-House Private Clouds	Schubert, Jeffery and Neidecker-Lutz (2010) Claburn (2009) White papers: Oracle (2009); Vmware (2010) Note: Hull (2009) – supporting the same idea although he is based on microeconomic points of views only.
All-In-One Enterprise	Lazonick (2005) Weinhardt et al., (2009)
One-Stop Resources and Services	Jassen and Joha (2010); Kiu, Yuen and Tsui (2010) White paper: CSTransform (2009)
Government Funding	Lazonick (2005); Educause (2008)
Venture Capital	Hunt et al., (2003); Lazonick (2005)
Entertainment and Social Networking	Madhavapeddy et al., (2010), Maranto and Barton (2010) White paper: IBM (2009), RightScale (2010) Popular products: Apple iPhone; iPad; TV; iPod nano and Facebook (where the press has much more articles and updates than papers)

To classify the business models and processes, Chang et al. (2010 a; 2010 b) classify all Cloud business models into eight types and they use Cloud Cube Model (CCM) to represent the good practices in Cloud businesses supported by case studies. They also explain strengths and weaknesses in each business model which collaborators and investors have found useful. Table 2 shows advantages and disadvantages of eight Cloud business models (Chang et al., 2010 a).

Having the winning strategies also greatly influences decision-makers from traditionally non-cloud organisations. Wolfram is a computational firm providing software and services for education and publishing, and apart from using CCM, it has considered adopting the second business model. Upon seeing revenues in iPhone and iPad, they added a new model, the eighth model, by porting their applications onto iPhone and iPad. Similarly MATLAB, adopted the first and second model, and began the eighth model by porting their application to iPhone and iPad in order to acquire more income and customers.

Table 2. Advantages and disadvantages of each of eight business models (Chang et al., 2010 a; 2010 b)

No.	Business Models	Advantages	Disadvantages
1	Service Providers and Service Orientation	This is a main stream business model, and demands and requests are guaranteed. There are still unexploited areas for offering services and making profits.	Competitions can be very stiff in all of infrastructure, platform and software as a service. Data privacy is a concern for some clients.
2	Support and Service Contracts	Suitable for small and medium enterprises who can make extra profits and expand their levels of services.	Some firms may experience a period without contracts, and they must change their strategies quickly enough.
3	In-House Private Clouds	Best suited for organisations developing their own private clouds which will not have data security and (permanent) data loss concerns.	Projects can be complicated and time consuming.
4	All-In-One Enterprise	Can be the ultimate business model for big players Consolidating different business activities and strategies, including an ecosystem approach or comprehensive SaaS.	Small and medium enterprises are not suitable for this, unless they join part of an ecosystem.
5	One-Stop Resources and Services	A suitable model for business partnership and academic community. Can get mutual benefits through collaboration.	All participating organisations or individuals should contribute. If not managed well, it may end up in other business models or a community breaking apart.
6	Government Funding	Government can invest a massive amount, and this is beneficial for projects requiring extensive R&D, resources and highly trained staff.	Only affluent governments can afford that, and also top-class firms and universities tend to be selected.
7	Venture Capital	Can receive a surplus that is essential for sustainability. Useful for start-ups, or organisations nearly running out of cash.	It can be a prolonged process without a guarantee to get anything.
8	Entertainment and Social Networking	If successful, this model tends to dash into a storm of popularity and money in a short time.	Teenage social problems and a few extreme cases seen in the media.

There were start-ups such as Parascale using the seventh model to secure their funding, and they adopted the first model by being an IaaS provider. They moved into the second model to generate more revenues. The National Grid Service (NGS) has used the sixth model to secure funding, and their strategy is to adopt the fifth model by becoming the central point to provide IaaS cloud services for the UK academic community. Facebook has used multiple business models; the first, seventh and eighth model to assist their rapid user growth and business expansion.

Guy's and St Thomas' NHS Trust (GSTT) and Kings College London (KCL) spent their funding on infrastructure and resources to deliver a PaaS project. Knowing that outsourcing would cost more than they could afford financially together with the possibility in project time delays, they decided to use the third business model, "In-House Private Clouds", which matched to cost-saving, a characteristic of Cloud. They divided this project into several stages and tried to meet each target on time. In contrast, other NHS projects with more resources and funding, have opted for vendors providing the second and forth business models, "Support and Service Contract" and "All-in-One Enterprise Cloud".

5. STAKEHOLDERS' POINTS OF VIEW: RISKS FOR ORGANIZATIONAL ADOPTION AND HOW RISKS ARE RELATED TO CLOUD ADOPTION CHALLENGES

Before considering or deploying organisational adoption, different types of benefits and risks should be identified so that mitigation approaches can be proposed. This is useful for project management to maximise the extent of benefits and to minimise the risks. There are two steps involved. The first step is to tabulate the types of risks and determine their impact, with the ones with high impact factors being classified as adoption challenges. The second step is to analyse the benefits of adoption and explain how these benefits can address those challenges. Khajeh-Hosseini et al. (2011 a) performed a similar survey on Cloud users and clients. Based on their analysis, they tabulate different types of risks while adopting or outsourcing to Cloud presented in Table 3. Related details will be presented in Section 8.2.

Table 3. Different types of risks for organisational adoption of Cloud (Catteddu and Hogben, 2009; Khajeh-Hosseini et al., 2010 a, 2010b; 2011a)

ID	Risks	Mitigation approaches and potential indicators	References
R1	Organisational: Loss of governance and control over resources which might lead to unclear roles and responsibilities.	Clarify roles and responsibilities before cloud adoption.	Catteddu, and Hogben (2009); Dibbern et al., (2004); Khajeh-Hosseini et al. (2010 a, 2010 b); Jurison (1995).
R2	Organisational: Reduced staff productivity during the migration as changes to staff work and job uncertainty lead to low staff morale and anxiety spreading in the organisation.	Involve experts in the migration project so that they have a sense of ownership.	Khajeh-Hosseini et al. (2010 a); Grudin (1994).
R3	Organisational: Managing a system deployed on several clouds can make extra management effort compared to deploying systems in-house.	Make management aware of the extra effort that might be required.	Aubert, et al., (2005); Dibbern et al., (2004); Buyya et al. (2010 b)
R4	Organisational: Changes to cloud providers' services or acquisitions by another company that changes/terminates services.	Use multiple providers.	Catteddu, and Hogben (2009)

Table 3. (Continued)

ID	Risks	Mitigation approaches and potential indicators	References
R5	Technical: Performance is worse than expected. It might be difficult to prove to the cloud provider that their system performance is not as good as they promised in their SLA as the workload of servers and network can be variable in a cloud.	Use benchmark tools to investigate the performance of the cloud under investigation before decision making. Use monitoring tools to independently verify the system performance.	Aubert, et al., (2005); Armbrust et al., (2009); Durkee (2010); Jurison, J. (1995).
R6	Technical: Interoperability issues between clouds as there are incompatibilities between cloud providers' platforms.	Use cloud middleware to ease interoperability issues.	Catteddu, and Hogben (2009)
R7	Financial: Actual costs may be different from estimates, this can be caused by inaccurate resource estimates, changing prices or inferior performance resulting in more results to be required than expected.	Monitor existing resource usage and use estimation tools to obtain accurate cost estimates of deploying IT systems on the cloud. Check results of performance benchmark.	Aubert, et al., (2005); Khajeh-Hosseini et al., (2011 b); Dillion et al., (2010)
R8	Financial: Increased costs due to complex integrations. Inability to reduce costs due to unrealisable reductions in system/support staff.	Investigate system integration issues upfront, avoid migrating highly interconnected systems initially.	Dillion et al., (2010); Herbert and Erickson (2011); Kotsovinos (2010).

5.1. How Those Risks Relate to Cloud Adoption Challenges

All these risks present a number of adoption challenges, although some can be overlapped or related to one another. For example, both financial risks (R7 and R8) can be classified as cost estimate risks for which a prediction model can be used to calculate business performance including the return on investment (ROI) as accurately as possible.

Rosenthal (2009) report that Cloud Computing offers a new business paradigm for biomedical sharing and the impacts of such adoption have a significant effect on the way biomedical research can go forward. The added value is regarded as 'risk and return analysis', in which Youseff et al. (2008), Weinhardt et al. (2009 a) and Hugos and Hulitzky (2010) acknowledge the importance of measuring return and risk with their rationale presented. However, their approaches do not include key metrics for a systematic calculation. They do not demonstrate a process and methodology which can be reproduced by the commercial and research communities. This presents the first challenge as "model and analyse risk and return on adoption of a large computer system systematically and coherently".

Organisational risks (R1, R2 and R3) and technical risk (R5) present problems related to people, system and policy as a result of service migration to Cloud. Those risks are directly involved with migration, since a change in service model has implications in terms of lack of control, staff morale, system management, service availability and benchmarking. All these terms can be summarised as "risk mitigation for migrating to a new system including Cloud", as those problems arise due to service migration to Cloud. Services should be delivered efficiently after migration. To ensure organizations have a smooth transition to system adoption including Cloud adoption, it will be useful to provide detailed descriptions about how to mitigate risks of migrating to Cloud.

Organisational risk (R4) and technical risk (R6) present an interesting case that different services and clouds should work together. This can ensure different clouds can communicate. However, current deployment is a challenge as integrations are not straightforward. An easy-to-use and innovative approach for cloud and service integration needs to be considered.

There are additional risks such as legal and security risks but neither is dealt with here since additional resources would be required. In addition, the current focus for organisations that are adopting Cloud such as University of Southampton, NHS, IBM and Commonwealth Bank of Australia (CBA) is to address technical, financial and organisational issues and related adoption challenges. The high-level question is how organisations should adopt or consider adopting Cloud Computing. If they decide to adopt Cloud, "how stakeholders can understand the benefits and risks for Cloud adoption easily" is the question stakeholders ask (Information Week Survey, 2010). This needs to include risk analysis as a critical factor (Misra and Mondal, 2011) as it brings significant impacts to the adopting organisations including organisational and technical risks (R1, R2, R3, R4, R5 and R6) as a consequence of adoption. Meeting the stakeholders' expectations and the evidence of worthiness of adoption is an important agenda for stakeholders (Khajeh-Hosseini et al., 2010 a, 2010b; 2011a). This means return and risk calculation needs to take technical and organisational factors into consideration and is not limited to financial factors. Presenting results of return and risk allows stakeholders to understand the status of benefits and risks, which also fulfil the strategic goal for organisational adoption.

5.2. Additional Cloud Adoption Challenges

There are researchers investigating adoption challenges such as Service Level Agreements (SLA) in Clouds (Brandic et al., 2009; Buyya et al., 2009) and Business Models and Classification (Chou, 2009; Weinhardt et al., 2009 a). SLA focuses on billing models and has direct implications on prices, but they focus on the prices paid for the duration of using Cloud. Business models and classifications tend to focus on the way organisations can obtain the profitability not limited to SLA. There are initiatives explaining how SLA can demonstrate cloud business models (Brandic et al., 2009; Buyya et al., 2009). A limitation about SLA is they only focus on operational levels and are not directly connected to strategic levels. Other aspects for successful Cloud delivery have to be investigated at a wider scale, particularly the alignment between the strategic and operational focus of Cloud adoption. There are good examples for how dominant Cloud vendors focus on strategic levels for Cloud adoption to get a greater share of benefits. These organisations include Microsoft, Google, Oracle, IBM and Facebook, all of which obtain more revenue through other forms of services.

To help organisations designing, deploying and supporting clouds, especially private clouds, considering both strategic and operational approaches for Cloud adoption is recommended. Armbrust et al. (2009) describe Cloud Computing technical adoption challenges and considered vendors' lock-in, data privacy, security and interoperability as the most important challenges. Khajeh-Hosseini et al. (2010 a; 2011 a) identify human-social issues in Cloud adoption to be resolved and explain their importance using case studies. This means adoption challenges need to take technical, financial and organisational issues into strategic consideration before adoption and implementation take place. Based on the discussion above, the most influential adoption challenges are summed up in Table 4 with their justification provided.

Table 4. Summary of Cloud adoption challenges

Adoption challenges	How do they relate to Table 2	Justification	Types of focus
Model and analyse risk and return on adoption of a large computer system systematically and coherently	R7 and R8 Additional literature: Youseff et al. (2008) Rosenthal (2009) Weinhardt et al. (2009 a) Hugos and Hulitzky (2010)	Useful for stakeholders to understand whether they should adopt Cloud and calculate their business performance after adoption to prove its worthiness.	Strategic
Risk mitigation to system adoption including Cloud	R1, R2, R3 and R5	Detailed descriptions about how to compute and reduce risk of system adoption including Cloud will be demonstrated to help organisations have a good management and control of Cloud projects.	Operational

6. A NEED FOR A FRAMEWORK FOR CLOUD COMPUTING

There are different types of clouds in the market targeting different types of groups, industry and services. With regard to orientation of businesses, all of clouds fall into one of three groups: Infrastructure as a Service (IaaS); Platform as a Service (PaaS) and Software as a Service (SaaS).

Foster et al. (2008) explain that Grids and Clouds offer common solutions to some research questions. However, this interpretation is not entirely correct as lessons learned cannot be resolved and transferrable in the same way. This is supported by Sobel et al. (2009) who argue that Grid and Cloud are different. In particular Web 2.0 is involved with Clouds from the beginning to the current status but this is not necessarily so for Grids. In contrast, Weinhardt et al. (2009 a) define the difference between Grids and Clouds as in the business models where Clouds can provide new business opportunities. This is supported by the observation that the number of organisations offering Cloud solutions and their variety has been increasing since 2007. Before deploying any type of Cloud Computing development, an essential step is to design and implement good quality Business Models and a Business Framework (Hosono et al., 2009; Weinhardt et al., 2009 a; 2009 b). Hosono et al., (2009) demonstrate Service System Modelling (SSM) and explain how SSM helps Business Models to be developed with Cloud Frameworks. Anstett et al. (2009) explain how Business Process Execution Language (BPEL) assists in developing a Cloud Framework to create a SOA-driven Business Model. Weinhardt et al. (2009 a) explain their definitions and importance of Cloud Business Models (CBM) and show how CBM can influence research directions for academic communities. Buyya et al. (2008, 2009) and Armbrust et al. (2009) define CBM and explain their rationales in terms of (i) pay-as-you go systems; (ii) cost saving calculations;

and (iii) SOA and SLA theories. However, the feedback from industrialists (Financial Times Book, 2009; Chee, Wong and Jin, interviews, 2009; Chou, 2009; Information Week Survey, 2010) is that the CBMs proposed by Buyya et al. (2008, 2009) and Armbrust et al. (2009) are too complicated to understand and as a result, these models cannot be used and applied easily and effectively in real-time cloud computing businesses and organisational Cloud adoption. In addition, there are few Cloud Business Frameworks that can accommodate different types of technical solution in relation to their businesses (Klems, Nimis and Tsai, 2008). Although IaaS, PaaS and SaaS are generally classified as three business models, there is no definite guideline for running successful and sustainable cloud businesses.

7. IDENTIFIED PROBLEMS WITH EXISTING FRAMEWORKS

There are existing frameworks to deal with IT services or architecture but none of them is designed for Cloud adoption with support of case studies. Eleven frameworks discussed in this section:

1) Cloud Business Model Framework (CBMF) by Weinhardt et al., (2009 a; 2009b)
2) Linthicum Cloud Computing Framework (LCCF; Linthicum, 2009)
3) Return on Investment (ROI) for Cloud Computing (Skilton, 2010)
4) Performance metrics framework (Assuncao, Costanzo and Buyya, 2010)
5) Oracle Consulting Cloud Computing Services Framework (OCCCSF; Oracle, 2011)
6) IBM Framework for Cloud Adoption (IBM, 2010)
7) CloudSim (Calheiros et al., 2009)
8) BlueSky Cloud Framework for e-Learning (BCF; Dong et al., 2009)
9) Hybrid ITIL V3 for Cloud (Heininger, R., 2012)
10) DAvinCi, a Cloud framework for Service Robots (Arumugam et al., 2010).
11) Cloud Computing Business Framework (Chang et al., 2011 b; 2011 c; 2012 a; 2013 a)

7.1. Cloud Business Model Framework (CBMF)

Weinhardt et al., (2009 a; 2009b) propose Cloud Business Model Framework (CBMF) as a strategic way for all organisations to be successful in cloud businesses. They present four core business cloud elements: Infrastructure, Platform, Applications and the Business Model. Each main layer is supported by its core functions and service providers, and is also stacked on top of another. However, there is a drawback in this proposal. CBMF assumes that each layer is independent and only connects directly to the Business Model layer. Some service providers or Cloud resources allow upgrading from one layer to the next level before moving onto the Business Model layer. For example, PaaS – when more applications are developed and tested in the Cloud environment, the final product can be delivered as a SaaS service (such as CRM and financial analysis) instead of PaaS. CBMF does not provide any details about how their framework can help organizations adopt Cloud Computing, and does not have any recommendations about how to run and maintain Cloud services, which are important to some adopting organisations.

7.2. Linthicum Cloud Computing Framework (LCCF)

Linthicum Cloud Computing Framework (LCCF) is focused on how organisations should offer their services based on his recommended architecture. He explains different types of services on top of each other and this rationale. However, there are not enough use cases and Linthicum (2009) appears to generalise his architectural framework based on his own experience. A valid Cloud computing framework should be applicable to a majority of practices and services. There are not enough details about whether organisations should continue adopting more Cloud resources and services, or simply run one service without opening new services or expanding existing services.

7.3. Return on Investment (ROI) for Cloud Computing

Skilton (2010) investigates Return on Investment (ROI) for Cloud Computing and provides cost impact analysis for adoption. He also states key factors affecting Cloud ROI with its key performance indicators (KPIs) to allow service-oriented business and IT to work together in harmony. However, Skilton (2010) does not show any details about how to calculate ROI or how to perform cost-benefit analysis. Stating KPIs without showing how to calculate ROI does not help stakeholders to understand whether they should adopt Cloud Computing or expand existing services.

7.4. Performance Metrics Framework

Performance metrics framework (Assuncao, Costanzo and Buyya, 2010) is used to evaluate and demonstrate cost-effectiveness for clouds and to perform experiments for validation. It is an extension of SLA framework based on work of Buyya et al., (2009) which explains how SLA framework works across public clouds. The performance metrics framework is an IaaS-only framework that focuses on SLA which is only a particular type of risk and return analysis. The rationale is that stakeholders have a more comprehensive view about the added values offered by Cloud adoption, and requires a high-level strategic plan for adoption. The performance metrics framework does not offer any measurement for other services such as PaaS and SaaS, nor does it deal with challenges in Cloud adoption such as risk mitigation to Cloud and integration with other services and clouds.

7.5. Oracle Consulting Cloud Computing Services Framework

Oracle Consulting Cloud Computing Services Framework (OCCCSF; Oracle, 2011) aims to help Oracle customers to implement Cloud solutions and has five major themes: Roadmap;

Standardise, Consolidate, Automate and Optimise. OCCCSF also outlines key factors for Cloud adoption and categorises these factors under their Oracle Cloud Domain Model. OCCCSF provides strategic plans for their client organisations to adopt Cloud. The major limitation is that it is difficult to see how this framework can be fully adopted and applied by non-Oracle customers. A robust and valid framework should allow customers to choose any technologies and vendors which can work under different types and conditions for Cloud implementation. In addition, a working framework should allow customers to choose their products and technologies for successful delivery, instead of just using one way for implementation.

7.6. IBM Framework for Cloud Adoption (IFCA)

IBM (2010) proposes IBM Framework for Cloud adoption (IFCA) which defines Cloud Service Levels and Cloud Delivery Models in relation to Cloud adoption. It divides Cloud services into four layers, with business process on the top, followed by SaaS, PaaS and IaaS at the bottom. IFCA contains different Cloud usage for Private Cloud and Public Cloud, where Exploratory Cloud, Departmental Cloud and Enterprise Cloud are part of the Private Cloud; and Exclusive Cloud and Open Cloud are part of the Public Cloud. There are three types of users in the IFCA: Consumer; Provider and Integrator. Each type of user has a different role and contributions to the IFCA.

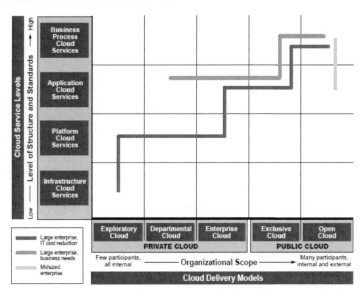

Figure 1. IBM Framework for Cloud Adoption (IFCA).

Figure 1 shows a generic adoption recommended by ICFA. In the large enterprise with cost reduction as their adoption focus, the Exploratory Cloud is focused on IaaS and PaaS since it fits for pilot studies. The Departmental Cloud is ideal for PaaS to work with different services in other departments, particularly data services. The Enterprise Cloud is focused on PaaS and SaaS. There are also different usages for "Large enterprise, business needs" and "Midsized enterprise" presented in Figure 1. IFCA provides a good recommendation and tries to provide a generic solution for all types of industries and all types of Clouds. Its major drawback is that there are no case studies or use cases. If there are real case studies to support the proposal, IFCA will be in a solid position as an established framework for Cloud adoption.

7.7. CloudSim

CloudSim is a software framework to demonstrate the implementation of Cloud data centres and services by the use of Java-based technologies (Calheiros et al., 2009). There are examples to demonstrate how CloudSim can be useful for implementations and these are supported by the use cases and experiments performed by CloudSim development team. It is well-known open source Cloud software with several good features. The lead author and co-authors' students have used CloudSim to provide proof-of-concept for Cloud implementations. The following limitations have been identified from their experience: key variables and values must be defined before the use of CloudSim and CloudSim is more suitable to use as stand-alone public clouds or public clouds that are distributed in different sites. There is insufficient evidence that CloudSim can be fully delivered for private clouds and hybrid clouds, as the challenges for Cloud adoption need to be resolved during the design stage of CloudSim. Buyya et al. (2010 b) propose and demonstrate InterCloud to address this issue. However, a working framework should always be valid and workable for different types of Clouds.

7.8. BlueSky Cloud Framework for e-Learning

Dong et al. (2009) explain challenges for e-Learning and propose the BlueSky Cloud Framework (BCF) to resolve challenging issues. They explain their framework architecture, including the components, layers and interactions between different components in different layers. However, it is a conceptual framework, as there is insufficient evidence to confirm that it has real implementations and case studies. There are no descriptions about the validation methods, and whether simulations and modelling are used for validation. There are no follow-up journal articles to explain the current status of their framework project yet.

7.9. The Hybrid ITIL V3 Framework for Cloud

The Information Technology Infrastructure Library Version 3 (ITIL V3) is a useful framework adopted by many organisations to understand good practices and allow different roles within the same organisation to streamline their processes. It is composed of five processes which are Service Strategy, Service Design, Service Transition, Service Operations and Continual Service Improvement (Chang et al., 2013 a). The ITIL V3 has been adopted by organisations to improve efficiency and communications between different departments, since members of staff can think and understand the same under the influence of the framework. However, ITIL V3 does not provide specific solutions for any types of Cloud adoption problems (Heininger, 2012). A valid criticism about ITIL V3 is that it offers key points and important concepts but expects organisations to resolve problems themselves. Limitations in ITIL V3 can be addressed by adopting other frameworks, which shows that ITIL V3 is not yet a complete framework for Cloud Computing. Cloud Computing has evolved and moved on quickly and the framework requires updating to include guidelines and recommendations for specific types of Cloud adoption such as Mobile Clouds. If an organisation decides to offer mobile-based Cloud services, adopting organisations will find no remedies or suggestions from ITIL V3.

7.10. DAvinCi: A Cloud Computing Framework for Service Robots

Arumugam et al. (2010) present DAvinCi, a Cloud framework for Service Robots. They explain their methodology, approaches, algorithm and experimental results. It is a working framework for Service Robots. But a working framework needs to present its most up-to-date results and improvements over existing adoption challenges and there have been no further publications. In addition, the framework is constrained to work only for robots.

7.11. Cloud Computing Business Framework (CCBF)

Chang et al. (2011 a; 2011 b; 2012; 2013 a) present the Cloud Computing Business Framework (CCBF), which is focused more on the literature, process and methodology that leads to the development of the conceptual framework and how it can be useful for organisations and businesses with selected case studies. There are case studies demonstrated by CCBF (Chang et al., 2011 a; 2011 b; 2012; 2013). While the framework has been used by Cloud-Adopting organisations, demands and efforts have been moved to how the framework can meet the requirements for the adoption challenges (described in Section 5), particularly case studies for successful Cloud adoption. Stakeholders from organisations that plan to implement Cloud feedback that they would like to see more case studies and recommendations. An improved version, Cloud Computing Adoption Framework (CCAF), is focused more on how organisations should do to resolve issues around Cloud adoption challenges. There is a detailed case study involved from design, implementation and user support for Cloud services (Chang et al., 2013 b).

7.12. Summary of the Section

Each of the Cloud Computing frameworks presented has some drawbacks such as insufficient detail of how organisations should adopt Cloud Computing; and if they adopt, what are the issues and priorities they should be aware of for delivery of Cloud deployment and services. Limitations of existing good frameworks are presented in Table 5, with the proposal for the development of a new framework to address those issues.

Table 5. What a proposed framework can offer for limitations of existing frameworks

Existing frameworks	Limitations of existing frameworks	What a proposed framework should offer
Cloud Business Model Framework (CBMF; Weinhardt et al., 2009 a; 2009b)	CBMF assumes that each layer is independent, and only connects directly to Business Model layer. CBMF does not provide any details about how their framework can help organisations to adopt Cloud Computing, and does not have any recommendations about how to run and maintain Cloud services.	A proposed framework will allow different service layers connecting to each other. For example, work developed for PaaS can be further improved to SaaS. The proposed framework has included case studies for how organisations adopt Cloud and sums up key lessons learned.
Linthicum Cloud Computing Framework (LCCF; Linthicum, 2009)	There are not enough use cases/case studies, as Linthicum appears to generalise his architectural framework based on his own experience. There are not enough details about whether organisations should continue adopting more Cloud resources and services, or simply run one service without opening new services or expanding existing services.	A proposed framework should include several case studies, which are used to show how organisations can calculate their Risk and return analysis and discussions about benefits of Cloud adoption supported by results. Examples can allow the finance industry to adopt Cloud and to perform multiple workloads such as calculating risks and pricing, achieving good accuracy without sacrificing performance, and also to perform large-scale simulations in a short period of time.
Return on Investment (ROI) for Cloud Computing (ROICC; Skilton, 2010)	ROICC does not show any details about how to calculate ROI (or return) and how to perform cost-benefit analysis. By stating KPIs without showing how to calculate ROI, it does not help stakeholders to understand whether they should adopt Cloud Computing or expand existing services.	A proposed framework can calculate risk and return analysis to Cloud for technical, cost and user focused projects for Cloud adoption for organisations that adopt Cloud. Results should be supported by case studies.
Performance metrics framework (PMF; (Assuncao, Costanzo and Buyya, 2010)	They only focus on one aspect of risk and return analysis, particularly SLA. There are other types of risk and return analysis they should look at. PMF does not measure other services such as PaaS and SaaS, and does not deal with challenges in Cloud adoption such as risk mitigation to Cloud.	A proposed framework can calculate risk and return analysis for three types of Cloud adoption, which include technical, cost and user aspects of risk and return analysis. It can calculate for IaaS, PaaS and SaaS.
IBM Framework for Cloud adoption (IFCA; IBM, 2010)	IFCA tries to provide a generic solution for all types of industries and all types of Clouds. However, there are no use cases or case studies at all since it has been available for more than 2 years.	A proposed framework has detailed case studies to explain the benefits of Cloud adoption. Stakeholders can understand the extent of return and risks for their Cloud adoption easily. A proposed framework can be fully adopted by non-IT sectors such as Healthcare and Finance to demonstrate that it is a generic solution working across sectors.

Existing frameworks	Limitations of existing frameworks	What a proposed framework should offer
Oracle Consulting Cloud Computing Services Framework (OCCCSF; Oracle, 2011)	It is difficult to see how OCCCSF can be fully adopted and applied by non-Oracle customers. A robust and valid framework should allow customers to choose any technologies and vendors which can work under different types and conditions for Cloud implementation.	A proposed framework allows customers to choose their hardware and software technologies. The proposed framework focuses on the delivery of their Cloud adoption and allows flexibility for adoption. The key focus can model risk and return analysis and demonstrate risk mitigation for Cloud adoption.
CloudSim (Calheiros et al., 2009)	Key variables and values must be defined before the use of CloudSim. Not all organisations that adopt Cloud should always need these variables. There are insufficient examples that CloudSim can be fully delivered for private clouds and hybrid clouds, as the challenges for Cloud adoption should be resolved. Their proposal of InterCloud may resolve some of these issues.	A proposed framework can allow any Cloud services working on public, private and hybrid Clouds, which are supported by publications and framework adopting-organisations.
BlueSky Cloud Framework for e-Learning (BCF; Dong et al., 2009)	BCF is a conceptual framework, as there are insufficient evidences to justify it has real implementations and case studies. There are no descriptions about the validation methods. There are no follow-up journal articles to explain the current status of their framework project.	A proposed framework will have real implementations and case studies to support its validity. There will be papers published each year to ensure the improvement of the framework is helpful to organisations that adopt Cloud.
Hybrid ITIL V3 Cloud (Heininger, 2012)	ITIL V3 does not provide specific solutions for any types of Cloud adoption problems and expects organisations to resolve problems themselves. There are no any guidelines and recommendations for specific types of emerging Cloud adoption such as Mobile Clouds.	A proposed framework should have details of how to help Cloud-adopting organisations to resolve adoption challenges and have hand-on experiences for implementations. Organisations can reproduce recommendation and steps proposed by the framework, which keeps up-to-date with the latest technological offers such as Mobile Clouds.
DAvinCi (Arumugam et al., 2010)	The project does not have any publication updates since 2010. A working framework should have updates to present its most up-to-date results and improvements over existing adoption challenges. In addition, a framework should also work for other domains and not just for robots.	A proposed framework has regular updates to report its progress and most up-to-date results, case studies and successful Cloud deliveries. It can work in a number of domains and organisations, and has a continuous life cycle after Cloud adoption.
Cloud Computing Business Framework (CCBF; Chang et al., (2011 b; 2011 c; 2012; 2013 a)	The framework focuses more on the literature, process and methodology that leads to the development of the conceptual framework and how it can be useful for organisations and businesses with selected case studies. More case studies and recommendations should be focused on Cloud adoption challenges and issues to resolve.	A proposed framework needs to offer more industrial feedback, case studies and demonstrations of proof-of-concept than CCBF. The proposed framework should offer more technical implementations for Cloud Computing, and recommendations to make good practices into repeatable steps for Cloud-adopting organisations. The proposed framework has more up-to-date summary of lessons learned from case studies and the process of Cloud development.

The eleven different Cloud Computing frameworks presented here have their own drawbacks such as insufficient details of how organisations should adopt Cloud Computing; and if they adopt, what are the issues and priorities they should be aware of. Since adoption is an important organisational decision and process, a relevant and valid framework should address those issues and adoption challenges. Limitations for each framework are stated and how the new proposal can overcome these limitations will be presented in the following section.

8. Discussions

Section 5 identified and discussed Cloud adoption challenges, and explained how work for these two adoption challenges can provide recommendations and workarounds for Cloud adoption. Two key areas for these research questions are identified which correspond to "calculate risk and return analysis of a large computing system adoption including Cloud adoption" and "risk mitigation to Cloud". Section 6 explains why it is better to have a framework approach to deal with Cloud adoption, where the summary with the support of literature review explains why a framework is necessary for Cloud adoption. Section 7 describes selected frameworks and highlights the limitations of each. It becomes apparent that there is a need for a new framework to address limitations of the existing frameworks.

8.1. Desired Characteristics for a Proposed Framework

The new framework needs to overcome limitations from other frameworks presented in Table 5.

**Table 6. How a proposed framework can meet the criteria
to be a Cloud adoption framework**

Criteria for a Cloud adoption framework	How to meet the criteria
Align technical activities with business models and strategies	Business model is at the top of a proposed conceptual framework to apply strategies and case studies approach. The Business process is on the strategic layer of the proposed framework. The objective is to align IT and business requirements and to fully translate the stakeholders' demands to design, deployment, data collection and analysis for Cloud adoption.
Be easily adopted by the industry or any organisations	There are several organisations that have used the proposed framework.
Integrate fully with activities of organisations that adopt Cloud	A proposed framework can demonstrate different levels of Cloud framework adoption. The level-four and level-three adoption are the highest, which are organisations that design the Cloud service from the beginning to the implementation and to the service delivery and support.
Compile all key lessons learned and recommendations which can be influential to academia and industry	All key lessons can contribute to recommendations which can be influential in academia and industry. There are organisations which have used CCAF to report contributions to their Cloud adoption. There are good-quality journals to be published.

It can be validated by quantitative methods including simulations, modelling and experiments, and also supported by qualitative methods that contain feedback from surveys and selective interviews. According to Chang (2013), a good framework should have the following characteristics:

- Align technical activities with business models and strategies
- Be easily adopted by the industry or any organisations
- Integrate fully with activities of organisations that adopt Cloud
- Compile all key lessons learned and recommendations which can be influential to academia and industry

Table 6 presents how a proposed framework can meet each of these criteria.

8.2. Future Challenges for Risk and Return Analysis

Risk and return analysis is a major challenge identified in Section 5 from the stakeholders' points of view. There are three types of risk and return analysis required: technical, costs and users (Chang et al; 2011 b; 2011 c; 2013 a). These are future challenges for a proposed framework to resolve.

8.2.1. Costs (Financial) Measurement for Risk and Return Analysis

There is a need to measure risk and return analysis in terms of its business benefits to aid the strategic decision of Cloud adoption. This will address the key financial risk that needs to be addressed when adopting cloud: R7 the risk of the actual costs being different from the estimates, this can be caused by inaccurate resource estimates, changing prices or inferior performance resulting in more resources spent than expected. This is mitigated by monitoring existing resource usage and using estimation tools to obtain accurate cost estimates of deploying IT systems on the cloud. (Aubert, et al., 2005; Khajeh-Hosseini et al., 2011b; Dillion et al., 2010). The type of risk and return analysis is focused on cost-saving and profitability. Inaccurate resource estimates can be reduced using precise cost calculations and consolidated resources to reduce operational costs. Precise and accurate calculations of profitability enable stakeholders to understand benefits due to Cloud adoption.

8.2.2. Technical Measurement for Risk and Return Analysis

Technical performance (R5) considers whether Cloud adoption can provide better performance such as completing requests more quickly or whether more work can be done in the same period of time. This relates to efficiency, and this type of risk and return analysis is focused on improvements in efficiency. The same number of jobs/requests can be completed quicker, or more jobs/requests can be done in the same time frame for Cloud systems comparing to non-Cloud systems.

8.2.3. Users (or Organisations) Measurement for Risk and Return Analysis

Organisational issues identified (R2 and R3) are concerned with adoption challenges which include whether the internal feedback is positive and the extent of user satisfaction rating. This is a measurement to reflect users and clients' rating about Cloud adoption, which is an important aspect to confirm the added values of using a new Cloud platform or application. This type of risk and return analysis is focused on User satisfaction ratings. An increased percentage of users (or clients) feel there is an improvement to the quality of products and services such as having a quicker response time, a higher proportion of jobs completed at the same time and a more efficient system/application to get their work completed, which results in a higher positive rating for Cloud adoption. In general, this is summed up as user satisfaction rating.

The proposed framework should be able to meet all these three requirements and allow stakeholders to understand the extent of return and risk of their Cloud adoption, regardless of whether they adopt a technical, costs or users focus.

8.3. Future Directions Related to This Research

Future directions are important to influence the way adoption framework is carried forward, and related areas are presented as follows.

- Integration: Integrations with different services are crucial to the organisations in their enterprise activities. The advantages of doing so allow them to improve efficiency and need not spend multiple resources to do multiple tasks. Instead, one single service can deliver requests for two services. Chang et al. (2011 d) firstly made a pioneering proof-of-concepts, Business Integration as a Service (BIaaS), to demonstrate how different services can work together as a single service. They expand their work by demonstrating architecture, computational analysis and methodology (Chang et al., 2012 b). Further to this, Chang (2013 a) demonstrate his BIaaS work for small and medium enterprises that adopt SAP. Those results can help organisations to analyse return and risk in one go, instead of inputting different data for each service and get two separate results which are not connected together. Integrations between services can reduce time, effort and funding to manage Cloud services.

- Big Data: The return and risk analysis is essential to Big Data research, which needs algorithms to process datasets, calculate complex modelling and present them in a way that can be understood easily by researchers and stakeholders. Some of the work has been demonstrated by Chang et al. (2012 c; 2013 b) to manage and analyse medical data including images, datasets and experimental results. A platform is required to help scientists analyse Big Data, process results quickly and accurately and present the results which can be interpreted easily. The use of BIaaS can help achieve these goals.

- Specialised disciplines for Cloud adoption: Some disciplines require highly sophisticated tools and services for Cloud adoption. Medical informatics is one of such area that needs integrations of different expertise and technologies. Chang (2013 b; 2013 c; 2013 d) demonstrate that Cloud Computing can be used in brain segmentation technology to understand the brain cell activities while relearning a skill such as dance. Advanced techniques can be applied to analyse thousands of datasets and process them at once between four and ten seconds.

CONCLUSION

This paper presents a review related to Cloud Computing focusing on the benefits of adoption and background to Cloud Computing. This is highly relevant to industry and academia as there are growing numbers of organisations adopting or actively using Cloud. Understanding Cloud usage and adoption is highly relevant, as it helps stakeholders to understand their risk and return analysis and the extent of added values (such as efficiency, cost-saving, profitability and user satisfactions) offered by Cloud adoption. Adoption challenges including risk and return analysis and risk mitigation to Cloud arise for organisations that adopt Cloud, particularly private clouds. The use of a framework can help to manage Cloud design, deployment and services much better. Existing frameworks all have their limitations and cannot meet requirements for Cloud adoption challenges fully. A new framework is required to deal with adoption challenges and offer solutions and recommendations in the shortcoming of other frameworks.

Technical, financial and user requirements and complexity in handling Cloud adoption challenges need a structured and well-organised framework to deal with emerging issues and provide solutions for others. A proposed framework needs to be dynamic and structured to help different types of Cloud services, whether risk and return analysis and risk mitigation to Cloud. Future directions are discussed, and innovative ways for integrations, Big Data and specialised disciplines for Cloud adoption will be the focus of the next-generation of Cloud adoption.

REFERENCES

A Vmware White Paper (2010), Eight Key Ingredients for Building an Internal Cloud VMware Private Clouds: Providing the Ability to Consume Resources, Regardless of Where They Reside.

Ahronovitz, M. et al., (about 70 authors, 2009), Cloud Computing Use Cases White Paper, Version 4.0, National Institute of Standards and Technology, July.

An IBM White paper (2008), IT service management to enable the fulfilment of your SOA strategy, IBM Global Services, October.

An Oracle White Paper (2009 a), Architectural Strategies for Cloud Computing, August.

An Oracle White Paper (2009 b), Platform-as-a-Service Private Cloud with Oracle Fusion Middleware, September.

An Oracle White Paper (2010), Oracle Cloud Computing, May.

An Oracle White Paper (2011), Oracle Consulting Cloud Services Framework, April.

Anstett T, Leymann F, Mietzner R and Strauch, S. (2009), Towards BPEL in the Cloud: Exploiting Different Delivery Models for the Execution of Business Processes", 2009 World Congress on Services, I, 6-10 July, Los Angeles, CA, USA.

Armbrust, M., Fox, A., Griffith, R., Joseph, A. D., Katz, R. H., Konwinski, A., Lee, G., Patterson, D., Rabkin, A., Stoica, I., Zaharia, M. (2009), Above the Clouds: A Berkeley View of Cloud computing, Technical Report, No. UCB/EECS-2009-28, UC Berkeley, February.

Arumugam, R., Enti, V. R; Liu, B., Wu, X., Baskaran, K., Kong, F. F., Kumar, A. S., Kang, D M., Goh, W. K., DAvinCi (2010), A cloud computing framework for service robots, 2010 *IEEE International Conference on Robotics and Automation* (ICRA), 3-7 May, Singapore.

Assuncao, M.D.D, Costanzo A.D. and Buyya, R. (2010), A cost-benefit analysis of using cloud computing to extend the capacity of clusters", Journal of Cluster Compute, 13: 335–347, April.

Aubert, B.A., Patry, M., and Rivard, S. (2005), A framework for information technology outsourcing risk management," ACM SIGMIS Database, vol. 36, Oct., pp. 9-28.

Boss, G., Malladi, P., Quan, D., Legregni, L. and Hall, H. (2007), Cloud Computing, IBM white paper, Version 1.0, October.

Brandic I, Music D, Leitner P and Dustdar S. (2009), VieSLAF Framework: Enabling Adaptive and Versatile SLA-Management, the 6th International Workshop on Grid Economics and Business Models 2009 (Gecon09), 25- 28 August, Delft, The Netherlands.

Briscoe, G. and Marinos, A. (2009), Digital ecosystems in the clouds: towards community cloud computing, the 3rd IEEE International Conference on Digital Ecosystems and Technologies, June 1-3, New York, USA, pp. 103-108.

Buyya R, Yeo C S and Venugopal S (2008), Market-Oriented Cloud Computing: Vision, Hype, and Reality for Delivering IT Services as Computing Utilities, HPCC 2008 Cloud Computing, keynote paper.

Buyya R, Yeo C S, Venugopal S, Broberg J and Brandic I (2009), Cloud computing and emerging IT platforms: Vision, hype, and reality for delivering computing as the 5th utility, *Journal of Future Generation Computer Systems*, Volume 25, Issue 6, June, Pages 559-616.

Buyya, R., Beloglazov1, A., and Abawajy, J. (2010 b), Energy-Efficient Management of Data Center Resources for Cloud Computing: A Vision, Architectural Elements, and Open Challenges, *PDPTA'10 - The International Conference on Parallel and Distributed Processing Techniques and Applications*, 12-15 July, Las Vegas, USA.

Buyya, R., Ranjan, R. and Calheiros, R. N. (2010 a), InterCloud: Utility-Oriented Federation of Cloud Computing Environments for Scaling of Application Services, Algorithm and Architectures for Parallel Processing, Lecture Notes in Computer Science, Volume 6081/2010, 13-31.

Calheiros, R.N, Ranjan, R., De Rose, C. A.F. and Buyya, R. (2009), CloudSim: A Novel Framework for Modeling and Simulation of Cloud Computing Infrastructures and Services, Technical report, *Grid Computing and Distributed Systems Laboratory*, The University of Melbourne, Australia.

Catteddu, D. and Hogben, G. (2009), Cloud Computing: benefits, risks and recommendations for information security, Technical Report, European Network and Information Security Agency.

Celik, A., Holliday, J. and Hurst, Z. (2006), Data Dissemination to a Large Mobile Network: Simulation of Broadcast Clouds, the 7th International Conference on Mobile Data Management (MDM) 2006, 10-12 May, Santa Clara University, USA.

Chang V, Bacigalupo D., Wills G., Roure D. D. (2010 a), A Categorisation of Cloud Computing Business Models, poster paper, CCGrid 2010 IEEE conference, Melbourne, Australia, May.

Chang V, Li C S, De Roure D, Wills G, Walters R and Chee C (2011 a), The Financial Clouds Review. *International Journal of Cloud Applications and Computing*, 1 (2). pp. 41-63. ISSN 2156-1834, eISSN 2156-1826.

Chang V, Mills, H and Newhouse, S (2007), From Open Source to long-term sustainability: Review of Business Models and Case studies, UK e-Science All Hands Meeting, Nottingham, UK, September.

Chang V, Wills G, De Roure D (2010 b), A Review of Cloud Business Models and Sustainability, IEEE Cloud 2010, the third International Conference on Cloud Computing, 5-10 July 2010, Miami, Florida, USA.

Chang, V. (2013 a), Business integration as a service: computational risk analysis for small and medium enterprises adopting SAP, International Journal of Next-Generation Computing, 4, (3).

Chang, V. (2013 b), Brain Segmentation – A Case study of Biomedical Cloud Computing for Education and Research. In Learning Technologies Workshop, Higher Education Academy (HEA), University of Greenwich, June.

Chang, V. (2013 c) Cloud Computing for brain segmentation technology. In, IEEE CloudCom 2013, 02 - 05 Dec, Bristol, UK.

Chang, V. (2013 d), A Framework for the Adoption of Cloud Computing in Organisations: Issues, recommendations and case studies, technical report, University of Southampton, February.

Chang, V., De Roure, D., Walters, R. J. and Wills, G. (2011 b), Organisational Sustainability Modelling for Return on Investment: Case Studies presented by a National Health Service (NHS) Trust UK. *Journal of Computing and Information Technology*, 19, (3).

Chang, V., De Roure, D., Wills, G. and Walters, R. (2011 c), Case Studies and Organisational Sustainability Modelling presented by Cloud Computing Business Framework, *International Journal of Web Services Research*, 8, (3), 26-53.

Chang, V., Walters, R. J. and Wills, G. (2012 b), Business Integration as a Service, *International Journal of Cloud Applications and Computing*, 2, (1), 16-40.

Chang, V., Walters, R. J. and Wills, G. (2012 c), Cloud Storage in a private cloud deployment: Lessons for Data Intensive research (Best student paper). In The second international conference on *Cloud Computing and Service Sciences* (CLOSER 2012), April, Porto, Portugal.

Chang, V., Walters, R. J. and Wills, G. (2013 a), The development that leads to the Cloud Computing Business Framework, *International Journal of Information Management*, 33 (3), June 2013 (Chang et al., 2013 a).

Chang, V., Walters, R.J. and Wills, G. (2013 b), Cloud Storage and Bioinformatics in a private cloud deployment: Lessons for Data Intensive research. In Cloud Computing and Service Science, Springer Lecture Notes Series, Springer Book.

Chang, V., Wills, G. and Walters, R. J. (2011 d), Towards Business Integration as a Service 2.0. In, IEEE International Conference on e-Business Engineering, The 3rd International

Workshop on Cloud Services - Platform Accelerating e-Business, Beijing, China, 19 - 21 Oct.

Chang, V., Wills, G., Walters, R. and Currie, W. (2012 a), Towards a structured Cloud ROI: The University of Southampton cost-saving and user satisfaction case studies. In Sustainable ICTs and Management Systems for Green Computing, IGI Global, page 179-200.

Chard, K., Caton, S., Rana, O. and Bubendorfer, K. (2010), Social cloud: Cloud computing in social networks, 2010 *IEEE 3rd International Conference on Cloud Computing*, 99-106.

Chen X, Wills G B, Gilbert L, Bacigalupo (2010), Using Cloud for Research: A Technical Review, TesciRes Report for JISC, June 2010.

Chou T (2009), Seven Clear Business Models, Active Book Press, 2009.

Christudas, B. D. (2008), Service Oriented Java Business Integration", Book, published by Packt, ISBN: 978-1847194404, February.

Claburn, T. (2009), Google Plans Private Government Cloud", technical report, InformationWeek, 16th Sep.

Creeger, M. (2009), CTO Roundtable: Cloud Computing, special article, Communications on the ACM, Vol. 52, No 8, August.

CS Transform (2009), Franchise Marketplace 2.0: A solution for citizen-centric government delivery, CSTransform White Paper.

Denaro G, Pezzè M and Tosi D (2009), Ensuring Interoperable Service-oriented Systems through Engineered Self-Healing, the 7th joint meeting of the European software engineering conference and the ACM SIGSOFT symposium on The foundations of software engineering, 26-28 August, Amsterdam, The Netherlands.

Dibbern, J., Goles, T., Hirschheim, R., and Jayatilaka, B.(2004), Information systems outsourcing: a survey and analysis of the literature," *ACM SIGMIS Database*, vol. 35, Nov., pp. 6-102.

Dillon, T., Wu, C. and Chang, E. (2010), Cloud Computing: Issues and Challenges, 2010 24th IEEE International Conference on Advanced Information Networking and Applications, pp.27-33, 20-23 April, Perth, Australia.

Dong, B., Zheng, Q., Qiao, M., Shu, J. and Yang, J. (2009), BlueSky Cloud Framework: An E-Learning Framework Embracing Cloud Computing, *Lecture Notes in Computer Science Volume* 5931, pp 577-582.

Dunn, T.(2010), Identity Management: Cloud and Virtualisation, keynote, Munich Cloud.

Durkee, D. (2010), Why cloud computing will never be free, Communications of the ACM, Vol. 53, May 2010, p 62.

Educause (2008), The Tower and the Cloud: Higher Education in the Age of Cloud Computing, ISBN 978-0-9672853-9-9, 2008.

Etro, F. (2009), The Economic Impact of Cloud Computing on Business Creation, Employment and Output in Europe, *Journal of Review of Business and Economics*, May.

Financial Times Book (2009), Managing in a Downturn: Leading Business Thinkers on How to Grow When Markets Don't, Financial Times, Prentice Hall, ISBN 978-023-73005-7.

Foster, I., Zhao, Y., Raicu, I., Lu, S.Y. (2008), Cloud Computing and Grid Computing 360-Degree Compared, *IEEE Grid Computing Environments* (GCE08), 12-16 Nov, Austin, Texas, USA.

Friedman, A. A. and West, D. M. (2010), Privacy and Security in Cloud Computing, Issues in Technology Innovation, published by the Centre for Technology Innovation, Washington DC, No 3, October.

Gillen, A., Grieser, T. and Perry, R. (2008), Business Value of Virtualization: Realizing the Benefits of Integrated Solutions, White Paper, the IDC, July.

Gillett, F. E. (2009), The Personal Cloud – How Individual Computing will shift from being Device-Centric to Information-Centric, July, Forrester Research White paper.

Heininger, R. (2012), IT Service Management in a Cloud Environment: A Literature Review, working paper, Social Science Research Network.

Herbert, L. and Erickson, J. (2011), The ROI of cloud apps, in A Total Economic Impact™ Analysis Uncovers Long-Term Value In Cloud Apps, Forrester.

Hobona G, Fairbairn D and James P (2010), Orchestration of Grid-Enabled Geospatial Web Services in Geoscientific Workflows, IEEE *Transactions on Automation Science and Engineering,* page 407-411, Volume 7, No. 2, April.

Hosono, S., Kuno, A., Hasegawa, M., Hara, T., Shimomura, Y. and Arai, T. (2009), A Framework of Co-creating Business Values for IT Services, 2009 IEEE International Conference on Cloud Computing, September 21-25, Bangalore, India.

Hugos, M. H. and Hulitzky, D. (2010), Business in the Cloud: What Every Business Needs to Know About Cloud Computing, Wiley Publishing, ISBN 978-0-470-61623-9.

Hull, J.C (2009), Options, Futures, and Other Derivatives, Seventh Edition, Pearson, Prentice Hall.

Hunt, F. H., Probert, D. R., Wong, J. C. and Phaal, R. (2003), Valuation of technology: exploring a practical hybrid model, PICMET 2003, July 20-24, Portland USA.

Hunter, J., Little, S. and Schroeter, R. (2008), The Application of Semantic Web Technologies to Multimedia Data Fusion within e-Science, Book Chapter, Chapter 8, *Semantic Multimedia and Ontologies*, Part 3, 207-226.

Hwang, K., Kulkarni, S. and Hu, Y. (2009), Cloud Security with Virtualized Defense and Reputation-based Trust Management, 2009 Eighth IEEE International Conference on Dependable, Autonomic and Secure Computing, 12-14 December, Chengdu, China.

IBM (2010), Defining a framework for cloud adoption, technical paper.

Information Week Survey (2009), Why do you use SaaS and private Clouds, results based on interview and surveys 250 managers and directors.

Jassen, M., and Joha, A. (2010), Connecting cloud infrastructures with shared services, Proceedings of the 11th Annual International Digital Government Research Conference on Public Administration Online: Challenges and Opportunities, May 17-20, Puebla, Mexico.

Jurison, J. (1995), The role of risk and return in information technology outsourcing decisions, *Journal of Information Technology*, vol. 10, Dec., pp. 239-247.

Kagermann, H., Österle, H. and Jordan, J. M. (2011), IT-Driven Business Models: Global Case Studies in Transformation, John Wiley & Sons.

Kangasharju J, Lindholm T and Tarkoma S (2008), XML Security with Binary XML for Mobile Web Services, *International Journal of Web Services Research*, page 1-19, Volume 5, number 3, July- September.

Khajeh-Hosseini A, Sommerville I, Bogaerts J, Teregowda P. (2011), Decision Support Tools for Cloud Migration in the Enterprise. IEEE 4th Int. Conf. on Cloud Computing (CLOUD 2011), Washington DC, USA.

Khajeh-Hosseini, A., Greenwood, D., and Sommerville, I. (2010 a), Cloud Migration: A Case Study of Migrating an Enterprise IT System to IaaS, 3rd IEEE International conference on Cloud Computing, *Cloud* 2010, 5-10 July, Miami, USA.

Khajeh-Hosseini, A., Greenwood, D., Smith, J. W., and Sommerville, I. (2011 b), The Cloud Adoption Toolkit: Supporting Cloud Adoption Decisions in the Enterprise, Software: Practice and Experience.

Khajeh-Hosseini, A., Sommerville, I., and Sriram, I. (2010 b), Research Challenges for Enterprise Cloud Computing, LSCITS Technical Report.

Kiu, C. C., Yuen, L. Y. and Tsui, E. (2010), Semantic Interoperability for Enhancing Sharing and Learning through E-Government Knowledge-Intensive Portal Services, *Journal of E-Governance*, Volume 33, Number 2, page 108-116, May.

Klems M, Nimis J and Tai S (2009), Do Cloud Compute? A Framework for Estimating the Value of Cloud Computing, *Journal of Designing E-Business Systems – Market, Services and Network*, Volume 22, Part 4, 110-123.

Lazonick, W. (2005), Evolution of the New Economy Business Model, *Journal of Business and Economic History* (online version), Vol. 3.

Lesem, S. (2012), founder of Mezeo (founded in 2009), personal blog, http://cloudstoragestrategy.com/.

Lin, G., Fu, D., Zhu, J. and Dasmalchi, G. (2009), Cloud Computing: IT as a Service, IT Pro, March/April, *IEEE Computer Society*, 1520-9209/09.

Linthicum, D., "Defining the Cloud Computing Framework", *Cloud Computing Journal*, January 2009.

Madhavapeddy, A., Mortier, R., Crowcroft, J. and Hand, S. (2010), Multiscale not multicore: efficient heterogeneous cloud computing, Proceedings of the 2010 ACM-BCS Visions of Computer Science Conference, 13-16 April, Edinburgh, UK.

Maranto, G. and Barton, M. (2010), Paradox and Promise: MySpace, Facebook, and the Sociopolitics of Social Networking in the Writing Classroom, *Computers and Composition Journal*, Issue 27, page 36–47.

Marston, S., Li, Z., Bandyopadhyay, S. and Zhang, J. and Ghalsasi, A. (2011), Cloud computing - The business perspective, *Decision Support Systems*, Volume: 51, Issue: 1, Publisher: Elsevier B.V., Pages: 176-189.

Martino, L.D. and Bertino, E. (2009), Security for Web Services: Standards and Research Issues, *International Journal of Web Services Research*, page 48-74, Volume 6, Number 4, October-December.

Mohaisen, A., Towards Trustworthy Computing on Social Networks: Measurements and New Applications, PhD thesis, University of Minnesota, August 2012.

Moran, D., Vaquero, L.M. and Galan, F. (2011), Elastically Ruling the Cloud: Specifying Application's Behavior in Federated Clouds, 2011 *IEEE International Conference on Cloud Computing*, 4-9 July, Washington D. C., USA.

Overby, S (2003). The Hidden Costs of Offshore Outsourcing, keynote and technical report, CIO.com, September.

Paci, F., Bertino, E. and Crampton, J. (2008), An Access-Control Framework for WS-BPEL, *International Journal of Web Services Research*, page 20-43, Volume 5, number 3, July-September.

Papazoglou, M. P. and van den Heuvel, W-J. (2011), Blueprinting the Cloud, *IEEE Internet Computing,* Vol. 15 No. 6, November/December.

Rosenthal, A., Mork, P., Li, M.H, Stanford, J., Koester, D. and Reynolds P. (2010), Cloud Computing: A New Business Paradigm for Biomedical Information Sharing, *Journal of Biomedical Informatics,* Vol. 43, Issue 2, April, Pages 342–353.

Schubert L, Jeffery K and Neidecker-Lutz B (2010), The Future for Cloud Computing: Opportunities for European Cloud Computing Beyond, *Expert Group report*, public version 1.0, January.

Skilton, M. (2010), *Building Return on Investment from Cloud Computing*, White Paper, The Open Group, April.

Sobel, W., Subramanyam, S., Sucharitakul, A., Nguyen, J., Wong, H., Klepchukov, A., Patil, S., Fox, A. and Patterson, D. (2008), Cloudstone: Multi-Platform, Multi-Language Benchmark and Measurement Tools for Web 2.0, In Proceeding of Cloud Computing and its Applications (CCA 2008), 22-23 October, Chicago, USA.

Tian, Y., Song, B. and Huh, E.N. (2011), Towards the Development of Personal Cloud Computing for Mobile Thin-Clients, *IEEE International Conference on Information Science and Applications* (ICISA), Jeju Island, S. Korea, May.

Weinhardt C, Anandasivam A, Blau B and StoBer J (2009), Business Models in the Service World, *IEEE Computer Society selected paper*, March/April, 1520-9202/09.

Weinhardt C, Anandasivam A, Blau B, Borissov N, Meinl T, Michalk W, Stober J (2009), Cloud Computing – A Classification, Business Models, and Research Directions, *Journal of Business and Information Systems Engineering*.

Yee, G. O.M. and Korba, L. (2008), Security Personalization for Internet and Web Services, *International Journal of Web Services Research*, page 1-22, Volume 5, Number 1, January-March.

Youseff, L., Butrico, M, and Da Silva, D. (2008), Toward a Unified Ontology of Cloud Computing", *Grid Computing Environments Workshop* GCE '08, 12-16 Nov., Austin, TX, USA.

Part 2. Energy Efficient Cloud

In: Advances in Cloud Computing Research   ISBN: 978-1-63117-192-5
Editor: Muthu Ramachandran   © 2014 Nova Science Publishers, Inc.

Chapter 7

ESTIMATING EMISSION REDUCTIONS FROM LOW CARBON INFORMATION TECHNOLOGY: THE GEOCHRONOS RELOCATION PROJECT

Paul Steenhof[1], Chris Weber[2]#, David Aikema[3], Randall Robinson[4], Rob Simmonds[3] and Cameron Kiddle[3]*

[1]CSA Group
[2]Climate Change Advisory Services
[3]University of Calgary, Canada
[4]Rackforce Inc.

ABSTRACT

In this chapter we present an information and communications technology (ICT) project that involved moving virtualized applications between data centres in order to reduce greenhouse gas emissions. The emission reductions have been accounted for according to a protocol that is conformant with ISO 14064-2, an international standard for quantifying and reporting emission reduction projects. While the total amount of emission reductions attributable to the project were relatively small, the results of the article are important and illustrative as this may be one of the first examples of trying to quantify a specific project that aims to reduce emissions through the provision of low carbon ICT services. With rapid growth being experienced in the ICT services sector generally and rising energy and environmental impacts of the industry, the topic of low or zero carbon ICT services is of increasing importance from a number of perspectives. Two are subsequently discussed in this chapter, including the possible place of ICT within carbon markets and also the role of such ICT projects for helping large users of data management services reduce the environmental impact of the services that they require.

Keywords: Green ICT, virtualization and cloud computing, emission reductions

* paul.steenhof@csagroup.org
# chweber99@gmail.com

INTRODUCTION

Over the last two decades the global economy has been transformed by the increasing role of data across nearly every sphere of civil society, in turn contributing to rapid growth in the data centre industry as a provider of data processing, data storage, and other data services. With this growth, there has also been a parallel increase in the power requirements associated with the millions of servers and thousands of data centres now in existence. In the United States for example, the Environmental Protection Agency estimated power requirements from data centres doubled from 2000 to 2006 to equal about 61 billion kilowatt-hours (kWh), or 1.5 percent of the country's total electricity consumption (Energy Star, 2007). It was estimated then that by 2011 this figure would likely nearly double. Global estimates of electricity usage from data centres are similar. Kommey (2008) concluded that worldwide data center power demand in 2005 was equivalent (in capacity terms) to about seventeen 1,000 MW power plants. The rapid growth of the data centre industry and the subsequent increases in electrical requirements are also contributing to increases in the greenhouse gas emissions (GHG) associated with the electricity required by the data facilities. In 2002, the ICT sector in its entirety had an estimated global carbon footprint of 0.53 gigatonnes of carbon dioxide equivalent (Gt CO_2e), representing about 1.25 percent of global emissions, while by 2007, this equalled about 0.83 GT CO_2e, or about 2 percent of global emissions (Benowitz and Samuel, 2010). By 2020, it is projected that the global ICT footprint, of which datacentres contribute significantly, will equal 1.43 Gt CO_2e, representing 2.7 percent of the global total. Put another way, this represents a 170 percent increase in emissions in the 2002 to 2020 period, or 9 percent annual growth. There are a number of major technical changes which could help lower the energy and emissions footprint of ICT services in future years, particularly in terms of moving towards location-independent cloud computing and the benefits achieved through improving the energy and carbon performance of the data centre itself. The GeoChronos Relocation Project is an example of such activity where emission reductions have been achieved by moving computing services from a data centre located in Calgary, Alberta, situated in a carbon-intensive grid, to a data centre in Kelowna, British Columbia, situated in a low carbon grid.

CHAPTER PURPOSE

This chapter presents a case study of an ICT project that has been implemented to reduce emissions where we apply a protocol developed for quantifying and reporting emission reductions from ICT projects. The specific protocol used was developed to be conformant with the requirements of the international standard ISO 14064-2: "Specification with guidance at the project level for quantification, monitoring and reporting of greenhouse gas emission reductions or removal enhancements", and is entitled The ICT GHG Reduction Protocol (referenced to as the Protocol throughout) (CSA, 2011). The use of an ISO conformant protocol for quantifying and reporting emission reductions is important since most carbon markets and players within these require the use of accepted best practices or methodologies. ISO 14064-2 is widely viewed as one the preeminent international standards that provides guidance for GHG quantification and reporting. We conclude the chapter by hardware. At the University of Calgary datacenter, GeoChronos used (as of December 2010) the following hardware systems:

- A set of compute nodes that run VM's performing different tasks
- A file server to serve VM images
- A file server to serve data via NFS.

Each of the file servers were connected to a storage area network (SAN), while network switches were employed to move data between nodes and the file-servers and between the nodes and the external clients. In addition, as part of this project, once GeoChronos had been relocated to Kelowna, all the network and data traffic associated with GeoChronos users was still initially received at the University of Calgary and then redirected from the University of Calgary over a dedicated network link to RackForce.

CHRONOLOGICAL PLAN

Following project setup, the GeoChronos project was operational for eight months starting in February 2011, with data from the project monitored for three months starting in July 2011. Below is the detailed chronology of the GeoChronos relocation project:

- Mid-June - November 2010 – Setup, configure, testing of nodes and cloud infrastructure
- December 2010 - January 2011 - Migration of GeoChronos development environment and testing
- February 2011 - September 2011 - GeoChronos site run at RackForce
- July 2011 - September 2011 - Monitoring data collected at RackForce
- October 2011 - GeoChronos relocated back to the University of Calgary

DESCRIPTION OF DATACENTRES INVOLVED IN PROJECT

There are numerous datacentres operated at or for the University of Calgary, and the datacenter involved with this project is a legacy datacenter located in the basement a large university building. Although a new combined heat and power plant was in the midst of being built to service the campus, at the time of the project the campus and the datacenter purchased their power from the Alberta electricity grid with diesel generators serving as a source of back-up power for some circuits. The datacenter is cooled from water which is pumped from the Bow River via the Bow River Pumping Station to a chiller plant located on the campus. The Bow River loop is an open loop and runs through the chilling plant to remove heat from the closed campus cooling loop. The Bow River loop also provides cooling water to the Foothills Hospital. The campus cooling loop runs from the chilling plant to a variety of facilities on campus and is constantly recirculated back to the chillers which remove the heat from the cooling loop and transfer the heat to the Bow River water loop. Chilled water flows through building air handling units and computer room air conditioning (CRAC) units during the year to provide cooling to the building and the datacenter. GeoChronos was moved to a datacentre owned and operated by RackForce Networks. RackForce Networks is a privately held ICT service provider based in Kelowna B.C., Canada. Founded in 2001, RackForce supports thousands of customers from over 100 countries. The multimillion dollar GigaCenter™ facility uses a scalable and highly efficient modular design and is built to be among the greenest and most advanced data centers in the world.

IDENTIFICATION OF SSRS ATTRIBUTABLE TO THE PROJECT

A life cycle assessment was performed on the project to determine the sources, sinks, and reservoirs (SSR) of GHG emissions that are controlled, related or affected by the project. The SSRs occurring during the project were identified first, and products, materials and energy inputs/outputs were traced upstream to origins in natural resources and downstream along the life-cycle. This allowed for the identification of upstream and downstream related SSRs before, during and after project operation. It was then determined whether each of the identified SSRs was controlled by the project proponent, related to the project, or affected by the project.

The project boundary was defined by the RackForce datacenter. The datacenter shares a building with offices which support the business of RackForce, including sales, management and administration, but which are not directly related to operation of the datacenter. As such, these offices are not considered to be within the project boundaries. Although a natural gas heating system provides heat to the office portion of the building during winter months, it was not included in the description of the project as it is not part of the datacenter. One of the key assumptions is that the addition of a small amount of leased servers to the RackForce datacenter is a small insignificant increase in the amount of ICT services that RackForce will be providing and as a result there are no significant increases in any SSR's (e.g., waste disposal, coolant leakage etc) associated with the normal operation of the datacenter.

The SSRs associated with the project are illustrated in Figure 1, and described in Table 1.

Table 1. Description of the SSRs controlled, related or affected by the project

SSR Name	#	Description	Controlled / Related or Affected
Upstream SSR's before project operation			
Software development	P1	The development of the software that will be used to run the application on the leased servers and any applications needed to support the GeoChronos application, including supporting management software or cloud management software.	Related
Raw materials used in ICT equipment	P2	The acquisition and/or treatment of the raw materials used in the manufacturing of ICT equipment (e.g., silicon, lead, copper, etc.).	Related
Manufacture of ICT equipment	P3	The manufacturing of the compute, network, storage and supplemental equipment (KVM, monitors, workstations) needed to support the GeoChronos application at RackForce.	Related

Table 1. (Continued)

SSR Name	#	Description	Controlled / Related or Affected
Upstream SSR's before project operation			
Transportation of ICT equipment to facility	P4	Transportation of the leased servers and related ICT equipment to RackForce for installation.	Related
Installation of ICT equipment, rack/cabinets	P5	Installation of all ICT equipment, including racks/cabinets, to support GeoChronos in RackForce.	Related
Production of diesel fuel	P6	Extraction and refinement of crude oil to produce diesel used for backup power.	Related
Upstream SSR's during project operation			
Electricity from the BC Hydro power grid	P7	Electricity generation including transmission line losses needed by the data centre for operation and provision of ICT services including any electricity required for the supporting infrastructure that is not provided by onsite electricity.	Related
Network Traffic	P8	The network traffic that users of GeoChronos generate in using the application at the RackForce datacenter	Related and Controlled[1]
Onsite Project SSR's			
Back-up Diesel Generator	P9	Operation of the diesel back up generator as needed to provide backup power to the RackForce datacenter.	Controlled
Power source maintenance (P9)	P10	Maintenance of the back-up power source.	Controlled
ICT equipment maintenance	P11	Additional maintenance of the servers and related ICT equipment and supporting infrastructure as a result of the supporting GeoChronos at RackForce.	Controlled
HVAC system	P12	Additional use and leakage of refrigerant associated with operation of the HVAC at RackForce as a result of the GeoChronos relocations. Also includes any additional maintenance of the HVAC system, particularly to meet the cooling requirements of the data centre.	Controlled
Downstream SSR's after project termination			
ICT disposal and recycling	P13	Disposal and demanufacturing of servers and related ICT equipment being used to support GeoChronos for recycling purposes, shredding of the hard drives, and transport of this equipment to recycling or waste facilities.	Related
Green ICT takes off	P14	The project's success spurs a large growth of similar low carbon ICT services. (market impact).	Affected

---

[1] Part of the network between the University of Calgary datacenter and the Rackforce datacenter in Kelowna is controlled by the project proponent and their partners and part of it is not controlled or a related SSR.

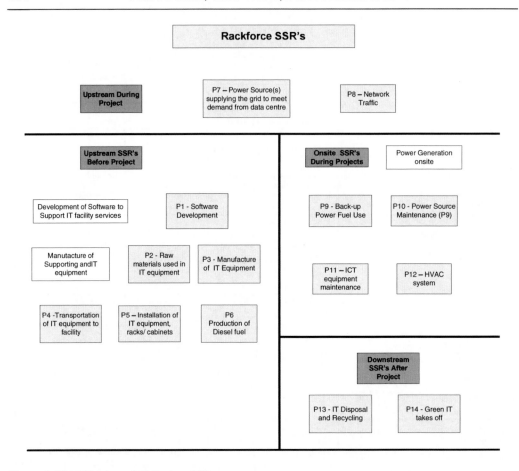

Figure 1. Identification of all Project SSRs.

SELECTION AND JUSTIFICATION OF THE BASELINE SCENARIO

As stipulated in ISO 14064-2, the baseline represents what would have occurred in the absence of the project, inclusive of energy sources and the technologies used. Here, the baseline technology must be able to provide the same product or service as the technology in the GHG project so that they may be directly compared.

As stated, based on the project typology outlined in the ICT Greenhouse Gas Reduction Protocol, this project involved a Type 2 use case 2 project activity. For these project types, the process for determining and quantifying emissions reductions is outlined as follows;

Type 2: Project activities involving improvements to ICT services

This project Type includes project activities where emission reductions are achieved from an improvement in the delivery of ICT services This could involve physical improvements in information and communication technologies so as to achieve higher workload efficiency or the migration of machines, applications, or other services from one ICT environment to another, including virtualization and consolidation projects.

(2) Leased Machines: The proponent's original collection of physical machines at the original facility is replaced by a leased collection of physical machines at a lower carbon facility. The software packages are equivalent in the original and new implementations; however the assignment of software packages to physical machines may be different, and the physical machines comprising the new collection may be different in number and type from the original collection.

The baseline for this type of project activity has been specified in the Protocol as the following;

"The standard baseline comprises substitution of the original physical machines with up-to-date commonly available physical machines at the baseline facility, using the project's assignment of software packages if possible.

In the case of this project, following the requirements of the protocol it therefore has been assumed that the project proponent would have, in the absence of moving the application to RackForce, installed up-to date commonly available physical machines at the current datacenter. These machines would have replaced the older original physical machines while remaining at their current facility at the University of Calgary. The baseline facility was assumed to be the current IT facility at the University of Calgary where GeoChronos is currently being hosted as operated and supported by the Grid Research Centre.

IDENTIFICATION OF SSRs ATTRIBUTABLE TO THE BASELINE

As was done in the project case, a life cycle assessment was performed on the baseline to determine and identify the SSRs of GHG emissions that are controlled, related or affected. The SSRs occurring during the baseline scenario were identified and a mass and energy balance was done on the various components to determine the upstream and downstream related SSRs before, during and after the baseline. These are illustrated in Figure 2, and described in Table 2.

Table 2. Description of the SSRs controlled, related or affected in the baseline

SSR Name	#	Description	Controlled / Related or Affected
Upstream SSR's before project operation			
Software development	B1	The development of the software that will be used to run the application at the Grid Research Center and any applications needed to support the GeoChronos application, including supporting management software or cloud management software.	Related
Raw materials used in ICT equipment	B2	The acquisition and/or treatment of the raw materials used in the manufacturing of ICT equipment (e.g., silicon, lead, copper, etc.).	Related

Table 2. (Continued)

SSR Name	#	Description	Controlled / Related or Affected
Manufacture of ICT equipment	B3	The manufacturing of the compute, network, storage and supplemental equipment (KVM, monitors, workstations) needed to support the GeoChronos application at the Grid Research Center.	Related
Transportation of ICT to facility	B4	Transportation of the servers and related ICT equipment to GRC for installation.	Related
Installation of ICT equipment, rack/cabinets	B5	Installation of all ICT equipment, including racks/cabinets, to support GeoChronos at GRC.	Related
Production of diesel fuel	B6	Extraction and refinement of crude oil to produce diesel used for backup power.	Related
Upstream SSR's during project operation			
Electricity from electricity grid in Calgary (EPCOR)	B7	Electricity generation including transmission line losses needed by the data centre for operation and provision of ICT services including any electricity required for the supporting infrastructure that is not provided by onsite electricity.	Related
Water Cooling of Data Center	B8	The datacenter at the University of Calgary which supports GeoChronos is cooled with water taken from the Bow River. There emissions result from the energy (electricity) used to cool the water, power the air conditioners, withdraw the water and pump it through the loop to the university and the datacenter and back to the Bow River.	Related
Network Traffic	B9	The network traffic that users of GeoChronos generate in using the application at GRC.	Related
Onsite Project SSR's			
Back-up Diesel Generators	B10	Operation of a diesel back up generator as needed to provide backup power to the University of Calgary Datacenter.	Controlled
Power source maintenance (B10)	B11	Maintenance of the back-up power sources.	Controlled
ICT equipment maintenance	B12	Additional maintenance of the servers and related ICT equipment and supporting infrastructure as a result of the supporting GeoChronos at GRC.	Controlled
HVAC system	B13	Additonal use and leakage of refrigerant associated with operation of the HVAC at GRC needed to support GeoChronos. Also includes any additional maintenance of the HVAC system, particularly to meet the cooling requirements of the data centre.	Controlled
Downstream SSR's after project termination			
ICT disposal and recycling	B14	Disposal and demanufacturing of servers and related ICT equipment being used to support GeoChronos for recycling purposes, shredding of the hard drives, and transport of this equipment to recycling or waste facilities.	Related

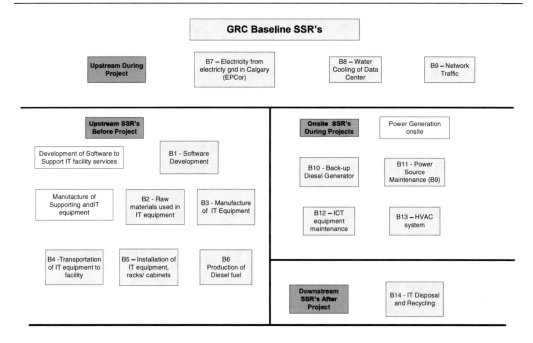

Figure 2. Identification of all Baseline SSRs.

SELECTION OF RELEVANT SSRs FOR QUANTIFICATION OR ESTIMATION OF GHG EMISSION REDUCTIONS

The protocol provides guidance in order to determine the relevant SSRs for quantification and reporting. The protocol's guidance was developed based on the following criteria that were applied according to the ISO 14064-2 requirements and principles:

(1) If the SSR did not result in GHG emissions it was considered not relevant except if the activity level for this SSR was necessary to calculate the emissions of another SSR.
(2) If the SSR was similar in both the project and the baseline scenario qualitatively and quantitatively then the SSR was considered not relevant since it would not have any impact on the GHG emission quantification
(3) If the SSR was similar qualitatively in the baseline and the project scenario, and the GHG emissions were greater in the baseline than in the project scenario then it was possible to consider the SSR not relevant since it is conservative to do so.

Additional criteria for removing GHG sources from estimation and measurement include if they are deemed to be minor and too difficult to measure. Using the information and criteria listed above the following SSRs were considered either relevant or not relevant for this quantification (see table 3).

Table 3. Comparison of SSR's and Selection of Relevant Ones

SSR Name	SSR # (Project / Baseline)	Controlled Related Affected	Relevancy and justification if not relevant
Software development	P1 / B1	Related	Not Relevant. This SSR does not have significant amount of greenhouse gas emissions associated with the move from the University of Calgary to RackForce.
Raw materials used in ICT equipment	P2 / B2	Related	Not Relevant. Some very small differences in the amount and type of raw materials that go into the manufacture of one type of server versus another. Same SSR.
Manufacture of ICT equipment	P3 / B3	Related	Not Relevant. The same amount of energy with very small differences go into the manufacture servers. There is no difference or a very small difference between the manufacture of a leased server versus an up-to date commonly available server. Same SSR or insignificant small differences
Transportation of ICT equipment to facility	P4 / B4	Related	Not Relevant. The differences in transportation are insignificant for a server going to Calgary vs. Kelowna. Same SSR or insignificant small differences
Installation of ICT equipment, rack/cabinets	P5 / B5	Related	Not Relevant. The same process of installation is required for a leased server as compared to an up-to date commonly available one installed in Calgary. Same SSR or insignificant small differences
Production of diesel fuel for backup)	P6 / B6	Related	Not Relevant. Same SSR or insignificant small differences
Power Source(s) supplying the grid to meet demand from the data centre	P7 / B7	Related	Relevant. The grid providing electricity to the two datacenters are significantly different, with one being primarily powered by coal-fired power plants and the other one being powered by hydropower. In addition, the amount of power being required by the IT facility and the ICT equipment to support the application could be different in RackForce as compared to the University of Calgary datacenter and could also be a source of emission reductions. This would be a Scope II emission or an electricity indirect emission reduction.
Water Cooling of Data Center	B8	Related	Relevant. SSR is only a source at the University of Calgary.
Network Traffic	P8 / B9	Related	Partially Relevant. All network traffic for GeoChronos is routed through the datacentre at the University of Calgary regardless if GeoChronos is actually at RackForce or at the University of Calgary. During the project the additional network traffic and associated energy use because of routing of the network traffic from the University of Calgary to RackForce in Kelowna via Vancouver using the CANARIE/BC Net network will need to be quantified. However, only the project SSR (P8) is actually relevant as the number of requests and the amount of traffic arriving at GeoChronos will be the same in the baseline and the project, but the project will have additional emissions associated with the network traffic to RackForce and back again. However, only part of the network is controlled by the proponent and it's partners.
Back-up Diesel Generator Power Fuel Use	P9 / B10	Controlled	Relevant. Same SSR, but there could be significant differences if the generator is used more in one location (different activity level). At the baseline facility, the emissions from the backup generators used in the baseline facility are minimal and can thus be ignored. Most of the equipment that would have been

SSR Name	SSR # (Project / Baseline)	Controlled Related Affected	Relevancy and justification if not relevant
			used at the baseline facility is not connected to generator-backed circuits. Only the storage array is connected in such a manner, and the GeoChronos project is only responsible for a small fraction of its use (1 TB of 20 TB total in the baseline scenario). Total carbon emissions during the time that the generator is operational appear unlikely to be significantly higher than at other times as the total power consumption decreases due to the remainder of the resources used by GeoChronos not consuming power at such times. The generator is also used to power much additional equipment - the critical services of the university- meaning that the storage array also accounts for a small percentage of generator output. The emissions from this SSR will only be calculated at the project scenario resulting in a conservative estimate of emissions for this SSR.
Power Source Maintenance	P10 / B11	Controlled	Not Relevant. Same SSR with insignificant small differences. Assume that the same power source maintenance (i.e., test runs) is carried out in the two locations and if there are any differences they would result in small differences in emissions.
ICT equipment maintenance	P11 / B12	Controlled	Not Relevant. Same level of ICT equipment maintenance will be required for the GeoChronos servers whether leased or at the University of Calgary. Same SSR or insignificant small differences.
HVAC system	P12 / B13	Controlled	Not relevant. The amount of additional impact on the HVAC system is minimal and comparable in both datacenters. Same SSR or insignificant small differences.
ICT disposal and recycling	P13 / B14	Related	Not Relevant. Same SSR or insignificant small differences.
Green ICT takes off (market impact)	P14	Affected	Not Relevant. Not an SSR in the baseline, may be a source of emissions in the project due to increased demand for Green ICT. This is actually negative leakage. Likely that the emission reductions are as a result of moving from another less green data centre to the new one. Will not be estimating the emission reduction because of difficulty in doing so and because it is negative leakage.

METHOD TO QUANTIFY/ESTIMATE GHG EMISSIONS AND/OR REMOVALS IN THE BASELINE AND PROJECT

Using the methodology as outlined in the Protocol, emissions in both baseline and in the project were determined based on the SSR's identified for both. The basic methodology for estimating emissions from the baseline scenario is formulized as follows;

$$t = p$$

$$EM(Ba) = (P_{ICT}(\text{Pr}) \times PUE(Ba) \times EF(Ba)) \tag{1}$$

where:

EM(Ba) = Emission associated with the baseline (in kg CO_2e)

P_{ICT} (Pr) = Power measured from the ICT equipment in the project, in GJ

PUE (Ba) = Power Usage Effectiveness (PUE) of the baseline ICT facility

EF (Ba) = Emission factor for source energy in the baseline, in kg CO_2e / GJ. This emission factor reflects all of the source energy used to provide the baseline facility's energy requirements

As stipulated in the Protocol, for project type 1 and the first three use cases for project type 2, ICT power is made equivalent between the baseline and the project – reflecting that emission reductions are related to the data centre environment and not the ICT equipment itself.

Emissions from the project scenario from the SSRs in the datacenter were similarly calculated as was done for the baseline. However, in addition to the SSRs identified for the baseline, for the project this also included the project SSRs identified with the network traffic from the University of Calgary datacenter to RackForce and back again over the CANARIE network. As a result of these additional SSRs, emissions from the project were determined as follows;

$$EM(\mathrm{Pr}) = (P_{ICT}(\mathrm{Pr}) \times PUE(\mathrm{Pr}) \times EF(\mathrm{Pr}) + (Energy_{Network} \times EF_{Network})) \qquad (2)$$

where:

$Energy_{Network}$ = The electricity required to operate and maintain the network for GeoChronos traffic between the University of Calgary and RackForce in Kelowna,

$EF_{Network}$ = The emission factor of the source power providing electricity to the network.

Each SSR as identified in table 15 in the previous section was matched with the values in the formula as shown below and each of these factors in the equations were measured, monitored or estimated to determine the emission reductions associated with the GeoChronos relocation project.

DETERMINING EMISSIONS IN THE BASELINE SCENARIO

Recall that emissions from the baseline scenario for all SSR's in the datacenter are calculated according to equation 1, as follows;

$$EM(Ba) = (P_{ICT}(\mathrm{Pr}) \times PUE(Ba) \times EF(Ba) \qquad (1)$$

The PUE captures the share of the total energy that contributes to directly powering the ICT equipment as well as the portion that contributes to the cooling and other supporting infrastructure of the datacenter. For the baseline, the PUE is therefore defined according to the energy sources used by the datacentre;

$$PUE_{Ba} = 1 + \left(\frac{Energy_{CRAC} + Energy_{CLOOP} + Energy_{Other}}{Energy_{ICTEquipment}} \right) \qquad (3)$$

where:

Energy$_{CRAC}$ = The amount of power used by the CRAC units in the datacentre
(kWh or GJ)
Energy$_{CLOOP}$ = The amount of power used by the cooling system (kWh or GJ)
Energy$_{Other}$ = The amount of power used by other supporting services such as lighting of
the datacenter (kWh or GJ).

Determining the PUE of the Baseline Facility

As indicated by equations 1 and 2, the PUE for both the baseline scenario and project was required in order to estimate emissions and emission reductions. While for the project facility this could be measured and monitored, there were a number of challenges for determining the PUE for the datacenter at the University of Calgary. One of the primary reasons was that the primary electricity feed to the datacenter was not dedicated as it also provided power to neighboring university infrastructure (i.e., a parking lot where block heaters are source of power consumption in the winter). As a result, it was not possible to determine the total amount of energy supplied to the datacenter from the various energy sources (i.e., the electricity grid, the cooling loop and any back-up generator) in a cost-effective manner. In addition, it was not possible to determine the amount of energy used for powering the ICT equipment at the datacenter or for determining what amount of energy was devoted to cooling and providing other support services for the data center.

It is also important to note that the baseline datacentre from which Geochronos was moved had been retrofitted a number of times with new overhead cooling units as well as more efficient CRAC units.

Therefore, based on a survey of literature investigating the PUE of datacentres as well as consideration of the technical characteristics of the University of Calgary facility, a number of assumptions were made to arrive at a conservative estimate for the data centre. In surveying relevant literature, a 2007 Report to Congress assumed an average PUE of 2.0 for US data centers for the period from 2000 to 2006 in order to estimate the total energy use attributable to datacenters (Energy Star, 2007). The average PUE of 2.0 was based on an energy use benchmarking study of 22 datacenters performed by the Lawrence Berkeley National Lab. In the same report, the EPA states that they expected the average PUE to decline to 1.9 by 2011. Other data from authoritative organizations which make conclusions based on the EPA study are similarly aligned, including from the Green Grid who state that PUE values of 2.0 are achievable with proper design (Green Grid, 2008). Digital Realty Trust, meanwhile, conducted a survey of about 300 data centers which was reported in 2011 concluded that the average reported PUE energy efficiency rating for respondents' data centers was 2.9 and that one in six respondents report PUE ratings of less than 2.0 for their facilities (Digital Realty Trust, 2011). With this and the above analysis in consideration, we assume that the PUE at the University of Calgary is 1.7 and that for the reasons stated above this can be considered to be a conservative assumption of PUE (i.e., it is conservative to have a lower estimate of the PUE of the baseline facility as this will mean a lower estimate of baseline emissions).

Determining the Weighted Emission Factor of Source Energy

The datacenter at the University of Calgary receives energy from three sources; the electricity grid, the backup generation and the cooling loop. These must all be considered when deriving the weighted emission factor of the facility. The sources of energy for the University of Calgary datacentre are shown schematically in figure 3;

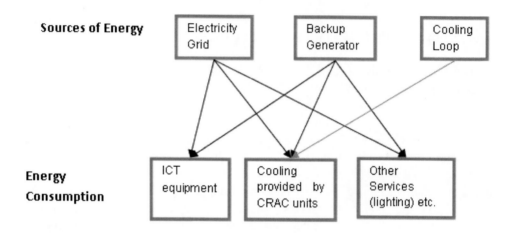

Figure 3. Sources of energy to University of Calgary datacenter.

For the baseline, we have assumed that the backup generator does not provide significant power to the datacenter. As a result, the sources of energy to the datacentre are in actuality the electricity grid and the cooling loop.

To determine the emission factor of the cooling loop, we required the following information:

- The total amount of power provided to the Bow River Pumping Station to draw the water from the Bow River
- The amount of water from the Bow River water loop that is provided to the campus relative to the total amount that is drawn from the Bow River
- The power needed by the pumps along the Bow River loop to get the water to the chillers
- The amount of power needed by the chillers to chill the water in the campus loop by transferring the heat from the campus loop to the Bow River loop (or by transferring the cold from the Bow River loop to the campus loop)
- The power needed by the pumps along the campus loop to circulate the water around the campus
- The total amount of cooling provided to the campus by the chilled water loop

Since the electricity used within the pumping and cooling process is from the Alberta electricity grid, the grid electricity factor was used to derive emissions from purchased electricity. In order to estimate emissions associated with the cooling loop, 12 months of data was collected on each of the parameters listed above. The resulting power usage and emission calculations are summarized in the table below (see table 4).

Table 4. Calculation of Emission Factor for the Campus Cooling Loop

Month	Bow River Pumping Station	Percent sent to campus	Chillers	Total	Emissions	Total Campus Chilled water	Emission factor
	KWh	%	KWh	KWh	Kg CO_2 e	KWh	g CO_2 e per KWh
10-Jun	174,736	76.22	1,053,344	1,186,528	1,044,145	4,945,880	211
10-Jul	239,699	85.51	1,396,703	1,601,669	1,409,469	6,375,229	221
10-Aug	220,748	81.91	1,230,080	1,410,895	1,241,587	5,591,572	222
10-Sep	139,229	76.34	716,381	822,668	723,948	3,279,696	221
10-Oct	149,035	74.44	776,391	887,332	780,852	3,577,909	218
10-Nov	159,245	67.6	143,030	250,679	220,598	1,671,349	132
10-Dec	139,910	69.32	0	96,986	85,347	1,461,166	58
11-Jan	143,183	64.93	0	92,969	81,812	1,473,520	56
11-Feb	129,629	63.52	0	82,340	72,459	1,309,239	55
11-Mar	152,301	65.01	0	99,011	87,130	1,565,719	56
11-Apr	176,170	71.57	46,600	172,684	151,962	1,559,662	97
11-May	152,014	70.29	542,017	648,868	571,004	2,955,381	193
Total	**1,975,899**	**72.22**	**5,904,546**	**7,352,629**	**6,470,313**	**35,766,322**	**180.91**

As shown, the average annual emission factor of the energy supplied via the cooling loop equaled 180.91 grams/kWh. This is roughly ¼ of the emission intensity of the power grid in Alberta, reflecting in part that during the coldest months of the year additional cooling of water from the Bow River is not required. In arriving at a combined emissions factor, sources familiar with the university's datacentre suggested that 70 percent of the datacentres total energy should be attributed to electricity purchased from electricity grid and 30 percent attributed to energy from the cooling loop. Based on the grid average emission factor, this would suggest a combined emission factor for source energy of 680.3 g CO_2e per kWh.

DETERMINING EMISSIONS FOR THE PROJECT

Recall that emissions at the project will be determined by:

$$(2) \quad EM(\text{Pr}) = (P_{ICT}(\text{Pr}) \times PUE(\text{Pr}) \times EF(\text{Pr}) + (Energy_{Network} \times EF_{Network}))$$

where:

EM(Pr) = Emission associated with the project (in kg CO_2e)

P_{ICT} (Pr) = Power measured from the ICT equipment in the project, in GJ

PUE (Pr) = Power Usage Effectiveness of the project ICT facility

EF (Pr) = Emission factor for source energy in the project, in kg CO_2e/GJ

Energy$_{network}$ = The electricity required to operate and maintain the network for GeoChronos traffic between the University of Calgary and RackForce in Kelowna,

$EF_{network}$ = the emission factor of the source power providing electricity to the network. This is expected to be based on the emission factor of the grid in Alberta and B.C.

where the PUE is determined by:

$$PUE = 1 + \left(\frac{Energy_{Total}}{Energy_{ICTEquipment}} \right) \quad (5)$$

Therefore five variables need to be determined in order to estimate the emissions associated with the project – project ICT power usage, the PUE of the project facility, the emission factor of source energy for the ICT facility, the energy used by the network involved with transferring data, and the emission intensity of the electricity used for the network.

Determining the Project ICT Power Usage

The GeoChronos application was hosted on the following pieces of hardware at RackForce;

- A storage area network on a rack,
- A dedicated server on a rack with other servers,
- A virtual machine running in the cloud environment at RackForce on shared hardware and,
- Two blade servers on a chassis with a total of 8 blades.

The power to each of these pieces of equipment was monitored as follows;

Storage Area Network

For the SAN, the circuits providing power to the rack was monitored at the Power Distribution Unit (PDU) using specific power management software called Power Xpert. The amount of power used by GeoChronos at the SAN was apportioned based on the amount of storage used (or allocated) to GeoChronos. The same method was used to determine the amount of power used by GeoChronos at GRC attributable to the SAN.

Dedicated Server

A Raritan managed powerbar was used to measure the power used by this dedicated server. This data will be taken weekly by logging into the IP based interface on the powerbar. The power reading was then multiplied by the number of hours in the week to provide a number in kWh. The reading was taken when the workload on GeoChronos was not at a low level or possibly at a high level in order to be conservative.

Virtual Machine

GeoChronos also made use of a virtual machine (VM) in a shared cloud environment at the RackForce Gigacenter datacenter. In reviewing the shared resources in the cloud (i.e., RAM and CPU), it was seen that CPU assigned to any particular VM or group of VMs was typically underutilized or oversubscribed by as much as 300% whereas RAM was generally fully utilized (greater than 80%) by these same VMs and was not oversubscribed. Therefore RAM has been determined as a reasonable proxy to determine the fractional power usage for the GeoChronos VM on the cloud. The total RAM assigned to the cloud segment where the GeoChronos VM resides was divided by the RAM assigned to the GeoChronos VM.

This ratio was multiplied by the amount of power used by the cloud. Power readings were taken from the internal management systems that are built into the blade center computers that are used to provide compute resources to the cloud. These readings were taken weekly and the watts multiplied by the hours in a week in order to provide a number in kWh.

Blade Servers

The power used by the blade servers was measured in the following manner;

- Internal management systems built into blade servers provide power consumption in real time
- The chassis power consumption was also measured using the internal power measurement and management software of the chassis.
- The chassis power consumption was subtracted from the power consumption of all of the blades in that chassis and the difference was the amount of overhead power to be allocated to each blade (split equally across each blade).

The results showed that each blade used 10 watts per hour while the chassis used 88 watts per hour. After allocating the overhead power to the 2 blades used by GeoChronos, this meant that the application was responsible for 22 watts per hour or 3.7 kWh per week.

Determining the PUE of the Project Facility

The total energy provided to the project datacenter is from two sources; electricity from the power grid as well as energy from the back-up diesel generator. Each of these were monitored and/or estimated at the project scenario site during the project in terms of both total energy use and the energy used specifically for ICT equipment. In particular, the amount of electricity provided by the electricity grid was determined by monthly utility bills from Fortis BC. Meanwhile, the load time of the generator was used to determine the amount of electricity generated from the diesel generator in order to support the datacenter as well as information about the total fuel used. Monitoring these showed that RackForce had a PUE of 2.0. Here, it should be emphasized that this is higher than the baseline facility largely because at the time of analysis was relatively underutilized relative to its full potential. Thus, there was a much large overhead of support services (cooling, etc.), compared to when the facility will be more fully utilized. At that point, it is expected that the PUE of the facility will fall well below that of the average data centre. Nonetheless, for the purposes of this analysis a PUE of 2.0 has been used.

Network Traffic Emissions Source

As indicated in equation 2, an additional relevant SSR which contributes emissions in the project scenario is the network between the University of Calgary datacenter and the datacenter in Kelowna. In the baseline, any user requests for GeoChronos go to the University of Calgary datacenter and are processed by the GeoChronos application. In the project, all of the requests associated with GeoChronos continue to be directed to the University of Calgary datacenter. They are then redirected to the RackForce datacenter in Kelowna. This additional network traffic is the source of addition power consumption and emissions. Consequently this source of additional emissions needs to be quantified in the project.

The network between the University of Calgary and RackForce is provided by two service providers, CANARIE and Shaw with equipment being owned by three organizations. CANARIE has a dedicated 10 Gbps wavelength (pipe) which is active and up 24 hours a day. CANARIE dedicated 10 % of this (1 Gbps) for the GeoChronos relocation. The CANARIE network handoffs any GeoChronos traffic to a transfer switch owned and operated by RackForce in the Vancouver station. The RackForce switch then hands-off the GeoChronos traffic to another service provider (Shaw) for the transfer of data from Vancouver to the RackForce Kelowna datacenter.

To determine the power consumption and emission for the CANARIE network between the University of Calgary and Vancouver, since the CANARIE wavelength pipe is always operating and the GeoChronos lightpath is similarly always open, power usage can be approximated by a constant.

We have used the maximum power specifications for all the equipment and stations on the CANARIE wavelength to estimate the power consumption attributable to this SSR. In addition, based on the location of the station, we have multiplied by the emission factor associated with the power grid in that province. We applied similar logic for the RackForce owned and operated network component.

QUANTIFICATION OF GHG EMISSION REDUCTIONS AND REMOVALS

Emission calculations are shown for the baseline, the project, and the emission reductions associated with the project.

Quantifying Emissions for the Baseline

Based on the monitoring done at the baseline and the project, and based on the methodology laid out in section 7, the data and emissions for the baseline are shown below:

Table 5. Estimate of baseline emissions

Emission Factor (Grid) (g CO_2e / kWh)	PUE	Power Grid Share	Cooling Loop Share	Emission Factor (Cooling Loop)	Weighted Emission Factor (g CO_2e / kWh)	P ICT (kWh)	Emissions (Baseline) kg
880	1.7	70	30	180.91	670	2042	2,738

Over the life of the monitored portion of the project (13 weeks), the baseline emissions would have been 2,738 kg of CO_2e.

Quantifying Emissions for the Project

The project operated from June 28, 2011 to September 25, 2011 for a total duration of 13 weeks. Emissions associated with the project occurred in two locations, the datacenter and the network. The datacenter emissions are shown in the table below;

Table 6. Estimate of project datacentre emissions

Emission Factor (Grid) (g CO2e / kWh)	PUE	P ICT (kWh)	Emissions (Project) kg
20	2.0	2042	81.68

Emissions from the network are shown as follows:

Table 7. Estimate of project network emissions

Province	Power consumed per week (kWh)	Emission Factor (g CO_2e/kWh)	Emissions per week (kg CO_2e)	Emissions Network (13 weeks)	Emissions (project) kg
Alberta	201.92	880.00	177.69	2,309.97	230.99
BC	488.66	20.00	9.77	127.01	12.70

Total emissions from the network over the length of the project attributable to GeoChronos totaled 243.69 kg of CO_2e. When factoring in emissions from the data centre, total emissions from the project over the 13 weeks totaled 325.37 kg of CO_2e.

ESTIMATED EMISSION REDUCTIONS

Emission reductions are estimated as the difference between the project and the baseline. These are estimated to equal 2,412 kg of CO_2e over the 13 week project. Therefore, if the

GeoChronos Relocation Project was run for a full year, the project would result in total emission reductions of 11,405 kg of CO_2e.

CONCLUSION AND DISCUSSION OF RELEVANCE FOR CARBON TRADING AND CORPORATE SUSTAINABILITY

In this chapter we have presented a quantification of emissions and emission reductions resulting from an ICT-related project. This is a complex topic involving emerging technologies and processes. However, the topic is of one of growing importance seeing the increasing role of ICT across the economy, the importance of data management for specific industries as well as the rising energy requirements for ICT and associated increases in GHG emissions,. This leads to a final discussion of the relevance of ICT and ICT projects, such as was presented in this chapter, for the broader topics of carbon trading and improving corporate environmental sustainability

In regards to carbon trading, this might include any activities tied to regulatory frameworks such as the Kyoto Protocol and regional trading systems tied to government climate change programs. However, increasingly, carbon markets are being impacted by voluntary actions to improve carbon performance, and it is here likely where ICT related projects will fit in.

On the demand side, the voluntary carbon market is largely made up of entities choosing to voluntarily purchase offsets to lower the carbon footprint associated with their activities, while on the supply side, this involves providers of verified emission reductions selling into this market. The market is therefore intertwined and reinforced by rising public awareness of environmental issues such as climate change as well as by organizations and businesses undertaking efforts to lower their carbon footprint or claim carbon neutrality through the purchase of carbon offsets.

In 2009, suppliers of emission offsets in the voluntary market transacted 93.7 million metric tonnes of carbon dioxide equivalent ($MtCO_2e$), worth about \$387 million in value, with expectations that the transactions could be as large as 1,200 $MtCO_2e$ by 2020 (Hamilton et al., 2010). Rising demand will likely be driven by the processes described above, namely the increasing public attention placed on the reduction of carbon in regards to the products they consume and the services they use. This will continue to drive corporations and other entities to lower the carbon footprint of their operations and products, in turn underpinning demand for offsets originating from sources such the delivery of lower carbon ICT.

Further to the use of emission reductions for carbon trading, sourcing low or zero carbon ICT services may come more and more on the radar of large corporations, institutions and users of data services. This is particularly relevant when considering the widespread inclusion of carbon in corporate sustainability reporting as well as the thousands of organizations who measure and disclose their greenhouse gas emissions and climate change strategies through efforts such as the Carbon Disclosure Project (PricewaterhouseCoopers, 2010). It is also relevant when considering the potential for the large-scale adoption of cloud computing and the rapid increases in the outsourcing of ICT services that has occurred during the last number of years and decades.

One approach to understanding the potential scale of a large scale ICT project or initiative is to consider the power use requirements attributable to the operation of datacentres directly owned and operated by a large corporation or organization. While in the past such information was often difficult to obtain and often not disaggregated from the power and energy use footprint of the corporation, increasingly, corporate environmental reporting has been including more details on the corporation's environmental impact. In 2010, for example, the Royal Bank of Canada (RBC) reported that the datacentres owned and operated by the company required nearly 92,250 MWh of electricity (RBC, 2010). If theoretically all of these were located in grids with an emissions factor equalling 0.50 kg CO_2e/kWh (representative of a grid that is a mix of fossil fuels, renewables, etc.), then this would mean that the datacentres owned and operated by this large bank would result in emissions equalling over 46,000 tonnes per year. This scale of emissions and potential emission reductions therefore helps indicate that focusing on lowering the carbon impact of ICT could in fact result in large emission reductions for a company or organization, thereby improving their environmental performance.

With burgeoning requirements for data management, the ICT services industry has been experiencing rapid growth in recent years. While cloud computing and virtualization are key technological processes that will likely continue and even accelerate this growth, these also link into actions that could help reduce the carbon intensity of data management. This chapter has focused attention on one example of how to lower or eliminate the carbon and environmental impacts of ICT services. However, there are many more, as stipulated in the protocol used and sourced in this chapter. Thus, in the future heightened attention could be given to the sector in terms of contribution to climate change mitigation.

REFERENCES

Benowitz, M. and S. Samuel, 2010, Green Information and Communications Technology (ICT) for Eco-Sustainability Overview. *Bell Labs Technical Journal* 15 (2), 1-5.

Canadian Standards Association (CSA) (2011). ICT Greenhouse Gas Reduction Project Protocol: Quantification and Reporting (version 1). Canadian Standards Association, Mississauga, Ontario. Canada

Digital Realty Trust, 2011, Accessed September 2011 from http://investor.digitalrealtytrust.com/phoenix.zhtml?c=182279&p=irol-newsArticle&ID=1398538&highlight=

Energy Star, 2007, Report to Congress on Server and Data Center Energy Efficiency Public Law 109-431, Accessed September 2011 from available from http://www.energystar.gov/ia/partners/prod_development/downloads/EPA_Datacenter_Report_Congress_Final1.pdf.

Green Grid, 2008, Green Grid Data Centgre Power Efficiency Metrics: PUE and DCIE, Accessed October 2011 from http://www.thegreengrid.org/~/media/White Papers/White_Paper_6_-_PUE_and_DCiE_Eff_Metrics_30_December_2008.ashx?lang=en.

Hamilton, K., M. Peters-Stanley and T. Marcello (2010). Building Bridges: State of the Voluntary Carbon Markets 2010, Ecosystem Marketplace, Bloomberg.

Koomey, J. G., 2008, Worldwide electricity used in data centers. *Environmental Research Letters* 3 (3),

Pricewaterhouse Coopers (2010). Carbon Disclosure Project 2010: Global 500 and S&P 500 Report Highlights. London, PricewaterhouseCoopers: 1-10.

Royal Bank of Canada (RBC) (2010). RBC 2010 Corporate Responsibility Report and Public Accountability Statement - Full Report, Royal Bank of Canada.

In: Advances in Cloud Computing Research
Editor: Muthu Ramachandran

ISBN: 978-1-63117-192-5
© 2014 Nova Science Publishers, Inc.

Chapter 8

ENERGY EFFICIENCY OF THE CLOUD COMPUTING SYSTEM

Francis Owusu, Colin Pattinson and Muthu Ramachandran*

Leeds Metropolitan University
School of Computing, Creative Technologies, and Engineering
Faculty of Arts, Environment and Technology
Leeds Metropolitan University, Leeds LS6 3QS, UK

ABSTRACT

Cloud computing has been hailed as the achievement of the long-held dream of computing as a utility and has the potential to transform a large part of the Information and Communication Technology (ICT) industry. Cloud computing is currently the buzz word of the Information Technology industry. But cloud computing has had its share of controversy; ranging from the definition of cloud computing to its energy efficiency. This chapter looks at one area of controversy; the energy efficiency of cloud computing. While some are advocating and touting the energy saving potential of cloud computing, others have questioned all the hype on the energy efficiency of cloud computing. The energy demand of data centres, communication networks and the Internet are predicted to grow. We outline previous contributions to the discussion on the energy efficiency of cloud computing and investigate the energy efficiency of cloud computing through simulations.

Keywords: Cloud computing, energy efficiency, energy consumption, data centre, communication network, internet, simulations

INTRODUCTION

Cloud computing is an infrastructural paradigm sweeping across the Information and Communication Technology (ICT) sector and has become the buzz word in the Information

---

* Email: f.owusu@leedsmet.ac.uk.

Technology (IT) industry. Cloud computing has been presented as the delivery of computing as a utility, with the potential to transform a large part of the Information and Communication Technology (ICT) industry (Armbrust et al., 2009). Cloud computing offers a new computing model whereby resources such as storage, computing power, networking infrastructures, and online applications can be provided and shared as services over the Internet. The mainstream popularity of cloud computing has been growing since 2006 and it is currently the most talked about technology in the ICT industry. Cloud computing is a business as well as an economic model, a paradigm shift by which the IT industry is fundamentally shifting from product based to service based. Other than technology and products that cloud computing offers, this fundamental shift is being driven by additional factors such as the wide availability of mobile devices and the shift towards mobile computing and growing popularity of social networks like Facebook and Twitter. The advent of cloud computing has been likened to the industrial revolution (Scott, 2010).

Cloud computing has had its share of controversy; ranging from its definition to its energy efficiency. The confusion over the definition of cloud computing was clearly manifested when twenty one Information Technology experts gave twenty one different definitions for cloud computing (Geelan, 2009). Daley and Woods (2010) noted that the issues around the energy efficiency of cloud computing are complex and there is need for more discussion and research on the subject. The importance of energy efficiency of ICT as a whole and cloud computing in particular has generated lots of discussion, with contributors ranging from environmental activists such as Greenpeace to government agencies such as the United States Environmental Protection Agency, and from IT industry giants such as Google to professionals of the Climate Savers Computing Initiative (Greenpeace, 2010; EPA, 2007; Climate Savers Computing Initiative, 2010).

Many studies and research have been conducted into the energy efficiency of cloud computing but most of them used the energy efficiency of data centres as their measurements (Koomey, 2007; Miller, 2010; Pike Research, 2010; Accenture, 2010; Nucleus Research, 2010; Baliga et al., 2010). But we have found the need to include communication networks which are used to provide data transportation for cloud computing services in any research and study of the energy efficiency of cloud computing. Our research focuses on the energy efficiency of cloud computing looking at data centre network architectures, how the location of data centres impact on the energy consumption in cloud computing environment and how the energy efficiency of cloud computing can be improved.

CLOUD COMPUTING TECHNOLOGY

Cloud computing is an evolution of different technologies including grid and utility computing and application service provision (ASP). The latest computing paradigm to be proposed and adopted to fulfil the long awaited vision of utility computing is cloud computing which has been predicted to transform the computing industry. Morgan Stanley (2008) identified cloud computing among the prominent technology trends. Gartner (2012), one of the leading IT research and advisory companies in the world said cloud computing has the potential to impact all aspects of Information Technology and how applications, information and business services are accessed by users.

Cloud computing is a fundamental shift from traditional 'desktop-as-a-platform' to 'Internet-as-a-platform' whereby computing platforms are deployed in clusters of servers hosted in dedicated data centres to achieve infinite scalability, guaranteed performance and availability (Singh and Vara, 2009). The personal computing era that flourished from the early seventies made desktop computing the norm for the last 30 years, but networking computers together and the building of massive data centres to service them have changed the dynamics, bringing cloud computing to the foreground and predicted to relegate desktop computing to the background. The centre of computing is shifting from the processing unit (desktop) to the network (cloud).

In cloud computing paradigm, programs or software that were traditionally installed on desktop computers and laptops are now accessible from the Internet. Cloud computing provides financial advantage by enabling the sharing of IT resources and cost among different users by offering multi-tenancy. Han (2010) wrote that cloud computing fundamentally changes how institutions and enterprises manage their computing needs as it enables the starting of an IT project with low cost, cost-effective management of computing resources, and the exploration of new computing possibilities. An organisation can increase its computing capacity as its needs increases and can also reduce its capacity as its computing requirements decreases. Cloud computing enables the moving of IT spending from Capital Expenditure (Capex) to Operational Expenditure (Opex) that could be ideal for organisations whose budgets are limited.

The spread of ICT and mobile communication is changing the way people communicate, relate and manage their daily lives (Greenpeace, 2010). There is now instant access to information not only on fixed devices such as desktop PCs but also on mobile devices such as smartphones, tablets, and netbooks. Cloud computing has enabled the current global delivery of entertainment and media through service providers such as YouTube, Facebook, Google, Apple, Twitter and Yahoo. This shift to digital technology is the beginning of a much larger shift as many companies in the service economy are moving from conventional business delivery models to new models delivered through the cloud.

CLOUD COMPUTING ADOPTION RATE

The adoption of cloud computing is growing as more companies and organizations embrace the technology. Beckman (2010) wrote that a study by a software and technology research firm found that 80% of participants plan to spend more on cloud computing in the next three years.

The study surveyed 500 IT executives and conducted 40 in-depth interviews to find the value of cloud computing to businesses. The study found that enterprises will be moving applications to the cloud at a rapid rate over the next few years. The study also found that 97% of respondents have cloud initiatives in progress and 18% of them plan to deploy mission-critical projects in the cloud. Meanwhile Gartner (2010), forecasted worldwide public cloud services revenue to reach $68.3 billion in 2010, a 16.6 percent increase from 2009 revenue of $58.6 billion. The forecast of Gartner was exceeded by $7 billion as shown in Figure 1 below (Forbes, 2013).

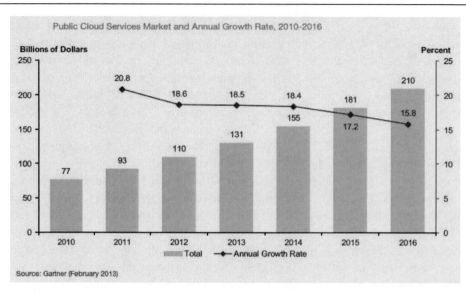

Figure 1. Public Cloud Computing Services Market and Annual Growth Rate, 2010-2016.

The cloud services industry will have strong growth through 2016, when worldwide cloud services revenue is projected to reach $210 billion. Gartner wrote that there was an acceleration in the adoption of cloud computing and cloud services by enterprises in 2010 together with an explosion in supply-side activity of cloud computing and estimated that enterprises alone will spend $112 billion on cloud computing by 2015. Meanwhile Verdantix (2011) projected that, companies in the United States will increase their Cloud Computing adoption in the next ten years from 10% to 70% of their total IT spend. They said that cloud computing is the IT solution for the 21st century and that businesses are looking for ways to operate more sustainably so as to increase their competitive edge. ICT is seen as a key area of focus for achieving sustainable goals.

COMPONENTS OF THE CLOUD COMPUTING SYSTEM

For the purpose of this research we describe cloud computing as a system with three main components. Figure 2 shows the cloud computing system comprising the data centre network, the communications network (including the Internet) and the cloud computing user network. Figure 2 shows the networks connecting to one another and the various user devices such as tablets, smartphones, laptops and desktops that cloud computing users use to access services.

DATA CENTRES

Data centres in the early dot-com era were made of mainframe-like servers of exclusive computing with concentrated power, designed and priced for enterprises. Google is credited with revolutionizing the modern data centre by changing from a network of a small number of high-power and very expensive servers to deploying cheap, commodity hardware in large numbers (Weiss, 2007). Secrecy among data centre operators makes it impossible to know exactly how many servers they operate. The Climate Group (2008) say there were 18 million data centre servers worldwide in 2007 but there will be 122 million servers by 2020 if growth continue in line with demand. However IDC say US server shipments declined 3% and 15% in 2008 and 2009 due to the economic recession but grew 20% in 2010 as seen in Figure 3 (Thibodeau, 2011).

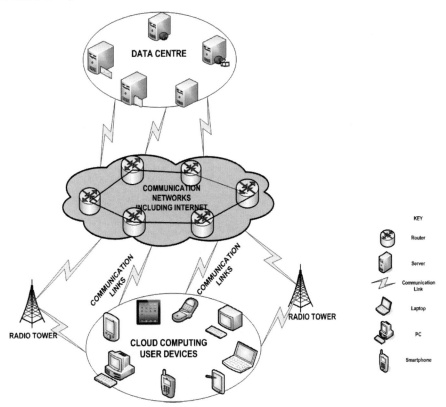

Figure 2. Components of the cloud computing system.

Year	Shipments	Change
2006	2.87 million	--
2007	2.96 million	3%
2008	2.87 million	-3%
2009	2.45 million	-15%
2010	2.95 million	20%

Source: IDC

Figure 3. U.S. Server Shipments by IDC.

Data centres have become the heart of Information and Communications Technology (ICT) and essential to the function of communications, business, academic, and government systems. Data centres have become common and essential as the world economy shifts from paper-based to digital information management and there has been a high growth of data centres due to the increasing demand for data processing and storage. This increasing demand for computing resources and the subsequent growth of data centres has led to an estimated doubling of the energy used to power the massive servers and cooling infrastructure that supports them (EPA, 2007). Loper and Parr (2007) wrote that data centres have been causing concerns because of the increasing amount of energy they consume.

However there have been improvements in the energy efficiency of data centres due to initiatives started by governments, organisations, enterprises and professionals to tackle the high energy consumption of ICT. In 2007 Google and Intel started the Climate Savers Computing Initiative (2010), an organization committed to making computers and servers more energy efficient. The Green Grid (2008) energy efficiency metrics focus on advancing energy efficiency in data centres and computing ecosystems. There is also The Climate Group (2010), a coalition of governments and some of the world's most influential businesses, all committed to tackling climate change through a low-carbon future. Another very important initiative is the Energy Star (2010) data centre energy efficiency program by the U.S Environmental Protection Agency and the U.S. Department of Energy. Energy Star aims to help individuals and organisations save money and protect the environment through energy efficient products and practices. The Energy Star (2012) labelling program has stringent total energy consumption levels for estimated annual energy use by desktop computers, laptops and servers.

Notwithstanding the gains made in the energy efficiency of data centres, there is the need to improve the energy efficiency of data centre networks and reduce their energy consumption and carbon dioxide emission to counter the rapidly growing demand for their services and future energy demand.

COMMUNICATION NETWORKS

Communication networks and the Internet are the backbone of cloud computing as they are used to transmit user requests to the cloud and to transmit responses back to the user. Since cloud computing services are based on remote servers in data centres, users can only access them if they have Internet access. Fixed and cellular broadband networks are used to transport data back and forth between the data centres and cloud users. The importance of communication networks to the success of cloud computing cannot be overemphasized as they hold the cloud together, connect the cloud to each other and send cloud services to users.

The energy efficiency of the Internet has come under intense scrutiny. Baliga et al. (2007) wrote that the exponential growth of the Internet brought with it the need for corresponding growth of equipment required to route the traffic. The consequence of this is a growth in energy consumption and carbon dioxide emissions. Baliga et al. (2007) again wrote that communication networks of broadband enabled countries consume 1% of the total energy consumption. Meanwhile Christensen et al. (2004) wrote that estimates for the energy consumption of the Internet by the United States of America range between 2% to 8% and said that there is the urgent need to improve the energy efficiency of the Internet as the improvement will enable cost savings as well as environmental benefits through reduction of greenhouse gas emissions. The cost of energy has been increasing as well as energy consumption increases.

It is not only fixed networks whose energy consumption is growing, Fettweis (2009) wrote that cellular networks consume 0.5% of the world's electricity. Of this consumption, mobile handsets account for only 1%, while the cellular networks accounts for 99% of the total energy consumption. Correia et al. (2010) wrote that mobile communication is increasingly contributing to global energy consumption and this is bound to continue because of the shift towards mobile computing due to the desire to access data and information on the move. Centre for Energy-Efficient Telecommunication (2013) wrote that because many people access cloud computing through the wireless network, the access network could become the main threat for cloud computing services sustainability. Centre for Energy-Efficient Telecommunication (2013) again wrote that wireless networks contribute disproportionately to the energy efficiency of cloud computing.

USER DEVICES

Velte et al. (2009) describe user devices as clients and classified them as *mobile devices* such as PDAs and smartphones; *thin clients* which are computers without internal hard drives that depend on the servers in the "cloud" to do all computations and display the information for users; *thick clients* which are normal computers that use web browsers to access "cloud" services.

There has been proliferation of user devices that can be used to access cloud computing services. There is now a shift from personal computers towards mobile devices to access cloud services on the move. Gartner (2010) predicted that mobile devices will become the dominant Internet accessing devices, saying there will be 1.78 billion PCs and 1.82 billion units of smartphones and browser equipped enhanced phones in use by 2013. The Climate Group (2008) meanwhile predicted that 50% of the world's population will own a mobile phone by 2020.

The International Telecommunications Union (ITU) wrote that the mobile-cellular market is the fastest growing telecommunication service market in history, saying there were 5.3 billion mobile-cellular subscriptions worldwide at the end of 2010 compared to the 4 billion of 2008 (ITU, 2011). Gartner (2013) said touch screen mobile devices will account for 58 percent of all mobile device sales worldwide and more than 80 percent in developed markets such as North America and Western Europe by 2013. Figure 4 illustrates the current data on user devices world-wide.

The growth in smartphones, notebooks, tablet computers, the Google phone, and the proliferation of mobile applications are compelling evidence of more users using mobile devices to access cloud computing services like emails and social networks. An IDC study found that 78%, 73%, and 70% of people use their smartphones for emails, web browsing and social networking respectively (Facebook, 2013). Perez (2010) on the other hand wrote that 91% of mobile phone users use their phones to access social networking sites compared to 79% of desktop users.

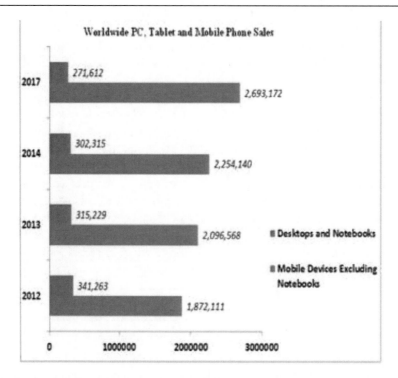

Figure 4. Worldwide PC, Tablets and Mobile Phone Sales.

IBM (2007) said personal computers (PCs) and laptops contribute to the high energy consumption and carbon footprint of ICT. Many PCs and laptops are not shut down at the close of work by employees but even when idle they consume between 60% and 70% of the energy they consume at peak load. IBM (2009) wrote that the combined energy consumption of desktops, laptops, printers, Local Area Networks (LAN), copiers, and other office equipment can be between 45% and 92% of the total energy consumption of the IT department.

These statistics point to the need and the importance of seeking for energy efficiency not only at the data centre but also on end user devices in order to sustain any gains made from improvements in data centre energy efficiency.

THE ENERGY EFFICIENCY OF CLOUD COMPUTING

The energy efficiency of ICT has come under scrutiny in recent years and there have been calls for the ICT industry to reduce its energy consumption and carbon footprint. Since ICT has become pervasive and demand for its services is growing, there are concerns for the sustainability of future energy demand of ICT. The introduction of cloud computing and the increasing use of the cloud has also brought concern for the implications of cloud computing technology on the energy consumption of the components of the cloud computing system. This has made the energy efficiency of cloud computing technology and the three components of the cloud system to become important in the search for energy consumption and carbon dioxide emission reduction in the ICT industry.

IMPORTANCE OF ENERGY EFFICIENT IMPROVEMENTS IN THE CLOUD COMPUTING SYSTEM

Energy Centre (2009) defines energy efficiency as doing an activity with less energy. Whereas Energy Consumption Rating Initiative (2010) defines energy efficiency as "energy consumption normalized to effective throughput". According to them a network system that can transport more data is more energy efficient than another system that transports less data but using the same amount of energy.

Energy efficiency improvements refer to a reduction in the energy used for a given task or activity (World Energy Council, 2013).Energy consumption reduction can result from better organisation and management but it is usually associated with technological changes. There is an increase in energy efficiency when energy used is reduced in performing a given task.

The goal of energy efficiency is to accomplish same task and function with less energy. The increasing adoption of cloud computing technology and the future predictions of cloud computing becoming dominant over desktop computing have propelled the energy efficiency of cloud computing to high importance. There is so much demand for data centre services that a survey of data centres found 40% of respondents saying they expect to run out of capacity by 2014 (Emerson Network Power, 2012). Cloud computing is the driver for the high demand for data centre services, therefore improving the energy efficiency of the cloud is not only important but urgent.

Moreno and Xu (2011) wrote that the energy consumption of ICT is causing serious economic and environmental problems because of pollution and the high cost of energy. Until recently the environmental impact of the use of ICT was relegated to the background because the focus was on processing speed, bandwidth, transfer rate, storage, and memory capacity. But this has changed due to the growing cost of energy to service the rapidly growing devices, peripherals, computers, data centres and digital communication. The rapidly growing energy consumption of data centres and communication networks, resulting in growing greenhouse gas emissions has become a critical issue. The energy demand of cloud computing due to widespread use represents a challenging problem in the future because of economic and environmental implications. Reducing energy consumption is a critical issue for service providers who have to meet increasing demand and performance expectations. Singh and Vara (2009) indicated that the energy consumption of data centres that provide cloud computing services is growing as demand for cloud service is increasing. The current trend of high energy consumption could make energy the dominant factor in the total cost of ownership. Concerns for the high energy consumption in data centres, the high cost of energy and its environmental impact have made the search of energy efficiency improvements in cloud data centres necessary.

Singh and Vara wrote that the focus is on energy efficiency opportunities through efficient application management, increasing efficiency of servers, power supply and distribution. But these approaches are not enough to deal with the energy consumption and environmental challenges of tomorrow. There is no mention of improvement in network energy efficiency as current approach to improve energy efficiency and this is an approach that we have explored as our contribution to the search for reducing the energy consumption in cloud computing environments. Controlling the energy consumption of data centres is a complex architecture problem that requires many methods. The current response to the energy consumption and energy demand of cloud computing will play an important role in meeting the energy needs of the future.

There is exponential growth in demand for cloud computing services making the energy cost and demand of providers to grow. This is evidence that the energy efficiency of cloud computing is important as it is the driver for the current services available for both fixed and mobile devices. Zhang et al. (2010) wrote that there is a growing consensus to put energy conservation at the top of the research agenda making energy consumption as one of the critical research issues. The carbon dioxide emission of ICT is bound to increase due to the increasing demand for Information Technology services. Lange et al. (2010) wrote that the problem of climate change has given rise to research on energy consumption and opportunities for energy efficiency improvement of ICT.

The importance of energy improvements can also be seen in the many past and current initiatives by governments, enterprises and organisations to improve the energy efficiency of ICT, especially the data centres in order to address the growing concerns about the high energy consumption and greenhouse gas emission. A survey of the Data Center Users' Group (DCUG), an association of data center, IT and facility managers formed by Emerson Network Power, found that 48% of data centre operators see energy efficiency as a major concern (Emerson Network Power, 2012).

The importance of energy efficiency was also shown in Symantec (2009) IT report, when 90% of organizations surveyed indicated that energy efficient IT is essential both to cut the cost of energy consumption and reduce environmental pollution. Gartner (2010) wrote that cloud computing is poised to dominate desktop computing as mobile devices become the dominant internet accessing device.

Pew Research (2010) in a survey found that majority of IT stakeholders and experts expect cloud computing to dominate desktop computing by 2020. The experts and stakeholders indicated that they expect to 'live mostly in the cloud' and not on the desktop, working mainly through cloud based applications accessed through their networked devices. By 2020 most people will access software applications online, share and access information through the use of remote server networks rather than depending mainly on applications and information stored on their personal computers. Many people will perform most computing and communicating activities through connections to servers operated by cloud computing service providers. A study found the value of cloud computing services growing at a high rate; $46.4 billion in 2008, $56.3 billion in 2009 and projected at $150.1 in 2013 (Gain, 2010).

The attention cloud computing is receiving, the trend towards widespread use due to the perceived economic benefits and the shift toward mobile devices make the energy efficiency of the cloud computing system very important. With the growth of the cloud comes an increasing demand for energy to store and transport data. The predicted growth in energy demand, energy consumption and carbon footprint of the cloud computing system cannot be ignored.

There is the need to mitigate those predictions through more energy efficiency improvement methods and mechanisms. Although there are many benefits for using cloud computing and service providers want its usage to grow, there is the need to ensure that these benefits are not outweighed by unsustainable energy consumption and carbon dioxide emissions.

SIMULATIONS ON DATA CENTRE ENERGY CONSUMPTION

In this research we used OPNET Modeler 14.5 as the simulation tool (Opnet, 2012). OPNET Modeler 14.5 provided the applications and devices for traffic generations. All the applications, user profiles, network devices (servers, routers and switches), and user devices were obtained from the object palette of OPNET Modeler. But the user and application profiles were modified and configured to suite our research needs. Web browsing which is a common cloud computing service was used in the experiments. We used web browsing to represent popular cloud computing services such as Facebook. Earlier we defined cloud computing as a system with three components making up of data centres, communication networks and user devices.

SIMULATION MODEL

Zhang, Cheng and Boutaba (2010) wrote that the basic foundation of data centre network architecture design is the layered approach, which has been used in some of the largest deployed data centers. They also wrote that currently most of the commercial clouds are implemented in large data centres and operated in a centralized fashion. Cisco (2012) also wrote that the data centre network has the core layer, aggregation layer and access layer. For the simulations for our experiments, two cloud computing systems were modelled and simulated based on Figures 5 & 6 show cloud computing models for simulation experiments with OPNET. Figure 5 demonstrates the standard cloud model whereas Figure 6 is the energy efficient cloud model.

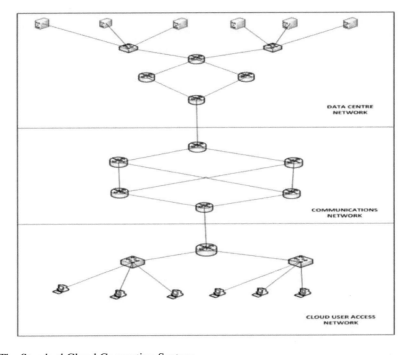

Figure 5. The Standard Cloud Computing System.

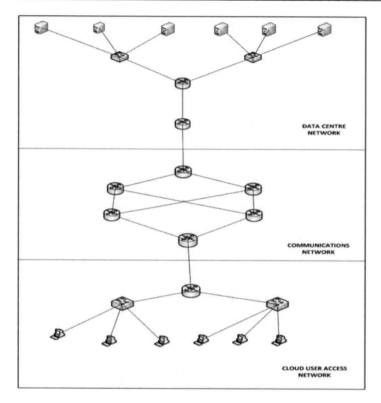

Figure 6. The Green Cloud Computing System.

Earlier we described cloud computing as a system and the Standard Cloud Computing System and the Green Cloud Computing System were modelled and simulated. The Standard Cloud Computing System was modelled based on the current data centre network architecture which has the core, aggregation and access layers. The standard architecture was optimized for energy efficiency to model the Green Cloud Computing System of which the core and aggregation layers were merged into one layer. Zhang, Cheng and Boutaba (2010) mentioned the network architecture design objectives that the current data centre network design have to meet. There was no mention of energy consumption because that has not been a major concern for data centre operators. But we strongly believe that energy consumption is an important issue that has to be considered by data centre network operators in the design of their networks.

SIMULATION EXPERIMENT 1

Experiment 1 was a test model and 2 scenarios were modelled. For scenario 1, an access network located in the United Kingdom where the cloud computing users were based was modelled and simulated. A data centre network located in U.S.A was modelled and simulated. For scenario 2, the access network in scenario 1 was duplicated and a data centre located in Europe was modelled and simulated. In our research we traced the route to a data centre of a popular cloud computing service provider and the data centre was located in U.S.A.

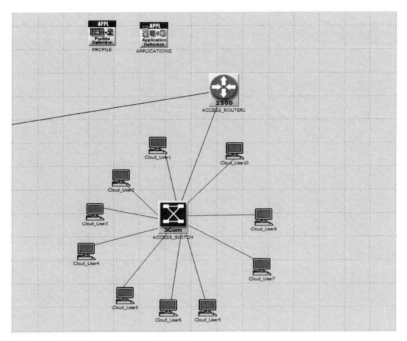

Figure 7. One Router UK Access Network Devices.

We therefore decided to locate one of the data centres in our simulations in U.S.A. The reason for locating the other data centre in Europe was to test a hypothesis that locating cloud computing data centres geographically near users to serve specific geographic regions can save energy. This is due to the fact that data transport in cloud computing environments has been found to consume lot of energy (Baliga et al., 2010). All the networks were modelled using the geographic location network modelling capability of OPNET Modeler. For Experiment, only one router was used in each network of the simulations.

The simulation results for Experiment 1 will be discussed in the next section of the chapter.

SIMULATION EXPERIMENT 2

In Experiment 2, we expanded and fine-tuned Experiment 1 and implemented our research idea to simulate the two cloud computing systems under investigation. There were two scenarios in Experiment 2; in scenario 1 the Standard Cloud Computing System located in U.S.A. was modelled with the numbers of router hops identified during the trace mentioned earlier. Based on the trace, the UK network was made of 4 routers for the access network and 6 routers for the communication network. There were 6 routers in the U.S.A. data centre network. In scenario 2, the Green Cloud Computing System with data centre located in Europe was modelled and simulated. The UK network and the communication network were the same as in scenario 1. The Europe data centre had 4 routers because of merging the core and aggregation layers into one layer. Figure 8 illustrates the cloud computing users' access network.

The results for Experiment 2 will be discussed in the next section of the chapter.

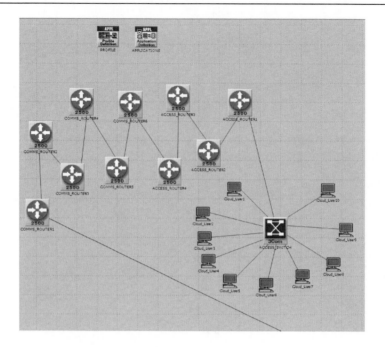

Figure 8. UK Access Network and Communication Network Devices.

SIMULATION EXPERIMENT 3

Experiment 3 was a duplicate of Experiment 2 but the IEEE 802.11 wireless access standard was implemented for the simulation. Figure 9 shows the access network of the experiment.

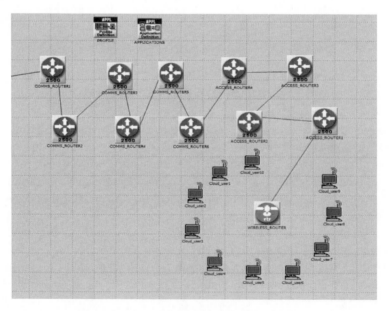

Figure 9. Wireless Access Network.

SIMULATIONS RESULTS ANALYSIS AND DISCUSSION

In this section we analyse and discuss the results obtained during the simulation experiments. This research project sought to answer some questions relating to the energy consumption and the energy efficiency of cloud computing. The results obtained and the data collected from the experiments have enable us answer those questions. The results of the experiments have also enabled us to prove hypothesis and test some assumptions that were made during the experiments. The results of the simulations which are the evidences for the experiments are presented in this section graphically with corresponding numerical data. The simulations results in the form of graphs were analysed through descriptive statistics and interpreted qualitatively. The descriptive statistics data analysis technique offer the most appropriate method to accurately and effectively present and explain the results of the simulations. Results were collected on Response Time at the access network and CPU utilization of the servers on the data centre network, routers and the cloud user devices. Data was collected on "Response Time" and "CPU Utilization" because they have been found to have a relationship to energy consumption in computing devices. We also collected and compared results on downloaded pages for the cloud users. The average response time is the time taken from when a request is sent, to the time when a response is received. In our experiments the average response time was the time elapsed between the cloud user sending a service request and receiving a response from a server at the data centre network.

RESPONSE TIME AND ENERGY CONSUMPTION

Hoxmeire (2000) defines response time as "the time it takes from the moment a user initiates an activity until result is displayed".

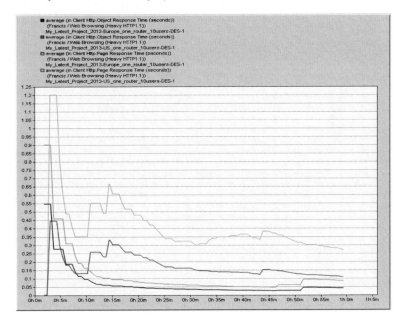

Figure 10. Response Time Experiment 1.

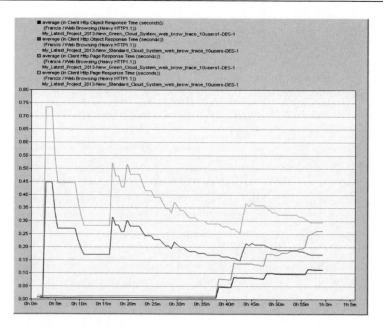

Figure 11. Response Time Experiment 2.

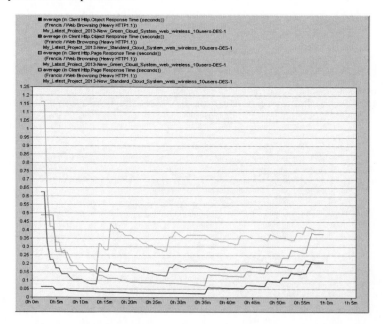

Figure 12. Response Time Experiment 3.

Response time was measured during the simulations because response time has a relationship with the energy consumption of computing systems (Albers, 2010; GHG Protocol, 2012). The higher the response time, the more energy is consumed and the lower the response time, the less energy is consumed. Therefore to improve the energy efficiency of the cloud computing system, there is the need to get a quick response time without increasing the speed of the processor of the device. GHG Protocol (2012) again wrote that response time can be used to calculate and estimate the greenhouse gas (GHG) emission of a network.

From Figures 10-12 above we observe that there was higher response time when services were accessed from the data centre located in U.S.A for all the experiments. Firstly this shows that locating data centres geographically near users to serve specific geographic regions saves energy and as such more energy efficient than locating data centres far away from users. Secondly, we see that merging the core and aggregation layers into one layer for the data centre network design is more energy efficient than having the core and aggregation layers separate.

CPU UTILIZATION AND ENERGY CONSUMPTION

Fan, Weber and Barroso (2007) and The Green Grid (2008) wrote that CPU utilization can be used as a single metric to estimate accurately the power consumption of a server as the CPU consumes a large percentage of the power to the server. By taking the average CPU utilization over a period of time, it is possible to calculate an estimate of the power consumed for that period. Furthermore, CPU utilization has a linear relationship with energy consumption and the power consumption of a server is proportional to its CPU utilization (Yamini, 2010; Tang and Dai, 2011; The Green Grid, 2008; Mazzucco and Dmytro, 2011)).

Figures 13 & 14 illustrate the CPU utilization result of the servers during the experiments. From Figures 13 & 14 we observe that the CPU utilization of the server of the data centre located in the U.S.A. is higher than the server of the Europe data centre. This means that the U.S.A. data centre server consumed more energy than the Europe data centre server because as stated earlier the higher the CPU utilization the more energy is consumed.

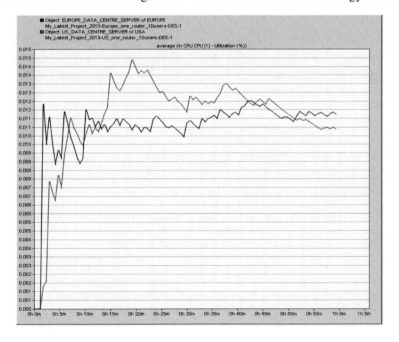

Figure 13. Server CPU Utilization Experiment 1.

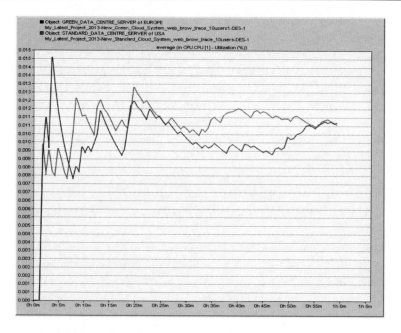

Figure 14. Server CPU Utilization Experiment 2.

COMPARING THE ENERGY CONSUMPTION OF THE CLOUD COMPUTING SYSTEMS

Earlier we wrote that for the purpose of this research we described cloud computing as a system with three components; data centre network, communications (including the Internet) network and cloud computing user network.

Therefore we decided to use the CPU utilization of the network devices of Experiment 2 to calculate and estimate the energy consumption of the Standard Cloud Computing System and the Green Cloud Computing System. To be able to get the energy consumption of each system we have to calculate the energy consumption of each device in all the components of each the system. We also observed from the simulation results that all the routers in the same system have the same CPU utilization.

Huang et al. (2011) confirmed that the power consumption of a server is directly proportional to CPU usage and that the energy consumption of a server can be represented by CPU utilization in a fixed processor frequency. Huang et al. (2011) wrote that the formula below can be used to calculate the power consumption of a server.

Power consumption (P) = 0.2782 X CPU utilization + 51.2765   (1)

Since routers and PCs have CPU utilization, we decided to use the numerical measurements CPU utilization of the servers, routers and PCs to compare the energy consumption of the two cloud computing system unser investigation. To obtain a whole number for the calculations all the CPU utilization measurements were multiplied by 1000. Tables 1 & 2 show the figures obtained for the various devices and used for the calculations.

Table 1. CPU Utilization of Network Devices

	Standard System	Green System
Data Centre Network Routers	22	18
Communication Network Routers	22	18
Access Network Routers	22	18
Data Centre Servers	11	18
User Device	7	7

Table 2. Number of Network Devices

	Standard System	Green System
Data Centre Network Routers	6	4
Communication Network Routers	6	6
Access Network Routers	4	4
Data Centre Servers	1	1
User Device	1	1

1. Standard Cloud Computing System Energy Consumption

Formula 1 above is used to calculate the power consumption of one device. Since we are calculating the power consumption of more than one device, the result has to be multiplied by the number of devices.

Power consumption (P) = (0.2782 x CPU utilization + 51.2765) n

Where n is the number of devices

Access Network Component
Power consumption of routers + power consumption of user device

= (0.2782 x 22 + 51.2765) x 4 + (0.2782 x 7 + 51.2765)
= 229.5876 + 53.2239
= 282.8115 watts

Communication Networks Component
Power consumption of routers

P = (0.2782 x CPU utilization + 51.2765)n
= (0.2782 x 22 + 51.2765) x 6
= 344.3814 watts

Data Centre Network Component
Power consumption of routers + power consumption of server

$P = (0.2782 \text{ x CPU utilization} + 51.2765)n + (0.2782 \text{ x CPU utilization} + 51.2765)$
$= (0.2782 \text{ x } 22 + 51.2765) \text{ x } 6 + (0.2782 \text{ x } 11 + 51.2765)$
$= 344.3814 + 54.3367$
$= 398.7181 \text{ watts}$

Total Power Consumption of Standard Cloud Computing System

Power consumption of data centre component + power consumption of communication networks component + power consumption of access network component

$= 398.7181 + 344.3814 + 282.8115$
$= 1025.911$

Since we are dealing with energy consumption which is different from power consumption, we use Formula 2 below to convert the results obtained using Formula 1 to energy consumed by the system.

$Energy\ Consumed\ (E) = Power\ Consumed\ (P)\ x\ time\ (t)\ in\ hours\ /\ 1000$ (2)

Energy Consumption in 24 Hours Using Formula 2

$Energy\ Consumed\ (E) = Power\ Consumed\ (P)\ x\ time\ (t)\ in\ hours\ /\ 1000$
$= 1025.911 \text{ x } 24/1000$
$= 24.62 \text{ kWh}$

2. Green Cloud Computing System

Access Network Component

$P = (0.2782 \text{ x CPU utilization} + 51.2765)\ n + (0.2782 \text{ x CPU utilization} + 51.2765)$
$= (0.2782 \text{ x } 18 + 51.2765) \text{ x } 4 + (0.2782 \text{ x } 7 + 51.2765)$
$= 225.1364 + 53.2239$
$= 278.3603 \text{ watts}$

Communications Network Component

$P = (0.2782 \text{ x CPU utilization} + 51.2765)\ n$
$= (0.2782 \text{ x } 18 + 51.2765) \text{ x } 6$
$= 337.7046 \text{ watts}$

Data Centre Component

$P = (0.2782 \text{ x CPU utilization} + 51.2765)\ n + (0.2782 \text{ x CPU utilization} + 51.2765)$
$= (0.2782 \text{ x } 18 + 51.2765) \text{ x } 4 + (0.2782 \text{ x } 11 + 51.2765)$
$= 225.1364 + 54.3367$
$= 279.4731 \text{ watts}$

3. Total Power Consumption of Green Cloud Computing System

Power consumption of data centre component + power consumption of communication networks component + power consumption of access network component

$$= 279.4731 + 337.7046 + 278.3603$$
$$= 895.538 \ watts$$

Energy Consumption in 24 Hours Using Formula 2
Energy Consumed (E) = Power Consumed (P) x time (t) in hours / 1000
$$=895.538 \ x \ 24/1000$$
$$= 21.49 \ kWh$$

From the calculations we observe that more energy was consumed by the Standard Cloud Computing System. We observe that the energy consumption of each of the components of the Standard Cloud Computing System was higher than their corresponding components in the Green Cloud Computing System. This shows the importance and necessity for making energy consumption an important consideration in network design to mitigate the growing energy demand and greenhouse gas emissions in cloud computing environments.

Based on the results of the simulations we observe that less energy is consumed when the two layer network design is implemented and data centres are located near users to service specific geographic regions. The Green Cloud Computing System provides the following advantages.

- *Switching of idle servers and network devices during low periods*
  This becomes easy due to the data centre serving specific regions and low usage is easy to identify and predict.
- *Reduced router hops*
  The shorter distance that transactions go means there are fewer router hops involve in the transaction.
- *Improved network and system performance*
  The lower response time shows an improved network and system performance.
- *Increased Productivity*
  The results of the simulations show that more pages were downloaded by the user device of the Green Cloud Computing System. This means that more work was done by the users on the green network than those on the standard network.

CONCLUSION AND FUTURE WORK

In this chapter we investigated the energy efficiency of the cloud computing system. Two models; the Standard Cloud Computing System and the Green Cloud Computing System were modelled and run by simulations. Results were collected on response time, CPU utilization and downloaded pages. The results of the simulations show that the Green Cloud Computing System has the lower response time meaning less energy was consumed on that system. We also compared the energy consumption of the two systems under investigation using the CPU utilization of the network devices. The results of the comparison show that our optimized system, the Green Cloud Computing System consumed less energy than the Standard Cloud Computing System. This supports our contention that energy efficiency should be a major consideration when designing the data centre network. The results also show the need to geographically locate and distribute data centres near users to serve users in specific geographic regions. The advantages for locating data centres geographically near users to provide cloud services for specific regions mentioned show that building small data centres and locating them geographically is more energy efficient than building large centralized data centres. Again the simulation results show that less energy is consumed when the network is optimized for energy efficiency as opposed to only the scale of the network. The simulation results also show that the growing energy demand of data centres can be reduced by making energy efficiency one of the primary goals of data centre network architecture design. In the future we hope to look at dynamic routing of users in cloud computing environments.

REFERENCES

Accenture (2010) *Cloud Computing and sustainability: the environmental benefit of moving into the cloud* [Internet], Accenture, Available from: <http://www.accenture.com/ SiteCollectionDocuments/PDF/Accenture_Sustainability_Cloud_Computing_TheEnviron mentalBenefitsofMovingtotheCloud.pdf > [Accessed 20 June 2011].

Albers, S. (2010) *Energy-efficient algorithms, Communication of the ACM*, 53 (5), May, pp. 86-96.

Armbrust, M., Fox, A., Griffith, R., Joseph, A. D., Katz, R. H., Konwinski, A., Lee, G., Patterson, A. D., Rabkin, A., Stoica, I., and Zaharia, M. (2009) *Above the Clouds: A Berkeley View of Cloud Computing* [Internet], University of California at Berkeley, Available from: <http://www.eecs.berkeley.edu/Pubs/TechRpts/2009/EECS-2009-28.pdf> [Accessed 5 April 2010].

Baliga, J., Ayre, R. W. A., Hinton, K., and Tucker, R. S. (2010) Green Cloud Computing - Balancing Energy in Processing, Storage and Transport *Proceedings of the IEEE*, 99 (1), August, pp. 1-19.

Baliga, J., Hinton, K., and Tucker, R. S. (2007) Energy Consumption of the Internet. *Conference on Optical Fibre Technology*, Melbourne, 2007, pp. 1-3.

Beckman, A. (2010) *Study Reveals Value of Cloud Computing* [Internet], Available from: <http://www.processor.com/editorial/article.asp?article=articles%2Fp3210%2F43p10%2 F43p10.asp&guid=64B96E522A1A4F31AB85D5DB0E4D313B&searchtype=0&WordL ist=CLOUD+COMPUTING&bJumpTo=True> [Accessed 28-09-10].

Centre for Energy-Efficient Telecommunication (2013) *the power of wireless cloud* [Internet], Available from: <http://www.ceet.unimelb.edu.au/pdfs/ceet_white_paper_ wireless_cloud.pdf> [Accessed 6 June 2013].

Christensen, K., J., Gunaratne, C., Nordman, B., and George, A., D. (2004) *The next frontier for communications networks: power management. Computer Communications,* 27 (18), December, pp. 1757-1902.

Cisco (2012) *Cisco Data Center Infrastructure 2.5 Design Guide* [Internet], Available from: https://www.cisco.com/application/pdf/en/us/guest/netsol/ns107/c649/ccmigration_09186 a008073377d.pdf [Accessed 4 October 2013].

Climate Savers Computing Initiative (2010) About [Internet], Climate Savers Computing Initiative, Available from: <http://www.climatesaverscomputing.org/about> [Accessed 10 August 2010].

Climate Savers Computing Initiative (2010) About [Internet], *Climate Savers Computing Initiative*, Available from: <http://www.climatesaverscomputing.org/about> [Accessed 10 August 2010].

Daley, B. and Woods, E. (2010) *Cloud computing energy efficiency, a good debate to have.* [Internet], GiGaom, Available from: < http://gigaom.com/cleantech/cloud-computing-energy-efficiency-a-good-debate-to-have/ > [Accessed 20 November 2011].

Emerson Network Power (2012) *Data Center Users' Group Special Report* [Internet], Available from: <http://www.emersonnetworkpower.com/en-US/Brands/Liebert/ Documents/White%20Papers/DCUG_Special_Report_sl-24668.pdf> [Accessed 9 May 2013].

Energy Centre (2009) How does one define energy efficiency? [Internet], Available from: <http://energycenter.org/index.php/technical-assistance/energy-efficiency/energy-efficiency-definition> [Accessed 16 May 2012].

Energy Consumption Rating Initiative (2010) *Network and Telecom Equipment – Energy Performance Assessment* [Internet], Available from: <http://www.ecrinitiative.org/ pdfs/ECR_1_0_4.pdf > [Accessed 26 April 2012].

Energy Star (2010) *Data Center Energy Efficiency Initiatives* [Internet], Energy Star, Available from: <http://www.energystar.gov/index.cfm?c=prod_development.server_ efficiency> [Accessed 22 October 2010].

Energy Star (2012) *Computers for Consumers* [Internet], Available from: <http://www.energystar.gov/index.cfm?fuseaction=find_a_product.showProductGroup& pgw_code=CO> [Accessed 1 June 2012].

EPA (2007) *Report to Congress on Server and Data Centre Energy Efficiency* [Internet], Energy Star , Available from <http://www.energystar.gov/ia/partners/prod_development/ downloads/EPA_Datacenter_Report_Congress_Final1.pdf?9e09-a353> [Accessed 20 May 2010].

Facebook (2013) *Always Connected - How Smartphones and Social Keep us Engaged* [Internet], Available from: <https://fb-public.box.com/s/3iq5x6uwnqtq7ki4q8wk> [Accessed 5 May 2013].

Fan, X., Weber, W. D., and Barroso L. A. (2007) Power provisioning for a warehouse-size computer. *Proceedings of the 34th annual international symposium on ccomputer architecture,* San Diego, June, pp.13-23.

Fettweis, G (2009) *ICT Energy Consumption: Trends and Challenges* [Internet], European Commission Information Society, Available from: <http://ec.europa.eu/information_ society/events/cf/ee09/document.cfm?doc_id=10510> [Accessed 10 November 2010].

Forbes (2013) *Gartner predicts infrastructure services will Accelerate cloud computing growth* [Internet], Forbes, Available from: <http://www.forbes.com/sites/louiscolumbus/ 2013/02/19/gartner-predicts-infrastructure-services-will-accelerate-cloud-computing-growth/> [Accessed 16 May 2013].

Gain, B (2010) Cloud Computing and SaaS In 2010. *Processor,* 32 (1), January, pp.12

Gartner (2010) *Mobile PC Market Experiences Strongest Growth Rate in Eight Years.* [Internet], Gartner, Available from: <http://www.gartner.com/it/page.jsp?id=1374913> [Accessed 7 June 2010].

Gartner (2010) *Worldwide Cloud Services Market* [Internet], Gartner, Available from: <http://www.gartner.com/it/page.jsp?id=1389313> [Accessed 18 July 2010].

Gartner (2012) *Gartner Outlines Five Cloud Computing Trends That Will Affect Cloud Strategy Through* 2015, [Internet], Stamford, Gartner, Available from: <http://www. gartner.com/it/page.jsp?id=1971515 > [Accessed 10 April 2012].

Gartner. (2008) *Gartner Says Contrasting Views on Cloud Computing Are Creating Confusion* [Internet], Gartner, Available from: < http://www.gartner.com/it/page.jsp?id= 766215 > [Accessed 15 June 2010].

Gartnet (2013) *Gartner says worldwide PC, tablet and mobile phone combined shipments to reach 2.4 billion units in 2013* [Internet], Available from: <http://www.gartner.com/ newsroom/id/2408515> [Accessed 16 May 2013].

Geelan, J. (2009) Twenty one Experts Define Cloud Computing [Internet], *Cloud Computing Journal,* Available from: <http://cloudcomputing.sys-con.com/node/612375> [Accessed 24 May 2010].

GHG Protocol (2012) *Guide for assessing GHG emissions of Cloud Computing and data center services,* [Internet], GHG Protocol, Available from: <http://www.ghgprotocol.org/ files/ghgp/Chapter_5_GHGP-ICT%20Cloud%20v2-2%2010MAR2012.pdf> [Accessed 10 March 2012].

Greenpeace (2010) *How dirty is your data,* [Internet], Greenpeace, Available from: http://www.greenpeace.org/international/Global/international/publications/climate/2011/ Cool%20IT/dirty-data-report-greenpeace.pdf> [Accessed 27 April 2011].

Greenpeace (2010) *Make IT Green Cloud Computing* [Internet], Available from: <http://www.greenpeace.org/international/Global/international/planet-2/report/2010/3/make-it-green-cloud-computing.pdf> [Accessed 15-05-10].

Han, Y. (2010) *On the Clouds: A New Way of Computing. Information Technology and Libraries,* 29 (2), June, pp. 87-92.

Hoxmeier, J. A. and DiCesare, C. (2000) *System response time and user satisfaction: An experimental study of browser-based applications,* [Internet], Available from: <http://citeseerx.ist.psu.edu/viewdoc/summary?doi=10.1.1.99.2770> [Accessed 6 September 2012].

Huang, Q., Gao, F., Wang, R., and Qi, Z. (2011) Power consumption of virtual machine live migration in clouds, *3rd International Conference on Communications and Mobile Computing,* Qingdao, April, pp.122-125.

IBM (2007) *Cutting the Carbon Footprint of IT* [Internet], IBM, Available from: <http://www-304.ibm.com/easyaccess/fileserve?contentid=119203> [Accessed 11 June 2011].

IBM (2009) *How much energy do your IT devices use?* [Internet], IBM, Available from: <https://www-935.ibm.com/services/uk/cio/pdf/howmuchenergy_lr.pdf> [Accessed 14 June 2011].

ITU (2011) *Measuring the Information Society* [Intenet], International Communications Union, Available from: <http://www.itu.int/ITU-D/ict/publications/idi/material/2011/ MIS_2011_without_annex_5.pdf> [Accessed 18 April 2012].

Koomey, J. G (2007) *Estimating Total Power Consumption by Servers in the U.S. and the World* [Internet], Pennsylvania State University, Available from: <http://citeseerx.ist.psu.edu/viewdoc/download;jsessionid=07D1EAC6629CF5A43F093D6CFEE610CB?doi=10.1.1.87.5562&rep=rep1&type=pdf> [Accessed 17 June 2011].

Lange, C., Kosiankowski, D., Weidmann, R., and Gladisch, A. (2010) Energy Consumption of Telecommunication Networks and Related Improvement Options. *Journal of Quantum Electronics*, April, 17 (2), pp. 285-295.

Loper, J. and Parr S. (2007) *Energy Efficiency in Data Centres: A New Policy Frontier, Environmental Quality Management,* 16 (4), June, pp.83-97.

Mazzucco, M and Dmytro, D (2011) *Optimizing Cloud providers revenues via energy efficient server allocation, Sustainable Computing - Informatics and Systems*, 2 (1), March, pp. 1-12.

Miller, R (2010) *Cloud Computing as an Energy Saving Tool* [Internet], Data Center Knowledge, Available from: <http://www.datacenterknowledge.com/archives/2010/05/17/cloud-computing-as-an-energy-saving-tool/> [Accessed 12 July 2010].

Moreno, I. S. and Xu, J. (2011) Energy-efficiency in Cloud Computing environments: towards energy savings without performance degradation, *International Journal of Cloud Applications and Computing*, 1 (1), pp.16-33.

Morgan Stanley (2008) *Technology Trends*, [Internet], Morgan Stanley, Available from: <http://www.morganstanley.com/institutional/techresearch/pdfs/TechTrends062008.pdf > [Accessed 10 April 2012].

Nucleus Research (2010) *Cloud Computing – It is Easy Being Green* [Internet], Nucleus Research, Available from: < http://nucleusresearch.com/research/notes-and-reports/cloud-computing-it-is-easy-being-green/ > [Accessed 28 December 2010].

Opnet (2012) *Network Simulation: OPNET Modeler Suite* [Internet], Available from: <http://www.riverbed.com/products-solutions/products/network-planning-simulation/Network-Simulation.html> [Accessed 16 July 2012].

Perez, S (2010) *Social Networking Now More Popular on Mobile than Desktop*. [Internet], Read Write Web, Available from: <http://www.readwriteweb.com/archives/social_networking_now_more_popular_on_mobile_than_desktop.php> [Accessed 20 July 2011].

Pew Research Centre (2010) *The Future of Cloud Computing* [Internet], Pew Research Centre, Available from: <http://pewinternet.org/~/media//Files/Reports/2010/PIP_Future_of_the_Internet_cloud_computing.pdf> [Accessed 18 July 2010].

Pike Research (2010) Cloud computing energy efficiency [Internet], Pike Research, Available from: <http://www.pikeresearch.com/research/cloud-computing-energy-efficiency> [Accessed 16 August 2011].

Scott, S. (2010) *Cloud computing - the next industrial revolution*. [Internet], CIO, Available from: <http://www.cio.com.au/article/365428/cloud_computing_-_next_industrial_revolution/> [Accessed 17 April 2012].

Singh, T. and Vara, P.K (2009) Smart Metering the Clouds *Proceedings of the 18th IEEE International Workshops on Enabling Technologies: Infrastructures for Collaborative Enterprises*, Groningen, June, pp.66-7.

Symantec (2009) *Green IT Report*, [Internet], Symantec Corporation, Available from: <http://www.symantec.com/content/en/us/about/media/GreenIT_2009.pdf > [Accessed 7 June 2010].

Tang C, J. and Dai M, R. (2011) Obtaining energy efficiency for computation intensive web services, *15th International Symposium on Consumer Electronics*, Singapore, 2011, pp. 643-646.

The Climate Group (2008) *Enabling the Low Carbon Economy in the Information Age* [Internet], The Climate Group, Available from: <http://www.smart2020.org/_assets/files/ 03_Smart2020Report_lo_res.pdf > [Accessed 14 June 2010].

The Climate Group (2008) *Enabling the Low Carbon Economy in the Information Age* [Internet], The Climate Group, Available from: <http://www.smart2020.org/_assets/files/ 03_Smart2020Report_lo_res.pdf > [Accessed 14 June 2010].

The Green Grid (2008) Data Center Power Efficiency Metrics: PUE and DCIE [Internet], *The Green Grid*, Available from: <http://www.thegreengrid.org/~/media/WhitePapers/ White_Paper_6_-_PUE_and_DCiE_Eff_Metrics_30_December_2008.pdf?lang=en> [Accessed 19 November 2011].

Thibodeau, P (2011) *Data centers use 2% of U.S. energy below forecast*, [Internet], Computer World, Avaialble from: http://blogs.computerworld.com/18738/data_centers_use _2_of_u_s_energy_below_forecast> [Accessed 18 April 2013].

Velte, A. T., Velte, T. J. and Elsenpeter, R. *Cloud Computing: A Practical Approach*, 1st ed., Wendy Rinaldi, Ed. New York, United States of America: McGraw Hill, 2009.

Verdantix (2011) *Cloud Computing – The IT Solution for the 21st Century*. [Internet], Carbon Disclosure Project, Available from: <https://www.cdproject.net/Documents/ Cloud-Computing-The-IT-Solution-for-the-21st-Century.pdf > [Accessed 10 October 2013].

Weiss, A. (2007) Computing in the clouds, Net Worker, December 11 (4), pp.16-25.

World Energy Council (2013*) Energy Efficiency Policies around the World: Review and Evaluation,* [Internet], Available from: <http://www.worldenergy.org/publications/ energy_efficiency_policies_around_the_world_review_and_evaluation/1_introduction/11 75.asp> [Accessed 12 April 2013].

Yamini, R. (2012) Power management in cloud computing using green algorithm, *Proceedings of the International Conference on Advances in Engineering, Science and Management*, Nagapattinam, March, pp. 128-133.

Zhang, Q., Cheng, L., and Boutaba, R. (2010) *Cloud computing: state-of-the-art and research challenges* [Internet], Available from: <http://download.springer.com/static/pdf/652/ art%253A10.1007%252Fs13174-010-0007-6.pdf?auth66=1382604973_184b4f8 ecf7c9f48e45d47a914d184fc&ext=.pdf> [Accessed 22 October 2013].

Zhang, Y., Chowdhury, P., Tornatore, M., and Mukherjee, B. (2010) Energy Efficiency in Telecom Optical Networks Surveys and Tutorials, July, 12 (4), pp. 441-458.

INDEX

D

E

F

G

H

I

T